Library of
Davidson College

SILHOUETTES

SILHOUETTES

BY
SIR EDMUND GOSSE

Essay Index Reprint Series

 BOOKS FOR LIBRARIES PRESS
FREEPORT, NEW YORK

First Published 1925
Reprinted 1971

INTERNATIONAL STANDARD BOOK NUMBER:
0-8369-2399-5

LIBRARY OF CONGRESS CATALOG CARD NUMBER:
78-156654

PRINTED IN THE UNITED STATES OF AMERICA

TO
CHARLES WHIBLEY
WITH THE ADMIRATION OF
AN OLD FRIEND

PREFACE

ANOTHER selection from the little sermons which I preach every week out of the pulpit of the *Sunday Times* asks for no less kind a reception than has been given to its predecessors. Like them, it skims lightly over a wide surface of criticism and biography, even of autobiography.

The only method which these swallow-flights can pretend to adopt is based upon curiosity and delight in all manifestations of literature. While the arrangement of the book is accidental, I may say for my own satisfaction that the little essay on Claudian comes first, because an eminent living author, who liked it, desires that it should.

July 1925.

CONTENTS

	PAGE
THE LAST OF THE PAGANS	1
BLUEBEARD AMONG THE AUTHORS	11
LYLY AND HIS "EUPHUISM"	21
CAMOENS	31
A SPANISH MYSTIC	41
CARY'S EARLY FRENCH POETS	51
WYCHERLEY	61
THE SIN OF WITCHCRAFT	71
AN APOLOGIST FOR ARCADIA	81
THE PORTRAIT OF ZÉLIDE	91
NATURE IN POETRY	101
MAKING OUR FLESH CREEP	111
THE CONFESSIONS OF A JUSTIFIED SINNER	121
A DOG WITH A BAD NAME	131
THE FABLE OF THE BEES	141
THE DIARY OF A COUNTRY CLERGYMAN	151
ANDREW LANG	161
ARTHUR O'SHAUGHNESSY	171
AUSTIN DOBSON	181
W. D. HOWELLS	191

Contents

	PAGE
MRS. HUMPHRY WARD	201
MR. SAINTSBURY	211
LAFCADIO HEARN	219
SHELLEY'S WIDOW	229
THE SORROWS OF OVID	239
A SURGEON'S RECOLLECTIONS	249
LOUIS COUPERUS	259
VAUBAN	269
ROMAN PICTURES	279
THE NERVES OF FRANCE	287
AMERICAN FOLK-SONG	297
THE BROTHER OF THE BRONTËS	307
LESLIE STEPHEN	317
THE CENTENARY OF A SPASMODIST	327
THE HOUSE WITH THE GREEN SHUTTERS	337
THÉODORE DE BANVILLE	345
HERMAN MELVILLE	353
A BELATED CAVALIER	363
THE SAVILE CLUB	373
MORALS AND MANNERS	381
THE CARPET AND THE CLOCK	391
INDEX	401

THE LAST OF THE PAGANS

THE LAST OF THE PAGANS

THREE hundred years after great poetry had seemed to cease in Italy, an exile from Egypt revived it during ten years of superb production. The writings of Claudian have not been very easy of access, the latest edition of the Latin text being one published in Leipzig thirty years ago, nor was there till now any translation in English except that issued at Sherborne in 1817 by a certain A. Hawkins, in heroic couplets, very dead and dreary, and none the livelier for being verbally rather close to the original. Hence inclusion of the great Milanese poet in the Loeb Library is particularly welcome, if only because Claudian is invaluable to historians.

It would be impertinent in me to appraise Mr. Maurice Platnauer's scholarship, but there is evident in his whole apparatus—his translation in prose, his manipulation of the text, his notes and his bibliography—an admirable competency. There is now no excuse for not reading the last of the ancients, of whom Gibbon said that "he was endowed with the rare and precious talent of raising the meanest, of adorning the most barren, and of diversifying the most similar topics." It is in the capacity of a lantern of information throwing radiance on the intrigues of a particularly obscure period of late Latin history, that Claudian has been chiefly examined. Historians, from Gibbon to Thomas Hodgkin, have revelled in his records, although the first-mentioned is careful to guard us against prejudice and violence in the partisan poet. I do not know why it is that Mr. Platnauer never once quotes

Gibbon, whose brilliant thirtieth chapter is full of eloquent tributes to the genius and memory of Claudian.

On one point only I venture, very timorously, to find fault with Mr. Platnauer. His performance of his task can have been attended with very little pleasure, since he seems to have no appreciation of the literary talent of Claudian. He talks about finding it " hard to withhold admiration " from the poet, but, nevertheless, he does withhold it. He says that his " faults are easy to find," and then proceeds to draw up a formidable list of them. He prints not one sentence in which there is any hearty praise of Claudian's poetry. Mr. Mackail, who has written on the subject too briefly, but with exquisite discernment, has praised in Claudian " a dignity and pathos that are worthy of the large manner of the classical period." This must disturb Mr. Platnauer, who would equally demur to Gibbon's praise of Claudian's " copious fancy, easy and sometimes forcible expression, and perpetual flow of harmonious versification." The disinclination of grammatical scholars to allow any pleasure to be taken in the works of the latest Latin authors is very curious. It is probably founded on a scholastic notion that it is bad for the young to read any Latin that is not of the most austere Augustan purity.

The objections, however, that are brought against the authors of the Decline are frequently based not on their individual genius, but on the passage of time. A certain effort is required to realise that Claudian was separated from Juvenal, whom we may consider as the latest " classic " writer of Rome, by a period of three hundred years—that is to say, that the elder was as remote from the younger as Shakespeare is from Mr. Kipling. During those centuries modifications were introduced not merely into the language, but into the manners of life and habits of thought of Italian society. The habit of literature may have become almost

The Last of the Pagans 5

extinct. But it seems the mere tyranny of a pedagogue to forbid admiration of an author simply because the style of that author bears the stamp of his own age. To refuse to recognise in Claudian a poet of a high order, the culminating point in a revival of brilliant accomplishment, and the most prominent literary feature of an epoch, is to sacrifice too much to the dignity of public school tradition.

It would seem that Claudius Claudianus was born at Canopus—that is to say, in Egypt—about the year 370. Nothing is known of him till he arrives, at perhaps the age of twenty-five, in Rome, towards 394 or 395. Hitherto it seems that he had written in Greek, but he shows himself to possess, from the first, a wonderful mastery of Latin. The poems he has left us, no doubt mere fragments of an immense poetical activity, bear the stamp of having been written between 395 and 405. This is not the place in which to dwell on the momentous events of this period in the stricken Empires of the East and of the West.

Those readers whose curiosity is stimulated by Mr. Platnauer's excellently concise account of the historical situation can gratify it by re-reading Gibbon's stately chapter on the Revolt of the Goths, or the still fuller history by the late Mr. Hodgkin. Claudian had probably just transferred himself to Milan when the Emperor Theodosius died (January 17, 395), and he was no doubt already in favour with Stilicho, the general who appears at this moment of crisis like a god out of a machine. It was Stilicho who defended Italy against the invasion of the Huns, and who presided at the final and permanent division of the Empire under Arcadius and Honorius, the young sons of the deceased Emperor. It was a new world. As Gibbon says, "the spirit of Rome expired with Theodosius," but it came precariously to life again at Milan, where Honorius reigned and Stilicho ruled, and where Claudian, with extraordinary rapidity, rose to the highest honours in the State.

What were the style and temper of the new laureate may be discerned in his earliest surviving poem, the " Panegyric on Probinus and Olybrius." It has been observed that this has " no appearance of being a first effort," and doubtless Claudian had already written, and perhaps published, much that is lost. The wonder is that anything has survived. He begins with concentrated elegance, in the Alexandrian manner, by an appeal to the Sun, and there follows a beautiful passage, perhaps too artificially dragged in, about the Moon outshining the constellations. Then he expatiates in praise of the two consular brothers, who were quite young, and of Probus, their father.

What Mr. Mackail calls the " epical " manner of Claudian is illustrated by the way contemporary history is introduced. The love of Claudian for set pictures is evident in a piece displaying the two young Consuls, holding their sceptres and wrapped in their jewelled togas, as they call up Father Tiber from his oozy couch of sedge. There is a gorgeous scene where the Nymphs prepare tables set with gems in a watery palace, blazing with purple and gold. The scene closes with the ardent determination of the Hours to inscribe the names of the young Consuls on a garland of immortal blossoms, the whole being a tissue of fact and fancy that evidently dazzled the court, although to us it may seem artificial and metallic.

It is a very different Claudian who reveals himself in the satires which take up a large place in his surviving works. There can be no doubt that the diatribes against Rufinus and against Eutropius, published when those determined enemies of Stilicho had just fallen, produced an immense sensation. The Satire on Rufinus, that hypocritical creature of Theodosius, begins with a wild cry of triumph over the death of the oppressor. Python has fallen, laid low by the arrow of Phœbus, while the whole world shouted for joy, and Cephisus, which so often foamed with his poisonous venom, now flows pure and limpid. This rapture is justified by a catalogue of the crimes of Rufinus, who does, in fact, appear to have offered a remarkably offensive type of the low-born upstart. The poet is well acquainted with the life-history of his detestable hero, and he is careful that every image and trope shall add contempt to the wretched fallen figure of Stilicho's worst enemy: then he turns abruptly to an ecstatic eulogy of Stilicho himself. With Claudian there are no fine shades; white is snow-white and black is lamp-black.

If we take for granted that in this case blame and praise were alike deserved, the "Rufinus" is a fine example of legitimate satire, aimed at the chastisement of vice. It is not unworthy to be matched against "Absolom and Achitophel." The "Eutropius," on the other hand, is so distempered by passion as to be little better than a venomous lampoon. The poet's horror at the crimes of the court of Constantinople is unfeigned, but it is also unmeasured, and in this satire Claudian passes beyond the bounds of what is allowed even to political invective. Nor does there seem to me to be anything in the "Eutropius" so admirably written as the close of the first book of the "Rufinus," where the apotheosis of the Western world, flushing with ecstasy in hues of paradise, under the sacrificial sway of Honorius, is related in verse which is melody itself.

The most impersonal of Claudian's poems is that which Mr. Platnauer prints last in the collection. "The Rape of Proserpine" has not found much favour with the critics, against whose professional censure I am not anxious to pit my amateur opinion. Even Mr. Mackail, who has written more warmly of Claudian than anyone else, finds this piece a little "chilly and colourless." Yet the poet wrote it, for he says so, out of a full heart, violently moved by the majesty of an ancient exquisite story. He seems to have been acquainted with Sicily, and to have witnessed an eruption of Etna. That the style is Alexandrian is so obvious that German scholiasts have suggested that Claudian wrote it in Greek, and translated it into Latin. I do not see that there is any evidence of this. His genius was Egyptian, but we might as well conjecture that Mr. Conrad wrote his novels in Polish, and translated them into English.

"The Rape of Proserpine" presents a series of magnificent pictures, beginning with the king of Hell gloomy on his squalid throne, and culminating in the goddess among the flowers of the meadow, where Zephyr conjures Henna to welcome her with brighter roses, more azure hyacinths and violets purpler and sweeter than earth ever saw before. The soil of Sicily is all a dream-land of splendour and perfume. Proserpine is borne away after the earthquake, and is received by Pluto in an address which, it seems to me, is of a high order of poetry, full of a sort of royal tenderness, prodigal and flushed. "Think not thou has lost the light of day; other stars are mine and other courses; a purer light shalt thou see, a richer age, a golden race." And then, in the soft melody of the incomparable hexameters, Hell becomes like Earth, and Hesperus shines out in a twilight sky, propitious over the silent underworld.

Perhaps the best parallel to such poetry is that of the great Scottish writers of the fifteenth century. Theirs also is a stumbling block to critics, who are shocked at the loaded palette and "aureate" profusion of Dunbar, with its heaped-up colours and rainbow effects. No doubt, if we are possessed by the exclusive fallacy of the Romanticists, this gorgeous density of style repels us. It lacks, we are told, simplicity. But all things are not necessarily simple, and De Quincey reminded us long ago that simplicity was misplaced in a description of Sennacherib's Feast.

I do not think it has been observed how much Claudian's more splendid passages resemble the ornate style of Tennyson's old age. Some of " The Rape of Proserpine " might almost be taken out of " The Voyage of Maeldune." Compare the description of the crag of Etna towering up out of the cataract of crocus and daffodil—*ferratus lascivit apex*—with the scene in the Isle of Flowers where

> the whole isle-side flashed down from the peak without ever a tree,
> swept like a torrent of gems from the sky to the blue of the sea,

and it is hard not to believe that the English poet remembered his Milanese predecessor.

If splendour, if a prodigal profusion of radiant mythological reminiscence, is not to be frowned upon as dissolute and extravagant, the rapturous pictorial abundance of Claudian's fancy must be allowed its own meed of praise. " As a poet Claudian is not *always* despicable," says Mr. Platnauer. I should suppose not, indeed ! But when we read him we ought not be thinking about Burns, nor even about Horace, for there are many rooms in the house of Apollo.

The isolation of Claudian must strike the literary student with surprise. He appears like an obelisk rising from a plain ; we see him without predecessor, without contemporaries, without disciples. But this must be the result of accident, for he cannot have flourished in so complete a solitude. His poems are all addressed to a cultivated audience, evidently ready to seize every refinement of allusion and every delicacy of execution. The survival of the inscription which once ran below his vanished statue set up by Arcadius and Honorius in the Forum of Trajan, throws a curious flash of light over the darkness. We are told on this illusive memorial that Claudian was " above all a poet and the most famous of poets," yet this tablet and the text of a few of his writings are all that remain to testify to the elaborate culture of Northern Italy before it was engulfed in the onset of the Barbarians.

BLUEBEARD AMONG THE AUTHORS

BLUEBEARD AMONG THE AUTHORS

THERE is an amiable deception about the general appearance of Mr. Macnamara's collection of the royal writings, for which he is not seriously to blame. But it is needful to expose it, before we examine any further the claim of King Henry VIII. to literary distinction. If these " Miscellaneous Writings " were indited in the English tongue, that bluff monarch would be one of the precursors of our prose; if they were written as Mr. Macnamara prints them, the monarch would be proved a miracle of developed style. But, in matter of fact, nothing here is in the language used by the subjects of the king, or by himself, except perhaps the songs for music, to which I shall return. He composed his treatises in Latin, and most of his letters, I suppose, in French; at all events, he cannot be quoted as an English author.

This is a sad pity, since he flourished at a period of the greatest importance in English composition, when prose was just being made a living thing in the hands of Hugh Latimer and Sir Thomas Elyot, who were Henry VIII.'s immediate contemporaries. It was still very rough and clumsy, and it had hardly been yet put to directly literary uses, for Ascham was to be our earliest artist in prose. The best prose-writing in England was liturgical, and led up directly to the Bible in the versions of Cranmer and Tyndale. If Henry VIII., with his undoubted originality and activity of mind, had chosen to identify himself with the new English prose, he would be to-day with the precursors I have just mentioned. We might forgive him for his want of delicacy towards a series of unfortunate ladies if he had left us another " Governor " or another " Utopia."

But what Mr. Macnamara prints is neither an ancient nor a modern version. "The Assertion of the Seven Sacraments," as he gives it, is composed in beautiful English, but not at all like what would be used by anyone either in 1521 or in 1925. This version, in fact, was revised and published by a certain Thomas Webster in 1680, and it will be found an amusing exercise to compare its sentences, which are modern in form even for the end of the seventeenth century, with the cumbrous language of the early part of the sixteenth. If we could only prove that Henry VIII. wrote (let us say) page 46 of this reprint, there would follow a revolution in the history of literature. As it is, there is no question that the earlier contents of Mr. Macnamara's volume present traps for the feet of the unwary, while they illustrate the transformation of our tongue in curious ways.

The same is true of the " Letter to the Emperor," which was written in Latin in 1538; the version here is pure Queen Anne. The amusing Proclamations for the putting down and destroying of cross-bows and hand-guns were doubtless either written in English or translated at the time, but it is not likely that Henry VIII. had anything to do with them individually. They hardly count among his " Writings."

Our regret that Henry VIII. disdained the use of the vernacular is increased by what we are told of the excellence of his Latin style. His biographers are unanimous in praising it, and Gairdner says that " if his arguments were mean, his Latin was king-like." Indeed, it was so far above the level of what kings were supposed to be capable of,

that popular rumour attributed the composition of the
"Seven Sacraments" to Richard Pace, Wolsey's right-
hand man, who was supposed to inspire the King's foreign
policy. But evidence is all against this legend, and Henry
VIII. was quite clever enough to write his own thesis.

We must not think of him at the age of twenty-nine
as the huge barrel of a debauchee that the late Holbein
portraits represent. When he became " Defender of the
Faith," although, perhaps, already infected with disease,
he still appeared to be the type of all that was elegant,
active, and shining, as when Giustiniani watched him
playing tennis with incredible agility, " his fair skin glowing
through a shirt of the finest texture." He was the hand-
somest, the most learned, the most athletic and religious
monarch in Christendom in 1521; nothing in him predicted the bloated and besotted tyrant of 1557. He was
extremely modern, an epitome of the new-found and semi-
pagan charm of the Renaissance, and without ever having
experienced any spiritual elevation, he distinguished
himself, like other brilliant young men of that stirring
time, by his passion for the intellectual " spinosities "
of theology. As Mr. Pollard has said, he " could brook
no superior in whatever sphere he wished to shine in,"
and when he took up religion it was with the intention
of surpassing Erasmus.

The King's interest in dialectics, and his tentative
attitude with regard to Rome, were awakened by the
publication of a book which thrilled the whole of Christendom. He was already a Thomist, a practised student
of the Schoolmen, although it is probable that their controversies presented themselves to his restless mind in a
certain light of futility. But his zeal might have continued
to be academic, if he had not been roused by his poet-
laureate, Bernard Andree, to watch the movements in
Germany of the new reformers and in particular of one

Martin Luther, who had become the centre of rebellious activity.

Henry VIII. was finally drawn into the controversy which was revolutionising Europe, by the issue of Luther's famous " Babylonish Captivity of the Church," a squib which blazed up into a volcano in 1520. The King, under suggestion from Andree and Wolsey, wrote to the Pope, Leo X., to tell him that he proposed to devote his leisure to " the defence of Christ's Church with his pen," and the Pope was enchanted, politically as well as ecclesiastically, at having found so brilliant a champion. On August 25, 1521, Wolsey wrote to Clerk that the King's book was completed, that is to say, evidently, was not merely printed but bound and ready for distribution. There is a copy at Windsor, signed by the King himself, which is doubtless the first which left the press. Mr. Macnamara's reprint is prefixed by a letter from the Pope, dated " the fifth of the Ides of October in the year of Our Lord's Incarnation *1501*." There is something wrong here; and even if the date is a misprint for 1521, I cannot make it agree with Clerk's account.

It must be borne in mind in reading the " Seven Sacraments " that Henry VIII. had at this time developed no definite antagonism to the Papacy. In fact, he instinctively disliked the new-fledged Protestantism of Germany, and had formed no objection to the supremacy of Rome. But Luther had in the past three years greatly extended the scope and vehemence of his attacks, and had now reached a point where forgiveness was impossible, so that Henry VIII., who had watched the wrangling with Tetzel and even the burning of the bulls with indifference, perhaps indeed with some mischievous amusement, was genuinely alarmed at the attacks on the Roman interpretation of the Sacraments contained in Luther's latest work.

The " Babylonish Captivity " reduced the seven Sacraments by four, and retained only baptism, the Eucharist and penitence. There was, as Tunstal shudderingly said, "much more strange opinion in it, near to the opinions of Bohemia," that is to say, of Huss. Against this wave of the incoming tide of Reform, it must be confessed that the "Seven Sacraments" of Henry VIII. was no more effectual than was the mop of Mrs. Partington when she tried to stem the Atlantic. One of the King's most eminent admirers has frankly admitted that the book "reproduced, without novelty or energy, the old common-places of authority, tradition and general consent." The conservative world, indeed, was vastly delighted with it, but Luther was contemptuous. He compared the "Pharaoh of England" to a fat swine and a nettle-eating ass. How rude these theologians are to one another!

Marriage was one of the Sacraments rejected by Luther as being merely *de jure positivo*, ordained by the Pope and not binding on Christendom, and in view of the remarkable freedom with which Henry VIII. treated this Sacrament in later life, it is probable that the modern reader will turn to this chapter of his rather dreary book with more anticipation than to any other. Poor Queen Katharine had long been the victim of the indifference and the scorn of her tyrannical consort, but he had not yet formed the definite design of putting her away. He says :—

"Let us consider God the consecrator of this Sacrament. Has he not consecrated Marriage with his blessing, when he joined together our first parents? For the Scripture saith, ' God blessed them, saying Increase and multiply.' Whose blessing having operated in all other living creatures according to their several capacities; who shall doubt but that he has infused the force of spiritual grace into the spirit of man, who alone is capable of reason, unless he did believe that God should be so sparing of his blessings to man, whom he created after his own image, that having regard only to his body, he should omit the soul, that breath of life which he himself has breathed, and by which he was most represented, without imparting any part of that great blessing to it?"

This seems a little confused in thought, but exemplary in sentiment. It is fair to admit that Henry VIII. to the end preferred a wife to a mistress, but whether in so doing he showed much reverence for the Sacrament of marriage, it must be left to the theologians to decide.

As the importance of Henry VIII.'s writings is considerably more anecdotal than positive, I am a little surprised that Mr. Macnamara does not tell the story of how the "Seven Sacraments" was received in Rome. Campeggio, who had been allowed to glance at the treasure, announced that the royal author had written more like an angel than a mortal. Wolsey immediately sent a copy, bound in cloth of gold, to the Pope, by the hand of Clerk; it had a Latin couplet written in it by the King's own pen. Clerk presented this treasure, in great secrecy, to Leo X., who immediately began to read it with every species of commendation, nodding and exclaiming that he "would not 'a thought that such a book should have come from the King's grace," a remark which was well meant, but might have been more felicitously expressed. The MS. verses were then pointed out to his Holiness, and, as the handwriting was very small and the Pope's eyesight defective, Clerk tactfully proposed to read them aloud. But his Holiness would not hear of such a thing, and almost snatching the volume back from the English envoy, read the verses out three times with extreme complacency. The Pope then asked for five or six more copies of the book, " to the intent he might deliver them to sundry cardinals learned." Later on he remarked that the book placed Henry VIII. on a level as a theologian with St. Augustine and St. Jerome, and, in consequence, on October 3, 1521, he conferred on the King of England the long-coveted title of "Defender of the Faith." I wonder whether the original copy, bound and clasped in rich gold, still exists in the Library of the Vatican?

We reach a very different order of ideas when we come to the letters addressed to Anne Boleyn. The character of this lady, still held so high in the eighteenth century, when Gray could write that,

> gospel-light first dawn'd from Boleyn's eyes,

has not worn well. We see in her a pretty young woman with little delicacy of instinct, and no strength of purpose. But the letters preserved in the Vatican by no one knows what strange chance, are curious documents. They contain no indication of time, and I am doubtful why Mr. Macnamara confidently dates the first six July, 1527, and the other twelve 1528, but I daresay he has good reason for the conjecture. Anne's replies have all been lost, which is no great matter for regret. Henry's are downright and amorous, but not so outspoken as would be gathered from Brewer and others, who have been scandalised at the "gross allusions" in them. One cannot but feel pity for the girl who came to such a wretched end eight years later, in strict conformity, however, with Henry's famous Sacrament of Marriage.

Mr. Macnamara's preface is an ingenious piece of special pleading, which will scarcely carry conviction with it. He says that Henry VIII. was "unsexual in character," which will be news to many historians. He also regards him, except in the legitimate Bluebeard capacity, as unspotted from the world. Has he read the report of the trial of the Duke of Buckingham? The notion of representing Henry

VIII. as a pure young man with a disinterested foible for the marriage state is very pleasing.

We have to consider Henry as an English poet. His claim rests upon the words which accompany the music privately printed by Lady Mary Trefusis in 1912. There seems to be no doubt that the airs, together with several anthems, were certainly composed by the King. Are the words also his? They strike me as later in style than lyrics would be before the day of Wyatt and Surrey, but I offer no opinion. The volume, which Mr. Macnamara has edited with evident care and enthusiasm, is very handsomely printed, but for my taste is too much a gift-book and not enough a monograph.

LYLY AND HIS " EUPHUISM "

LYLY AND HIS " EUPHUISM "

INSTEAD of discussing some vaporous point in morals or metaphysics, Lord Crawford has offered a good example to his colleagues, the other Chancellors of our universities, by addressing his students on a matter of solid literary history. He recalls to them, in an excellent essay, the efforts made for the improvement of the English language by the most interesting, but perhaps the most difficult, of Shakespeare's immediate predecessors. John Lyly, at a moment when English prose was still bound in fetters, and content to stumble on its path with a painful clank of iron, became " famous for facility in discourse." If we turn to the ordinary guides to knowledge we shall be surprised to find this harbinger of liberty dismissed as affected and obscure, and to be assured that his manner of writing was " a dangerous malady." His book has been called " a most contemptible piece of nonsense," yet when he died his world declared that few or none of those who survived him were, in their books, " such witty companions."

Here is a paradox, which Lord Crawford treats with acumen and humour, not confining himself strictly to Lyly, but taking him and his " Euphues " as vivid features of the variegated Elizabethan Renaissance. Lyly is particularly well suited to form the theme of a Rectorial address, because he stimulates discussion and naturally leads to a broad consideration of the principles of style. If we take other primitives, such, for instance, as Peele or Nash, we soon come to an end of what can be said about them, but Lyly stands at the cross-roads, like a signboard on which the directions are half erased, and the critics will wrangle about him for ever.

Like almost all the early Elizabethans, John Lyly is shadowy to us in his private relations. Lord Crawford accepts the customary outline, and he could hardly do otherwise, yet it is curious on what slender evidence most of our information rests. The approximate date of birth is certain, for Lyly himself says that he was "scarce born" when Mary I. came to the throne in July, 1553. Hence he was by a few months younger than Spenser and a little older than Greene, Lodge, and the others on whom he was to exercise great influence. At so tropic a time as was the close of the sixteenth century the vegetation of the mind advances with such rapidity that a year or two is as important as a decade would be to-day.

Lyly was of plebeian birth, a scion of the Weald of Kent, probably a farmer's son, but he found his way to Magdalen College, Oxford. We should note that, although his life was spent at Court, and although he was proud of his learning, he was essentially unacademic, and that, underneath his elaborate refinement, there was a firm democratic basis of common-sense. Before he was twenty-five he wrote that extraordinary book "Euphues, the Anatomie of Wit," published at the end of 1578. He sent the manuscript "to a nobleman to nurse"; this odd expression may mean that someone of influence effected its publication, or it may mean that Lyly submitted it for revision to one of the cultivated aristocrats who were flourishing at Court.

The success of "Euphues" was immediate and extraordinary. Lyly had put it forth with timidity, but it ran through English society like wild-fire. He had said that it was a book only "for an hour's reading," but the ladies learned it by heart, and flung phrases from it at one another. It became at once the "best-seller" of the

Lyly and his "Euphuism"

age. We find Lyly immediately appointed Vice-Master of the Playing Boys of the choir of St. Paul's. A continuation of the great romance appeared in 1580 as "Euphues and His England," and this was followed by a succession of plays, acted at Court, where Lyly presently became Controller of the Revels. In 1600 he offended Queen Elizabeth, which it was not difficult to do, but he was four times elected to the House of Commons before 1601, and died in 1606. This is really the sum of what we know; the rest is conjecture.

In that day, when the poets were all friends or enemies, in groups of partisanship, Lyly seems to stand alone. He influenced everybody, but hardly anyone is known to have been personally related to him. The success of "Euphues" long survived him, and the book went on being reprinted until thirty years after his death, when it seems to have gone into desuetude rather suddenly. But it had a glorious run of nearly sixty years, which is more than most works of fiction can boast. It was revived by that faithful lover of old fancy, the late Henry Morley, in 1861, and has attracted more and more attention ever since.

The reader who turns to "Euphues" in the hope of finding a sensational or even an amusing story will be disappointed. Perhaps the later and graver style of Henry James is nearer to it than any other modern example. Up to the time when Lyly wrote, the fashion of the novel had been founded on the old tradition of chivalry, with its violent incidents, its hyperbolic virtues and vices, and its incessant stir of adventure. Lyly conceived a new thing, the novel of character and analysis, where hardly anything happens externally, but all the interest is based on the clash of temperaments and the secret movements of the soul. Lord Crawford, in a particularly happy phrase, describes "Euphues" as being "in reality a genuine example of psycho-analysis," to which I would only add that the word must be used in its original and not in its Freudian sense, since Lyly has none of the disagreeable sexual taint so beloved in these days by our popular "psycho-analytic" novelists. The purity of his imagination is among his charms, and was undoubtedly one source of his success in the Elizabethan age, which preserved, or liked to affect, a sort of almost infantile delicacy, though that was often superficial enough.

One leading feature of "Euphues" was that it was the earliest English book which catered openly for the suffrages of feminine readers. Perhaps the most famous phrase in it is that in which the author says: "'Euphues' had rather lie shut in a lady's casket than open in a scholar's study." He flattered women with the tact of a fashionable confessor. He wheedled them to tell him their secrets, as Richardson did a century and a half later, and instead of betraying them, he defended them against all comers. He expanded in admiration of "the ladies in this blessed island," and pronounced them all to be as devout and brave as they were chaste and beautiful. The ladies had been accustomed to hear that they were beautiful and chaste, but it was a new thing for the most elegant of all students of the soul to pronounce them brave and devout. The poets and romancers had trumpeted their cruelty and loveliness to satiety, but it was arousing to be told by so acute an observer that the real qualities which animated their comely bodies were "temperance, modesty, mildness, and sobriety."

When a woman, a little weary of the chivalric boisterousness of the poets, read the scene of the coming of the Lady Iffida to the dying Fidus, in Lyly's second romance, I can conceive that she would feel that justice had for the first time been done to the tenderness of her sex. Lord Crawford is excellent on this point, to which sufficient attention has hardly been paid before. Everything that Lyly says about women has a sort of priestly unction; he expatiates in a sweet and consecrating tribute to female virtue, which had been misjudged in monkish times. He is like an indulgent and saintly prelate moving in the midst of a troop of exquisite women, all of whom seem to him to be princesses. Lord Crawford gives some notable instances; I will quote one which he does not name, because it seems to me to amplify the peculiar caressing tact in which Lyly was unique :—

" I would borrow, gentlewomen, so much leave as to resign mine office [as an exponent of the soul] to one of you, whose experience in love hath made you learned, and whose learning hath made you lovely. For me to intreat of the one, being a novice, or to discourse of the other, being a truant, I may well make you weary, but never the wiser, and give you occasion rather to laugh at my rashness than to like my reasons. Yet I care the less to excuse my boldness to you, who were the cause of my blindness."

Was ever before such a serpent such a dove? But Lyly was a fangless snake in the soft Elizabethan paradise.

Lyly's famous novel, however, can never be galvanised into a living force again. The loves of Philautus and Lucilla, and the reveries of the aged Eubulus, are as respectable as ever, but have ceased to be amusing. We must search elsewhere than in its plot for entertainment from "Euphues," and we find it in its style, which has been warmly praised and scoffingly censored. Dr. Landmann, in a commentary which was much discussed, thought he had traced the source of Lyly's very odd manner of writing to the study of Spanish, and in particular to the imitation of Antonio de Guevara, a Franciscan monk whose " Dial of Princes " was much read throughout Europe in the sixteenth century. There was considerable ingenuity in what Dr. Landmann said, but he pushed his parallels on too fast, as people will when they are riding a pet theory to market. Everybody who is really original owes something to a predecessor, and Lord Crawford is admirable when he says that he has not found " any convincing reasons that Lyly owed to Petrarch, Boccaccio, or Baldassare Castiglione, the famous author of ' Il Cortegiano,' more than the oblique tribute which scholars of a country just emerging into literary maturity would pay " to foreign authors of repute.

Lyly's style is his own, and its popularity had far-reaching results which were not wholly good and yet not wholly bad. It abounded to excess in antithesis, but this gave the author an opportunity to break up the leaden periods of his predecessors. Before we call Lyly dull, let us try to read Gosson or Harvey! It was an entirely new thing for English prose to be neat and clear, and we may forgive antithesis and what is called "affectation" in a writer who really does move on at a lively pace. As for Lyly's references to fabulous animals and plants, which have made some critics so crazy, they are not nearly so numerous as his enemies pretend, and for my own part I am amused to learn that "poison is taken out of the Honeysuckle by the Spider, venom out of the Rose by the Canker, and dung out of the Mapletree by the Scorpion." I am afraid Lyly did not write with his eye upon the object, yet it pleases me to be told that he who playeth on a tabor may, while that music continueth, stand upon a tiger in perfect safety.

The plays of Lyly have received less general attention than his romances, but they also exemplify the merits and demerits of his Euphuism. There are seven of them, or perhaps eight; except the blank-verse " Woman in the Moon," all are written in a prose that is elaborate and slow in movement, a light farcical prose, offered on a semiprivate stage to a learned audience, with incessant classical allusions. We should soon get very tired of these entertainments nowadays, although the dialogue is brisk and the diction simple enough. The subsidiary pieces are the most excessive; the Prologue to " Campaspe " is the very rant of Euphuism at its worst. The matter of the plays is all moonshine on the waters and cobwebs on the windows of real life; mere gossamer of fancy, but often very prettily and always very daintily expressed. The songs in Lyly's plays are easy and melodious, without a touch of what is called his " affectation." The songs in " Midas " are particularly limpid in style :—

> Nor flute, nor lute, nor gittern can
> So chaunt it as the pipe of Pan;
> Cross-gartered swains and dairy girls,
> With faces smug and round as pearls,
> When Pan's shrill pipe begins to play
> With dancing wear out night and day.

There is no trace of " Euphuism " here.

On the whole, we may sum up by admitting that Lyly was never spontaneous, never in direct touch with nature, but that he poured oil on the waves of language at a troublous time; that, when greater men than he were writing horrors like " Titus Andronicus," he was always on the side of the angels; and, not least, that he was a passionate and judicious lover of England for her own sake. Indeed, his mingling of devotion to exotic art, with a rapturous passion for all things English, is one of his leading characteristics.

CAMOENS

CAMOENS

PERSISTENT industry of research has not enabled Portuguese scholarship to fix the exact date of the birth of Portugal's greatest national author, but there seems little doubt that the year was 1524. We were therefore at liberty to celebrate the fourth centenary whenever we pleased, so that it does not slip our memory until after last December. Mr. Aubrey Bell—whose admirable studies in Portuguese, or (as we used to say) in the Portingall, language cannot be too warmly praised—marked the moment by publishing a succinct biography of the poet, which tells us all that is certainly known about him. This is an occasion for recollecting Froude's delicious impertinence about the Cornish saint, of whom he recounted " all we know, and more than all, yet nothing to what the angels know."

No writer has been, it appears, the victim of more fairy-tales than Camoens, and these are impatiently brushed aside by Mr. Aubrey Bell. But when all that is merely legend or fiction is cleared away, we are left feeling that the life of the author of " The Lusiads " must have been romantic far beyond the wont of literary lives. The spirit of the great navigators was in him; he wandered in Africa and Asia; he was a soldier and a lover and a sailor on the grand scale. He lived abreast of the heroic age of adventure. He was still a youth when King Manoel I. assumed the title Lord of the Conquest, Navigation and Commerce of India, Ethiopia, Arabia, and Persia. Camoens belonged to that epoch of empire; he did not merely sum it up in immortal verse, but he fought and suffered in the pulse and flood of it. His life is like a gateway in some stupendous piece of Manoelian architecture, such as the startled tourist sees to-day at Batalha or Thomar.

It seems strange that we know little that is positive about the career of a writer so famous and so representative as Camoens. Sir Richard Fanshawe, who was no mean writer of verse, put into the poet's mouth this summary :—

> Spain gave me noble birth; Coimbra arts,
> Lisbon a high-placed love and courtly parts;
> Afric a refuge when the Court did frown;
> War, at an eye's expense, a fair renown;
> Travel experience, with no short sight
> Of India and the world.

Mr. Bell will not hear of Spanish birth. The Galician family of the poet's ancestor, Vasco Perez de Camoens, had been settled in Portugal for upwards of a century and a half. The birth is claimed by Santarem and by Lisbon and by Coimbra, and Mr. Bell's arguments, expanded at great length, tend to make the last conjecture the most probable. The earliest editor of Camoens' lyrics roundly declared that " he was born in this our city of Coimbra." The visitor to that ancient and romantic university, the centre of Portuguese learning, likes to think that the author of " The Lusiads " saw the light in one of these terraced streets which still rise so elegantly over the curved waters of the Mondego. It is even more certain that he was educated in that Western Athens, where it is highly likely that he attended the lectures of the shining and acid Scottish exile, George Buchanan. It is believed that in 1543 the young poet left Coimbra for Lisbon.

In Lisbon, and in a church, on Good Friday, 1544, Camoens first saw Catarina de Ataide, who was then a lady-in-waiting to the Queen. This lady became to him what Beatrice had been to Dante and Laura to Petrarch.

As in those cases, so in the famous Portuguese romance, it is difficult to know how much was personal passion and how much a poet's tribute to the fashion of gallantry. Mr. Bell, however, presents Camoens to us as a sort of Paris, with three Caterinas all ambitious for the apple of immortality. Mrs. Browning—who was particularly interested in Caterina—would have been scandalised :—

> When the palace ladies, sitting
> Round your gittern, shall have said :—
> " Poet, sing those verses written
> For the lady who is dead "—
> Will you tremble,
> Yet dissemble,—
> Or sing hoarse, with tears between,
> " Sweetest eyes, were ever seen ? "

It would have been disconcerting indeed if the poet had been obliged to ask Which of the three ladies do you mean? Mr. Aubrey Bell even distracts us with a fourth, the Infanta Maria, daughter of the formidable King Manoel himself. This may be well enough; but we turn in indignation from a fifth suggestion, that Caterina was a Chinese slave-girl. The poet was doubtless rather light of love. What really matters is that the infatuation, to whomever it was directed, inspired what is, by the unanimous verdict of all good judges, the best lyric poetry written in Portuguese up to the present hour.

The incidents of the next few years are shrouded in a most bewildering obscurity. There is no lack of record, but the stories confute one another to a surprising degree. Set out in the dry light of Mr. Bell's scepticism, they awaken the doubt whether there ever was such a person as Camoens at all, or whether he was not a solar myth. Happily, we can put our feet down firmly on " The Lusiads " as on a solid deck. Suddenly we emerge from among the floating débris of legend and are in open water. In disgrace with the King, probably about some too impertinent dramatic petulance, Camoens was exiled to Africa in 1547. Here he spent two years as a soldier in the fortress of Ceuta, and here, in a battle with the Moors, he lost an eye. In 1549 he went back to Portugal, and lived for some years in Lisbon as a swashbuckler. He made himself disliked by the ladies, who called him the " One-Eyed Devil," and at last, during the Corpus Christi procession, he fought a Court official in the street and nearly killed him. This was the end of his rowdy period, for he was thrown into prison for eight months. In these unseemly adventures, Camoens approaches Villon, that rapscallion of genius. He was released at length on giving a pledge that he would enlist for India, whither, " as one leaving this world for the next," he did proceed in March, 1553. He went, in his thirtieth year, as a common soldier, pledged for three years' service. He was nearly wrecked in a storm off the Cape of Good Hope, but after six months of hardship he duly arrived at Goa.

Camoens now launched out into such a life of activity in strange places as hardly any other poet has ever conceived possible. The dreamers have enormously outnumbered the doers among the bards of the world. There have been Byron and Agrippa d'Aubigné and the Duke of Montenivoso (formerly Gabriele d'Annunzio). Lamartine is the eminent political exception. In our own circle, the Poet Laureate, greatly daring, sailed away to Ann Arbor in his eightieth year. But, as a rule, the poets have sat beside their nectar, contemplating the panorama of life, but taking no share in it. For Camoens there was no bed of down. Scarcely arrived at Goa, he started on a punitive expedition to the coast of Malabar; presently he helped to scour the Red Sea of pirates; then he hunted Turkish merchant-vessels in the Persian Gulf, he visited Malacca, he explored the Moluccas. No wonder that Mr. Aubrey Bell, though rigidly divesting himself of all credulous enthusiasm,

Camoens 37

cannot help exclaiming: " It is really extraordinary that, just as Camoens' works embrace the whole of Portugal's history, he should have visited in person almost without exception every part of the Portuguese Empire." Meantime, he was incessantly writing verses, no doubt the best that were ever composed on the Indian Ocean. Finally, we find him at Macao, in China, writing his epic of Portingall glory in a grotto on the seashore. On the way back, his ship was wrecked at the mouth of the Mekong River in Cambodia. Camoens lost all that he possessed in the world, except those cantos of the " Lusiads " which he had finished at Macao. He describes the incident in the tenth canto of the epic in terms which Fanshawe endeavours to render thus. After describing the Mekong, the poet continues :—

> Upon his soft and charitable Brim
> The wet and ship-wrackt Song receive shall Hee,
> Which in a lamentable plight shall swim
> From shoals and Quicksands of tempestuous Sea.

The exhausted poet, clutching his manuscript, landed on the shore of " Cauchinchina," in a grove that " smelt hot of Calambuco wood," where Buddhist priests took pity on his parlous condition.

His adventures were not ended, but they must be pursued in his biographies. He was finally imprisoned at Mozambique, of all places in the world, and accidentally succoured there by literary friends, who paid his debts and brought him home to Lisbon. In 1572 he succeeded in publishing his " Lusiads," and the fame of it spread through Europe. The splendid " Aminta " of Torquato Tasso was printed in the same year, and compliments passed between the Italian and the Portuguese poets, the two most eminent writers of the day. Camoens does not seem to have been known in England, where Shakespeare was a child at Stratford, but he was famous in Spain, where some of his poems were published in Castilian. Lope de Vega, like Shakespeare, was an infant, but we can "place" Camoens by remembering that Cervantes was his younger contemporary. The end of all the brilliant adventures was sad enough. Camoens died of the plague, in abject poverty, in 1579, and the stray note of a Spanish Carmelite monk has preserved the only record of the event. That is what Fray José Indio wrote: "How grievous to see so great a genius brought so low! I saw him die in a hospital at Lisbon, without so much as a sheet to cover him, after having won success in India and sailed 5,500 leagues of sea." The preservation of this note in a copy of the "Lusiads" now belonging to Lord Ilchester is in itself a romantic tale, fully told by Mr. Bell in his appendix.

Although the "Lusiads" is one of the most famous poems of all literature, it is not really well known in this country. The editions, commentaries, criticisms, and general effusions which Portuguese scholars have expended on Camoens seem to be innumerable. He is the one great intellectual glory of their country. But, in English, there is no really standard edition. Sir Richard Fanshawe's rough and spirited version, a handsome folio of 1655, has never been reprinted; Mickle's, of 1776, gives no real impression of the poem. Sir Richard Burton produced a harsh translation, said to be accurate, but very difficult to read. J. J. Aubertin's rendering, line by line, is much more satisfactory. It would be an excellent thing for some young English poet to devote himself to a version of the "Lusiads," which is not very long for an epic, not half so long as the "Jerusalem Delivered." What is wanted would be the power to transfer to English the mingled vigour and voluptuousness of the Portuguese. When Camoens describes what appear to be the Azores, this is how Fanshawe transfers the landscape:—

A thousand gallant Trees to Heav'n up-shoot
   With Apples odoriferous and faire;
The Orange-tree hath in her sightly fruit
   The colour Daphne boasted in her Haire;
The Citron-tree bends almost to her Root
   Under the yellow burthen which she bare;
The goodly Lemmons with their button-Caps,
Hang, imitating Virgin's fragrant Paps.

The savage-trees (That doeth Forest there
   With leavie Haire innoble and adorn)
Are, Poplars of Alcides; Laurels, deare
   In vain into the Golden God Unshorn;
Myrtles of Venus; the proud Pine severe,
   That Cybele for meaner love did scorn;
The speared Cypress, from this vale of Vice,
Stands pointing at Celestial Paradice.

This was well enough in 1655, but a stout young Georgian would do better in 1925.

A SPANISH MYSTIC

A SPANISH MYSTIC

WHEN the earthquake of the Reformation had rent the body of Christianity in twain, and when the seismic disturbance had begun to subside, there was at first in the Catholic Church a tendency to hold aloof from mystical experience, and to abide with docility in the plain paths of doctrine. The Dutch and German prophets had, unconsciously, prepared the hearts of their disciples to turn against scholasticism in suspicion and then in open hostility. The Anabaptists had frightened even the Reformers, and Luther had denounced them in the mood of a moderate Socialist of to-day with his anxious eye on Moscow.

If this was the case in the green tree, what would it be in the dry, and all over the south of Europe in the fifteenth century mystical enthusiasm was looked upon with dread and disfavour? But in the next age it assumed large proportions in Spain, where a school of mystical theology existed for a few years, and was illustrated, in quite a unique way, by a group of metaphysical poets, on to whose life and labours, long obscured, a great deal of light has lately been thrown.

The names of the principal planets in this constellation are St. Teresa of Jesus, Fray Luis de Leon, and St. John of the Cross. With these, Spanish critics associate Miguel Sanchez, author of the "Song of Christ Crucified," of whom, however, little has hitherto been said outside Spain. But St. Teresa has been revealed to us in a biography by the late Mrs. Cunninghame-Graham, while Luis de Leon was the subject of one of Fitzmaurice-Kelly's elaborate essays. St. John of the Cross, on the other hand, although acknowledged as being the greatest of these religious lyrists of Spain, has not, until now, received, even in his own country, anything like the attention his genius deserves.

The Spanish mystics of the sixteenth century lived in an ecstatic vehemence of vision. They showed none of the independence of authority which led the saints of pre-Reformation times to draw as near as they could to the Absolute by a system of symbolic images. That would have seemed cold and formal to St. Teresa, while, on the other hand, the intellectuality of Eckhart and his followers would have left her quite indifferent. All speculative character, as Professor Pringle-Pattison has remarked, is found to have faded out of the Spanish mystics, or, rather, to have been " crushed out by the tightness with which the directors of the Roman Church now held the reins of discipline." St. Teresa and her friends lived in a condition of ecstasy, which they imagined to resemble that in which St. Paul found himself when he knew not whether he was in the body or out of the body. They believed that by an effort of concentration they could incorporate themselves with God, become a part of the divine essence and melt, through a crisis of mystical anguish which they compared with the dissolution of a leaf in a flame of fire, into the very being of the Deity.

Their experiences, which by a singular and happy chance they embodied in prose and verse of enchanting beauty, were wholly sensuous, and had no reference to doctrine. They were inspired by a species of spiritual delirium, and their trance was illuminated by flashes of electric ecstasy. St. John of the Cross declared that he only lived, and certainly he only wrote, when his soul was torn with vehement anguish and his voice broken with moans of love. The strange thing is that out of these hysterical paroxysms there came forth prose and verse of extreme lucidity and melody.

A Spanish Mystic

The poems of St. John of the Cross were known only to a limited circle, who read them in manuscript, until after his death. When his "Spiritual Writings" were published at length, in 1618, all the group of Carmelite doctors had passed away, and the Inquisition had triumphed. The latter had adopted the much more popular and shallow visions of Luis de Granada as a means of satisfying the hankerings of the populace after mystical ravishment, and the hour of worship for the real mystics had not dawned. Hence, the texts of St. John of the Cross were neglected and mislaid, but they were not destroyed. It appears that there still exists in Spain an immense mass of material. For ten years past, a French scholar, Dr. Jean Baruzi, has dedicated his whole time and energy to the work of following St. John of the Cross through the rapture of his visions and the torment of his prisons. He has now published a "Saint Jean de la Croix et le problème de l'expérience mystique," and for the first time, in his capable and accurate hands, the astonishing author of "The Ascent of Mount Carmel" and "The Dark Night of the Soul" is placed before the world in an intelligible light.

It would be difficult to over-estimate the value of Dr. Baruzi's work, which completely supersedes all that had been hitherto published with regard to this great saint and poet. It is only right to explain that the purpose of Dr. Baruzi is philosophical no less than critical or biographical. He examines with great care the question which occupies many earnest minds to-day: What is the real psychological significance of such experiences as St. John of the Cross and our own exquisite Crashaw have crystallised in perfect verse?

The real name of St. John of the Cross in the world was Juan de Yepes. Even Dr. Baruzi has not been able to discover the exact date of his birth, but the year was 1542.

He was the son of a nobleman, Gonzalo de Yepes, who for some reason had been repudiated by his family; they "abhorred" him, and he had sunken into extreme poverty in the village of Fontiveros, where he struggled for a living as a weaver. He could not make both ends meet, and died, when his widow migrated, with the infant Juan, to Medina del Campo, now much decayed, but then a rich commercial city. Juan learned to read and write, showed some precocity in carving statuettes, and at the age of fourteen found employment in a fever hospital. His merit was recognised, and he was educated at the College of Medina, where the Jesuits had just begun to teach Latin. On leaving the hospital, Juan de Yepes was invited to enter the priesthood, but he declined; he preferred to become a Carmelite monk in the Convent of St. Anne in Medina, and he changed his name to Juan de Santa Matía. He was still in touch with the world, but gave up all secular relations at the age of twenty-five, when he passed through a crisis of revulsion and entered into the realm of spiritual dreams. But by this time he had met Teresa de Jesus and had left Medina del Campo for Salamanca.

The critical fact in the history of St. John of the Cross was the arrival of Teresa of Jesus at Medina del Campo on August 14, 1567. She describes in her autobiography how she appeared at midnight, and immediately took up her abode in a dismantled house in the town, which she proposed to turn into a convent of barefoot Carmelites.— She consulted Antonio de Heredia, who came over from Salamanca to discuss the plans with her, and brought with him "another religious, a young monk, called Brother John of the Cross, who told me," says St. Teresa, "marvellous things of his manner of life." She was fifty-two, the young monk less than half her age, and there was something of the relation of spiritual mother to child in the friendship which instantly sprang up between them.

A Spanish Mystic

Teresa of Jesus was a prodigy of genius, of whom our own English mystic, Crashaw, who celebrated her in burning numbers, said that she was " a woman for angelical height of speculation, for masculine courage of performance more than a woman." This priestess of the Flaming Heart, this " sweet incendiary," set fire to the passion of Brother John, and he became her disciple, her champion, and the greatest of her successors. Teresa was amazed to find in the young man an austerity which equalled her own, and long she put him to the test, without discovering any imperfection in him. But Dr. Baruzi, in an exhaustive examination of the documents, discovers in the attitude of St. Teresa to St. John of the Cross a slight element of hostility and even of fear. She speaks with a more cordial effusion of several other holy persons than she allows herself to do of St. John of the Cross, and yet none of them approached him in the qualities which she could appreciate better than any one else. This must always remain mysterious, especially as the correspondence of these two wonderful persons has not been preserved.

It was, however, in strict accordance with the ideas of St. Teresa that her young friend adopted the laws of her Reform, and, towards the close of 1568, in association with two other monks, founded a humble monastery at Duruelo. The rigour of their austerity was so excessive that Teresa, ever eminent for good sense, prevailed upon them to reduce it to what she called " a little agreeable suffering." Far less agreeable were the senseless persecutions which presently began to fall upon herself and her associates. The party of the Inquisition gained a malign influence over the dark and feeble character of Philip II., and their leaders in Madrid at last gathered courage to act. The Discalced Carmelites were denounced as apostates and threatened with excommunication. The Inquisition suppressed the writings of St. Teresa, of which every copy which could be found was destroyed, and on the night of December 3, 1577, armed men broke into the monastery, seized John of the Cross, and carried him, as "a malefactor," to a secret prison in Toledo, where he lay in great suffering until the following summer. The story of this persecution, of the mental misery of Teresa and the physical tortures of John of the Cross, are told in very great fullness by Dr. Baruzi, who has had access to all the secret records. We can but marvel at the strange, dark passion which tore the religious heart of Spain in the sixteenth century, and resulted in acts performed in the name of Christ which were even more stupid than they were savage.

We see in St. John of the Cross one of those rare natures in which suffering, physical and moral, instead of quenching genius, actually awakens and inflames it. The precious testimony of a witness, Mother Magdalena of the Holy Ghost, who visited him in the horrible prison where he was tortured, in Toledo, informs us that the greatest of all his poems, the astonishing "Night of the Soul," was composed in the midst of humiliations and pains which it makes the cheek burn to read of after three hundred years. St. John of the Cross bore his disgusting punishments " with patience and love," but, what is more wonderful, it was in those last months of isolation and misery in the prison of Toledo that his lyrical powers rose to their height.

How he escaped from his confinement, and how he found an asylum at Beas in the College of Baeza, must be read extensively in Dr. Baruzi's story. But it is very interesting that, at the moment of recovering physical calm, the lyrical fervour of St. John of the Cross appears to have abated. He set himself, not to write new poems, but to annotate the old ones. Later still, at Granada, in 1582, he gave final form to his imaginings, and it was here that he completed and polished the verses which, it is probable, he only composed and could not write down in prison, although the testimonies on this point are conflicting. Those images drawn from nature, which give an extraordinary charm to the lyrics of St. John of the Cross, were, in Dr. Baruzi's opinion, added at Granada. "Nous pouvons," he says, " le suivre goûtant la fraîcheur des eaux surabondantes, les jeux d'une lumière claire, le charme des neiges perpétuelles sous un ciel brûlant, les contrastes d'âpreté et de joie." It is pleasant to think so.

St. Teresa died on October 4, 1582, and with her something seemed to fade out of the life of St. John of the Cross. The Pope had decided in favour of the Carmelite Reform, and the frenzy of the local Inquisition had accordingly died down for the moment. Schemes of monastic administration occupied the mind of the poet, who wrote no more verse. His passion for solitude grew upon him, and something formidable daunted those who met him walking under the green oaks of the Sierra Morena. At last he was released " by a loving fever," to use his own strange expression, from the burden of life, on December 14, 1591, in the mountain village of Ubeda. He had survived the other great mystic poet of Spain, Luis de Leon, by four months. Their enemies were just combining for fresh attacks and persecutions.

Some of the poetry of St. John of the Cross was translated into English by Mr. David Lewis, but the best impression of it is that given by Mr. Arthur Symons. His versions are very fine, but perhaps it would need a blend of Christina Rossetti and Coventry Patmore to reproduce the melody, fire, and purity of these astonishing rhapsodies. St. John of the Cross was one of the most ethereal of transcendental dreamers. How extraordinary is the temper of theologians! The only thing Spanish ecclesiastics of the sixteenth century could think of doing with this wholly orthodox and harmless mystic was to lock him up in a privy and scourge him at intervals.

E

CARY'S EARLY FRENCH POETS

CARY'S EARLY FRENCH POETS

In recalling to light the forgotten volume of Cary's Early French Poets, Mr. T. Earle Welby has not said too much in praise of it, but has rather under-estimated its relative or historical importance. Taken as a plain introduction to the early, or Renaissance, poetry of France, Cary's chain of little prose chapters of biographical criticism, starred with graceful translations, is pleasant reading, but thin, occasionally inexact, and sometimes without penetration. That is to speak of it as though it were written to-day. But the importance of the work is its pioneer quality, which was much greater than even Mr. Welby seems inclined to recognise. The critic who first swims out into a new ocean, guided solely by his own genius of appreciation, deserves the most loyal support, and should be spared the censure which grows more and more easy to offer the more hackneyed becomes the treatment of his subject. We are not apt enough to give the credit of discovery to those who, in the face of universal detraction or ignorance, have insisted on proclaiming the unknown beauty.

This praise is pre-eminently deserved by Cary, who has been rewarded by it in a single direction. His famous translation of Dante, produced at a time when that poet was forgotten or detested, was slowly recognised as a masterpiece, and continues, though followed by such a cloud of parallel experiments, to be accepted as one of our minor classics. But this, though the only example remembered, was but one of Cary's feats in intelligent translation. The book Mr. Welby has reprinted for the first time is another. But its central significance lies in its date, which is more astonishing than Mr. Welby has realised. These essays were written, he says, " with very little French and no English guidance." Yes; but they were written in 1821, and therefore with no French guidance and in the face of violent English prejudice.

Henry Francis Cary was a contemporary of Byron and Shelley, as well as of Napoleon and other obstreperous public characters. But he resembled none of them. He was a mild, shy, impecunious, and almost painfully domestic clergyman, of whom it was justly said that, although, under strong provocation, he once wrote a very rude letter to the Lord Chancellor of the day, he was on every other occasion " adorned, more than most men, with the purest and most gentle virtues." He was Parson Adams, only more refined and less absurd. It seems a pity that he did not know Jane Austen, but I am afraid she might have made fun of him.

What distinguished him, however, in an age when the English clergy were almost instinctively scholars was his absorbing passion for poetry. All his life he was thirstily imbibing vast draughts of literature, foreign and home, ancient and modern. He kept a Literary Journal, which one of his sons printed after his death, and we find that the amount of what he read was Gargantuan. He " finishes " Porphyry, runs through Calderon, " resumes " Apollonius Rhodius, and " examines " Muratori all within a month. There is no pause; throughout his innocent life Cary never flagged; we watch him reading as he runs. Sir Philip Sidney, and Valerius Flaccus, and modern Italian tragedy, and Cicero, and Doctor Parr, all are jumbled together, and all are drained dry with the ecstasy of a wasp settled in a ripe peach. Cary beat his younger contemporary Macaulay in his sheer inexhaustible relish for the printed

Cary's Early French Poets

page. He only paused when he paraphrased what peculiarly delighted him, and in 1797 he very fortunately determined " to make the coming age his own " by translating into English verse the " Divina Commedia." This he finished in 1812, and the fortunes of that book make a very curious story, which, however, is not to be told here.

The ultimate and lasting success of the " Dante " led Cary to make other experiments in translation, among them a " Pindar " in the style of Gray. Some of these were faintly admired by his friends S. T. Coleridge and Charles Lamb, but they are forgotten now, except by Mr. Welby. Most completely forgotten of all are these essays on the Early French Poets, which nevertheless deserve and even demand resuscitation as a real curiosity of criticism. Their importance, as I must repeat, depends mainly on the date of their composition, since that of their belated publication, 1846, two years after Cary's death, is of no importance. They were written in the autumn or winter of 1821, and it is necessary to remind ourselves what the estimation of French poetry in England and that of early French poetry in France was at that date.

In the former country, the long Napoleonic wars had produced a spirit of exasperation against all French mentality, which may be compared with, but which greatly exceeded, what the late war brought forth here against German literature. Even Coleridge was disdainful, and we may search Hazlitt without finding a trace of sympathy with French imagination. Landor, who never said things by halves, declared that one third of the " Orlando Furioso," though disfigured by " a portion of extremely vile poetry," contained " more of good than the whole French language." De Quincey, who always writes of France like an angry maniac, said that French poetry marked " the lowest expression of senile? no, of *anile* imbecility." We see, then, what Cary had to fight against in 1821.

But the attitude of French criticism towards the poets in whom Cary showed so vivid an interest was even more curious. At the time of the Congress of Vienna, no doubt, poetical taste in France reached its lowest ebb. It was given up to the spirit of routine and imitation, to the superannuated conventions of a supposed classical tradition. Nothing earlier than Malherbe, nothing unrecognised by Boileau, was allowed to possess any merit. I wish Mr. Welby had pointed out how miraculously Cary was the pioneer in France as well as in England. I do not dwell on the fact, interesting enough in itself, that his investigations preceded by a single year the appearance of Hugo, Vigny, and the grand Cénacle generally, but I cannot refrain from observing that Cary reviewed Lamartine's first publication, the "Méditations Poétiques," immediately on the issue of that epoch-making little volume. His instinct was marvellous. But more to our present point is it to observe that the English clergyman recognised the beauty of the sixteenth century poets of France long before their greatest native prophet did so.

Here, again, dates are all-important. The beginning of a revival of taste in France was the famous and still invaluable " Tableau " of Sainte-Beuve. If we examine the facts closely we find that when, in August, 1826, that young writer for the *Globe* was tempted to compete for a prize offered by the French Academy on the History of French Language and Literature from the opening of the sixteenth century to 1610, he was still not merely ignorant of the subject, but, like all his countrymen, prejudiced against it. It is evident that such attention as was still paid to writers of the class of Marot and Ronsard was purely historical. Danou offered Sainte-Beuve " the benefit of his erudition," that is to say, the facts and the bibliography. Neither he nor anyone else had, in 1826, useful æsthetic advice to offer. But a shy English clergyman had possessed a shrewd intuition, entirely self-taught, since 1821.

By a tiresome accident, the Literary Journal of Cary, so very full where we do not need it, offers a gap here where we want it most. But, fortunately, we have a sufficient statement elsewhere from his own pen. In the chapter on Clement Marot, written late in 1821, he writes as follows :—

"In the course of this last summer I happened to reside for some weeks (from July 12 to September 25) in a place where I had free access to a large collection of books, which formerly belonged to the kings of France, but, like other Royal property, having been confiscated at the Revolution, still remains unreclaimed, and is now open to the use of the public."

This was the Library of Versailles, where we have to think of the English translator, straying, his own cicerone, from shelf to shelf, and "sampling" the quartos of sixteenth-century poetry which had not found a reader for two hundred years. In vain did Cary try to excite in his Parisian acquaintances any interest in these old poets; "the French of the present day," he complains, "set but little store on these revivers of the poetic art. Their extreme solicitude for what they call the purity of their language makes them easily offended by phrases the irregularities of which we should be ready to pardon in consideration of higher excellence." Cary was amazed at this barren fastidiousness of the French; and, with all European literature at his own fingers' ends, doubted whether "any other people have set up an exclusive standard of this sort." We may recall Keats' violent phrase about the "poor decrepid standard marked with most flimsey mottos, and, in large, the name of one Boileau."

From an examination of the original texts, without the slightest guidance from authority, it is not to be expected that the result could be final or implicitly correct. But there is no need to be unduly apologetic with regard to Cary's decisions. He brought from his English and Italian training a native sympathy with the irregularities of genius, and he treated these old French poets much as his friend Charles Lamb had treated the neglected Elizabethan and Jacobean worthies. His estimate of Ronsard is full and eminently sympathetic, although all Cary knew seems to have been taken from the contemporary life by Claude Binet, which, no doubt, he found with the other volumes on the neglected shelves at Versailles.

It was about this time that Keats gave several indications —he translated half of one of the " Cassandra " sonnets— of an interest in Ronsard. Keats was certainly an admirer and perhaps a friend of Cary. Is there here a link which has escaped his biographers? Cary, rather oddly, thought that Ronsard only " made himself ridiculous " by his devotion to Greek and Latin, and here he did not quite comprehend the noble poet's aim. But for Ronsard's gallant and picturesque sonnets and odes he was full of admiration. Here is Cary's version of Ronsard's famous greeting to Jean Antoine de Baïf :—

> Baïf, who second in our age to none,
>   Dost with free step to Virtue's summit mount,
>   While thou allay'st thine ardour at the fount
> Of Ascra, where the Muses met their son;
> An exile, I, where, sloping to the sun
>   Rich Sabut lifts his grape-empurpled mount,
>   Am fain to waste mine hours, and pensive count
> Loire's wandering waves as oceanward they run;
> And oft, to shun my cares, the haunt I change,
>   Now linger in some nook the stream beside,
>   Now seek a wild wood, now a cavern dim.
> But all avails not : wheresoe'er I range,
>   Love still attends, and ever at my side
>   Conversing with me walks, and I with him.

That Cary understood the Pléiade, and the earlier ingenious poets of the class of Marot, better than he did Villon and Pierre Gringoire is obvious, and Mr. Welby is even a little scandalised at his bewildered treatment of Villon. It is, indeed, a long cry from 1821 to the age of Rossetti and Swinburne. But Cary did not miss the ballade of the snows of yesteryear, though the "Testaments" not unnaturally puzzled him. His opinions are not always those which we hold to-day, but it is very remarkable with what an infallibility of instinct he pounces on what is still acknowledged to be best in some of the old authors. He read Amadis Jamyn, and instantly saw his most interesting lyric to be the "Ode sur la Chasse," just as in Joachim du Bellay he fell with almost uncanny promptitude on the "Vanneur de Blé aux Vents." If he did not see in this last all that Walter Pater saw in it sixty years later, small blame to him.

WYCHERLEY

WYCHERLEY

Justice is slowly being done to our classics of the end of the seventeenth century, and by no one more effectively than by Mr. Montague Summers. The record of this distinguished scholar is indeed already remarkable. We owe to him the first complete and accurate text of Buckingham, of Aphra Behn, and, still more important, of Congreve. But I am not sure that his latest effort, which lies before me in four quarto volumes, nobly produced by the Nonsuch Press, is not the most praiseworthy, as I think it must have been the most laborious of all.

The nineteenth century fought very shy of Wycherley, whose savage roughness alarmed all but the most dauntless critics, and the consequence was a timorous neglect of works which could not be despised, but were heartily disliked. Victorian criticism kept warily at a distance, as though Wycherley had been a tiger on a leash. The present generation, less squeamish than its predecessors, and with a kind of natural hankering after truculence, welcomes a Plain Dealer; and the recent successful performances of one of Wycherley's plays has proved that they are after all more witty than terrible. Let us not, however, fall into the opposite error, and deck out our beast of prey with bows of pink riband. Wycherley is a formidable figure, not very lovable, often not very supportable, a sort of Timon gnashing his teeth among the frolic poets; but he stands in front of them all in the matter of sheer strength, of resolute and unflinching realism.

It is characteristic that we know a good deal about

Wycherley, but almost all of it in the form of more or less violent anecdote. He came of an ancient and honourable family, long settled at Clive Hall, in Shropshire, where he was born in the winter of 1640. Mr. Summers, in his thorough way, gives an elaborate pedigree of the Wycherleys, which I must pass over, being interested only in the playwright. At the age of fifteen (according to Dennis, who was his friend) William was sent " for education to the western part of France, either to Saintonge or to the Angoumais." I take this to mean that he went first to La Rochelle and afterwards to Angoulême.

He was very handsome, as his portraits testify, and he was received into the best provincial society; more than that, he appears to have been the only Englishman ever admitted into what remained of the famous Hôtel de Rambouillet, where Mme. de Montausier still remembered the glorious days when all the best poets of France wove for her the Garland of Julie.

It is almost impossible that Wycherley failed to meet Des Réaux, tranquilly and secretly adding story by story to his " Historiettes," but if so the memoir-writer missed the chance of forging a link between French and English literature by preserving an impression of " le petit Huguenot." The five years of his youth which Wycherley spent in France exercised a powerful influence over his genius; he is the most French—with the France of the *ruelles galantes* of 1650—of all the English writers of the seventeenth century. To the effect of this early experience upon Wycherley's verse I will return in a moment.

The boy of fifteen left England a Protestant and became a Catholic in France, returning to the church of his native land when he came back as a man to England in 1659. Mr. Summers, who has a regrettable detestation of the Puritans, suggests that Wycherley felt " a little ridiculous " at being a Protestant in a Catholic country, and talks of the "dour ferocity" of the Huguenots. But Wycherley, in 1655, would not have been among Catholics at La Rochelle, where the leading families still belonged to the Reformed Religion. Moreover, there was no "dour ferocity" among the Protestants of France in 1650; they had become no less pleasure-loving and luxurious than their Catholic neighbours.

Mr. Summers should read the account of the annual Protestant conference at Charenton; there was no blight of the "Nonconformist conscience" over that lively ceremony. "De carrosse à carrosse, c'étaient lutte d'élégance et de pompe, conversations mondaines, rires et minauderies." The future author of "The Country Wife" would have resented nothing irksome in the "fastueux" Sundays of the Protestants of Saintonge. But when he moved to Angoulême he would find himself in a Catholic atmosphere of very much the same frivolity and intrigue, wit and parade. Through his whole life Wycherley shows no interest at all in religion; he is profoundly irreligious. He would suffer no inconvenience among Protestants in La Rochelle, none among Catholics at Angoulême, none in the Established Church in England. He was an intellectual Vicar of Bray, and cared for none of those things.

According to Anthony à Wood, Wycherley became a fellow commoner of Queen's College, Oxford, in July, 1660, but "departed" without any further observation of university statutes. We are further told that he "became a sojourner in Oxon for the sake of the Public Library," but also that he might be "reconciled" by Dr. Barlow to the Protestant religion. This vague remark provokes an astonishing tirade from Mr. Summers, who says that Wycherley "evidently" quitted Oxford in some disgust. I see no "evidence" of this, but Mr. Summers is betrayed by it into half a page of the most unmeasured invective against poor Dr. Barlow, whom he actually calls a

F

"thoroughly despicable and unworthy character." Barlow was librarian of the Bodleian, though Mr. Summers does not say so, and he was admittedly "an universal lover and favourer of learned men of what country or denomination soever." He was a strong Calvinist, indeed, and not a very courageous politician, and he was crazy about Popery, but Mr. Summers's abuse of him seems uncalled for.

I hope Mr. Summers will forgive me if I say that his violent prejudice against Puritanism is a defect which I should be glad to see excised from his writings. I am no lover of Puritanism myself, but to drag in attacks upon it on every possible (or impossible) occasion savours of a lack of historical philosophy. It marred, to my mind, Mr. Summers's notes on Congreve. It is still more disagreeably prominent in his treatment of Wycherley. What is the sense of railing against "red-hot ranters" in an essay on "The Country Wife"? Mr. Summers must know that we should be in even worse case to-day than we are had the Puritans never made their protest in favour of morals and piety.

Let us turn, however, to what is really important, the dramatic work which Mr. Summers has so ably edited. In his extreme old age Wycherley made a "confident and complaisant remark" to Pope, which Mr. Summers closely examines, but the importance of which I think he hardly realises. The dramatist told his youthful friend that he had written his four comedies at a very early age; he even stated the exact date of each. He said that "Love in a Wood," produced in 1672, had been composed in 1659, "The Gentleman Dancing-Master" (1673) in 1661, "The Plain Dealer" (1677) in 1663, and "The Country Wife" (1675) in 1665. Mr. Summers has no difficulty in showing that each of these plays contains references to an event later than the date which Pope reports. (But these may have been, surely, interpolated just before the perform-

Wycherley 67

ance?) What gives gravity to the pretension is that if we admit it we have to give Wycherley a claim to precedence in the history of comedy which he cannot otherwise deserve. In England it puts him before Etherege and before Dryden, both of whom, by the ordinary chronology, he follows.

But what is more serious is that it puts him on an exact level with Molière. Are we to believe that "Love in a Wood" was antecedent to the whole series of comedies, starting in 1659 with "Les Précieuses Ridicules"? The suggestion is absurd, unless we are prepared to acknowledge in Wycherley one of the supreme dramatic artists of the world. With all admiration of his gifts, this is impossible. My own theory is that Wycherley did make the claim which Mr. Summers doubts, and that he made it from vanity, vexed at its being so freely said that he followed Molière. Further back than 1659 he did not dare to go, but that was enough to support an entire independence of the influence of Molière. If he were in the west of France in 1658, it seems more than possible that Wycherley may have witnessed one or more of the performances given by Molière's troupe of actors while they wandered over France before settling at the Palais Royal. A very small spark would be enough to set fire to a theatrical faculty so inflammable as Wycherley's. But that, somehow, his talent was started by Molière's genius must be believed, Pope or no Pope.

It is comparatively little known that, besides his four famous comedies in prose, Wycherley wrote a vast amount of miscellaneous verse. This was not admired, even in his lifetime, and has never till now been reprinted. Mr. Summers has shown courage in editing it all, because he wished his edition to be complete, as an editor should. But from another point of view Wycherley's poems are welcome to the student. It is true that he lacked the poet's art, but, as was said of Oldham (but not with Oldham's excuse), "through the harsh cadence of a rugged line"

Wycherley constantly reveals the bias of his genius and that robust anger which made him the executioner of the fops and fine ladies. The prose preface to the collection of 1704, addressed to that " Malicious, Envious, Captious Coxcomb, O Damned, Damning Reader," is an amazing revelation of the author's temper.

No one, not Swift at his fiercest, railed upon his public as Wycherley did. The very titles of his poems suggest sketches for new " Plain Dealers " and still more reckless " Country Wives." Here are examples taken at random : " To a Sickly, Peevish yet Ambitious, Vain Malcontent " ; " To an Affected, Proud Jilt " ; " To a Lewd Woman of Affected Modesty " ; " To a Conceited Mistress." The poems are all of this order, brutal invectives in rough, galloping verse, mostly heroic ; they all reveal that scornful revulsion against society, as of one who had drained it to the lees and found them bitter, which makes Wycherley so unique in our dramatic world.

The reader, and no doubt the spectator, of Wycherley's plays must experience an uneasy feeling that he is not witnessing a scene of life which actually existed, except within a very restricted circle, in the England of 1670. Etherege gives us the genuine aspect of " high life," and Shadwell the shadow of low life, but Wycherley seems to move in a foreign atmosphere. The social manners he describes are much more those of Paris as he left it than of London as he found it. In the salon of Julie de Montausier he must have met the " peevish captious wits " and " handsome young women, who lov'd play, and sitting up at cards a nights." He gave them British names, and put rude, daring English speech into their mouths, but they were French in essence. Therefore, when he came to write his " Plain Dealer " he was tempted to give his own observation and hardihood the very colour of Molière's " Misanthrope."

Perhaps " The Country Wife " is the better play, as it is certainly the more English of the two, and the more humane, the less absolutely brutal. But for that very reason it is not so characteristic as " The Plain Dealer," where this playwright seems to roar with satiric passion. And we come back to France and to the " Miscellany Poems," where the accent is not so much that of the London of Charles II. as of the academic *ruelles* of Paris, with their inveterate pursuit of female frailty, their cruel wit, sparing neither friend nor foe, their total absence of sentimentality, their sophisticated " critiques " of everything in heaven and hell. Mr. Summers has recovered a lost mock-epic of " Hero and Leander," evidently belonging to Wycherley's youth. It is a rather horrible burlesque in the manner of Scarron, and would have been appreciated at the Hôtel de Rambouillet.

These rambling remarks must, however, be brought to a close; there is meat enough on the raw bones of Wycherley to load many a critical table. His expressed ideal was " The World Unmask'd," and he did his business so roughly that the sufferer stopped up both her ears. As his highly respectable contemporary, John Evelyn, wrote :—

> As long as Men are false and Women vain,
> Whilst Gold continues to be Virtue's Bane,
> In pointed Satire *Wycherley* shall reign.

He was not long on the throne, however, before he was exiled by a revolution of sentiment. There is talk of a restoration now, and it will be forwarded by Mr. Summers's labour. The conspiracy of neglect is over, and the savage playwright can at last be read in his entirety by all who can endure his snarl and his hot breath.

THE SIN OF WITCHCRAFT

THE SIN OF WITCHCRAFT

THE Witch of Endor has much to answer for. It would be rash to conjecture how many hundreds of poor women and afflicted children were tortured, drowned, hanged, and burned in the sixteenth and seventeenth centuries because Saul's Pythoness, as she was called, lifted the spirit of Samuel out of her mysterious recesses. The victory of Protestantism in England seems to have given impetus to the superstition, though I can think of no reason why it should do so. The great bishop of Salisbury, John Jewel, at the very close of his life, preached a sermon before Queen Elizabeth, in which he passionately warned her of the terrible spread of witchcraft in her dominions. He made a fervent appeal to her to stem this tide of wickedness, in which, he declared, " Your Grace's subjects pine away even unto the death, their colour fadeth, their flesh rotteth, their speech is benumbed, their senses are bereft."

The Queen was alarmed; she appointed a Commission, and the trials of witches began to be frequent and cruelly vindictive. The panic culminated in 1582 with the horrible execution of seventeen women from the village of St. Osyth, in Essex. It became extremely dangerous for anyone to cast doubt on the legality of such sentences, or to suggest that the phenomena were due to natural causes. But the excess of agitation and the perversion of justice were so marked that they began to produce a certain reaction in some just minds, and particularly in that of Reginald Scot, who published in 1584 a book which showed remarkable courage and not less remarkable humanity, his famous " Discoverie of Witchcraft."

It was not to be supposed that a man writing in England in 1584 would deny the existence of witches or would minimise their crimes. To have done so would not only have exposed himself to condign punishment, but would have been totally ineffective. Sober and instructed persons of every class were as certain that the Devil employed great numbers of old women to carry out his obscure and malignant designs, and that the malignity of these unhappy crones could only be checked by their being killed, as that the sun would set. Even so tolerant a man as Burton of " The Anatomy of Melancholy " was convinced that there were " white witches " in every Oxfordshire village.

Reginald Scot very clearly believed nothing of the kind, but he was careful not to say so. He tacitly acknowledged that, of course, there were witches, horrible creatures enough; but that in the great majority of cases brought before the magistrates it was the informers, " witch-mongers," as he calls them, who by their " lewd, un-Christian practices " extorted confessions from innocent people by inhuman terrors and tortures. There were some wicked witches, of course, but practically the wretches who were everywhere being dragged before the courts were perfectly harmless people, mainly of incomplete mentality, who surrendered their feeble intelligence and dim conscience to the thunders of their accusers. To dare to suggest so much as this was an act of signal moral courage, and Reginald Scot's book, besides being a compendium of extraordinary stories, was a lantern of humanity in a dark age. He had little of Montaigne's skill in writing, but he had much of his philosophical curiosity and temperance. From the moment when his " Discoverie " was published, although the horrors of witch-baiting did not cease for another century, it grew more and more possible to search for

The Sin of Witchcraft

a physical rather than a supernatural basis for the phenomena.

Elizabeth, who had acquiesced in the persecution of witches, was followed in 1603 by James VI. of Scotland, who had taken up, from his youth onward, a much more positive attitude. James differed in this matter from his predecessor. He had long been of opinion that a king should guide the intellectual life of his subjects, should be " the best clerk in his own country," and his literary productions show, almost pathetically, how confident he was of his power to carry out his duty in this respect. He read the treatise of Reginald Scot with horror, and was not deceived by it. He saw plainly enough that Scot, whatever he might say, maintained " the old error of the Sadducees, in denying of spirits." It therefore devolved upon the most pedantic, and one of the most learned, of monarchs to refute this sad heresy, and to show by a display of evidence that the powers of the Devil are infinite and are abundantly exercised by humble sorceresses in every Scottish hamlet.

As befitted one in so elevated a social station, King James sought to avoid the prolixity of the clergy, and the formality of the lawyers. His book, that it might be " more pleasant and facile," should be brief, lively, and as graceful as the monarch's limited gift of style permitted. It should be cast in the form of a dialogue, divided into three books, and while speaking with grave authority, it should aim at entertainment. The reader who takes in hand Mr. John Lane's very pretty reprint of the " Dæmonologie " should not compare it with modern treatises, but with the ponderous and stilted periods of the contemporary theologians. He will then admit that James I. is here doing his best to be bright. Moreover, he is carefully composing in English, and not in that crabbed Scottish vernacular which he sometimes affected. Certain passages, and in particular that in the Second Book, which describes the mode in which necromancers are transferred through the air from place to place, are vivacious beyond the wont of English prose in that day. But the whole thing is a nightmare, and so was the universal strong delusion.

The " News from Scotland," which completes this little volume, does not seem to be written by the Royal pen, but was composed with the full cognisance and probably published at the command of James VI. The " Dæmonologie " is a theoretical treatise, a sort of scientific summary of the principles of necromancy; the " News " is a report of proceedings taken, in the King's presence, against certain definite witches arrested in Scotland, and in particular of a very bad wizard, John Cunningham, whose name in sorcery was Fian. The whole thing began with the adventures of a certain Geillis Duncan, maid-servant to David Seaton, the bailiff of Tranent, who, finding that Geillis stayed out of the house every other night, promptly concluded that she must be a witch, and, in order better to try and find out the truth of the same, he did, " with the help of others, torment her with the torture of the Pilliwinckes upon her fingers." She would confess nothing, but the mark of the Devil was found in her " fore crag," the front of her throat. That was quite enough, and Geillis was thrown into prison, where she accused " innumerable others " of being notorious witches.

King James VI. now became interested, and sent for Geillis, who confessed that she had a small drum, on which, when she tattoed, everybody was obliged to follow her, like the Pied Piper of Hamelin. The King ordered her to perform on her drum, and to dance, and he took " great delight to be present " at this exhibition. But of all the persons accused by Geillis, the most deplorable was Agnis Tompson, who confessed so much and so glibly, that the King, credulous as he was, grew suspicious, and even told her that she was an " extreme liar." This piqued Agnis Tompson, who thereupon, " taking his Majesty a little aside, declared unto him the very words which passed between the King's Majesty and the Queen at Upsle in Norway the first night of their marriage, with their answer each to other." That produced a great impression on King James, who " swore by the living God that all the devils in Hell could not have discovered the same." Encouraged by her success, Agnis proceeded to invent the most ridiculous and unseemly chain of " confessions " that could be imagined. James believed every word of it, and gave thanks to Providence for having preserved him, on his return voyage out of Denmark, from the magic cat and the black toad and all the rest of the horrors.

Among those whom Agnis Tompson accused was one man of a superior order, against whom she had some grudge. This was the " Doctor Fian " already mentioned. He was the Master of the school in Saltpans, and at first he indignantly denied all complicity with the Tranent witches. But Agnis piled up her voluble accusations, and, to make sure of extracting the truth, Fian's head was " thrawed " with a rope, and he was put to the torture of the boot. Being made speechless by his sufferings, he was unable to use his voice, but the other witches, intensely zealous, advised the Court to look under his tongue, and there, sure enough, one of the Devil's charmed pins was found. That was quite enough, and in his dazed condition the poor wretch signed, in the King's presence, a " confession " of the most preposterous and immodest kind, which seems to me to bear upon it the stamp of Agnis Tompson's disordered imagination.

Having recovered a little from his tortures—the boot was not taken off him till he signed the confession—Doctor Fian promptly withdrew his statement. He was evidently in perfect ignorance of the pranks of his accusers. The

King was very much displeased at his obstinacy, and Doctor Fian was tortured again in a variety of horrible ways, the Devil supporting him through all " these grievous pains and cruel torments." Still he would confess nothing, and he was bustled into a cart, taken to the Castle Hill of Edinburgh, strangled, and then burned, " on a Saturday in the end of January last year, 1591." Agnis Tompson, of whom a portrait is given—an old woman on her knees, gesticulating, and swaying her fat body to and fro—was put in prison till His Majesty's pleasure. An edifying tale!

It has been conjectured that the Weird Sisters were introduced into " Macbeth " to which their incantations give its sinister tone, as a compliment to the newly-arrived King James, whose interest in witches was so notorious. But if the author of " Dæmonologie " saw the curtain rise on the " foul anomalies " dancing round the thunder-blasted heath, he would hardly recognise in them the vulgar objects of his suspicion. There is something majestic, something paradoxically noble, about Shakespeare's norns. They have little in common with the wretched old women over whose confessions and accusations His Majesty gloated and shuddered.

And there comes the great question in the midst of it: What did Shakespeare really think of the commotion which agitated the minds of those around him? He must have known all about the typical case of the three witches of Warboise, who were arraigned, convicted, and executed at the Huntingdon Assizes in 1593 for bewitching the five daughters of Mr. Robert Throckmorton. This trial thrilled the whole of English society; " the like," it was said, " hath not been heard of in this age." The Throckmorton children had epileptic fits, and they were nursed by a faithful old servant, who was devoted to them and was prepared to lose her " best blood to do them service." The children were

The Sin of Witchcraft

spiteful and naughty; wishing to get rid of their nurse, they said that she put toads and cats and devils into them. There was no real evidence, but the Throckmorton family, supported by a neighbour, Lady Cromwell, went into violent hysterics. Lady Cromwell died mysteriously. The Bishop of Lincoln was called in and was convinced that the Devil was at work.

Suddenly the old nurse, who had stoutly denied all the charges, collapsed and confessed her guilt in every senseless particular. " She was vapoured to that degree that they thought the Devil was in her." He was not; he was in the inconceivable gentry and clergy and lawyers who drove her into lunacy. The full report of this peculiarly monstrous case was scattered broadcast over England. One would like to know what Shakespeare thought of it; what King James VI. thought is a matter of indifference to anyone who reads the " Dæmonologie."

How slowly this public madness died is shown by no more dismal record than that of the trial of the witches of Bury St. Edmunds before Sir Matthew Hale in 1664. Here all the old sordid nonsense about toads and pins and taps and touches was brought forward, and no less a person than that great and wise physician, Sir Thomas Browne, came from Norwich solemnly to assert that the Devil had worked by his subtlety to urge on Amy Duny and Rose Cullender, who were duly hanged protesting their innocence. But the end of this craze was in sight. Bishop Francis Hutchinson, when incumbent of St. James', Bury St. Edmunds, had special opportunity for examining the evidence of what had passed there in his childhood, and, after a lifetime of consideration and comparison, he dared to publish his noble and courageous " Historical Essay Concerning Witchcraft, with Observations upon Matters of Fact," a volume which I should like to see reprinted. This, from a great divine, who was also a royal chaplain, produced a wide effect, and the horror subsided. But the credulity and cruelty of the witch-trials have thrown a blot on the whole of the seventeenth century in England, and we can only marvel at the indifference with which the great poets and philosophers of that age turned away their eyes from the shame of " all that lymphatical chimæra."

AN APOLOGIST FOR ARCADIA

AN APOLOGIST FOR ARCADIA

VAGUELY I seem to remember that some eminent Victorian clergyman burst into tears on learning that the possible number of musical airs is strictly limited. He wept to think that the time must come when nobody will ever find occasion to whistle a new tune. Mr. Ernest Newman would be able to give me the reference. And then there is the perennial shudder that results from being reminded that the coalfields of the world are exhaustible. But an alarm which comes more closely home to me than either of these is founded on the shrinkage of possible sources of literary criticism. What will the scholars and historians of fifty years hence find to do? Further and further excursions into the remote and the obscure threaten to deprive critical posterity of employment. What dole will be devised in 1973 for literary antiquaries anxious to work and yet incapable of finding a job?

These melancholy reflections are the result of reading Professor John G. Robertson's learned, exhaustive, and original study of the Italian sources of Romanticism. It sweeps in a new and interesting but extremely remote province of critical study, and dazzles us with a profusion of names, works, and controversies few of which any of us ever heard before. In future we have to pretend that we are familiar with Gravina and Crescimbeni, although in fact we may never until now have heard their melodious names. The ordinary histories of Italian literature do not so much as mention most of the protégés of Professor Robertson, with the exception of Vico, to whom ignorance clings as to a sheet-anchor. But what is this to the burden which will be put on the memory of students when our great-grandchildren are driven to write large books on Tibetan philosophy and the drama of Senegambia, because everything nearer home has been exhausted?

The central fact in modern literary history is that during the eighteenth century in every country of Europe Reason as the guiding principle in poetry was dethroned in favour of Imagination. What scholars continue to wrangle about is the date of this change, which can be shifted in England from Addison to Wordsworth and back again. But before the Age of Reason set in there flourished in the seventeenth century a curious heresy called Euphuism or Gongorism or Marinism, according to the country in which it flourished; this affected the literature of France and the feebler poetry of Holland and Germany and Portugal. In fact, it was universal, and we suffered from it here, not merely in such writers as Lyly, but later in Cowley and Crashaw. The youthful Dryden had a severe attack of it, but recovered. It had its merits, which are too often overlooked, but it was responsible for outbreaks of almost inconceivable bad taste. Everywhere in Europe there followed a revival of discipline which took the form of a rigorous adherence to rules derived from what was believed to be the doctrine of Aristotle.

By general consent the school of conceit and extravagance gave way before what was called " classic " taste, the nature of which was laid down by Boileau and Rapin in France and by Pope and his friends in England. The result of this was the adoption of an artificial but pure and logical manner of writing, almost unadorned except by the intellect, a style everywhere in favour during the eighteenth century. But running underneath this classic tendency, and more and more forcing itself to the surface, was the imaginative or, as it came to be called, romantic style, with which we are all

An Apologist for Arcadia

familiar. It has been customary to seek for the earliest manifestations of this style in the English literature of the age of Queen Anne. Professor Robertson, as the result of years of laborious investigation, proposes to transfer the credit, so far as we can call it creditable, to a set of forgotten Italian writers of the end of the seventeenth century.

Contrary to the usual view, in which England and France are seen interacting on one another in the struggle against neo-classicism, while other countries, such as Spain and Italy, are regarded as for the moment negligible or merely imitative, Professor Robertson claims the leading rôle for the Italian critics. In all discussion of this kind a difficulty arises from the incessant overlapping of movements in irregular ebb and flow. The great instance of this is the famous " Quarrel of the Ancients and the Moderns," which excited the whole of intelligent Europe at the end of the seventeenth century, and is supposed to have changed the face of literary history. The more closely we examine this great controversy, the more bewildered we are by the antiquity of the Moderns and the modernity of the Ancients. We perceive a certain trend of ideas, but when we descend to concrete examples we are lost. Racine is the very type of the poetry of reason, yet who is inspired by a more passionate imagination?

This difficulty besets the argument of Mr. Robertson, although he strives to persuade himself that it does not exist. Anything like a mathematical exactitude is impossible, and would only distress our vision if we could attain to it. Mr. Robertson's learned and persuasive disquisition cannot be held, even by a tyro in the subject, to give an exact, that is to say, a full, account of the trend of Italian taste at the close of the seventeenth century. It omits—it was bound to omit—too much to represent fairly Italian poetic art at that time. For instance, Redi is but briefly referred to, and Filicaja is not even, so far as I can discover, mentioned. But what is the poetry of Italy between 1675 and 1700 if the *canzoni* of Filicaja are ignored? Professor Robertson will say that they did not come within the frame of his picture. Very good, but then we must recognise the limitations within which he has confined himself.

This difficulty obliges the Professor to lapse into a certain injustice with regard to branches of investigation outside his scope. For example, I think he must be held to repeat too loosely the old charges against Marini. I went into this question last year in treating the essay of Professor Grierson, and need not amplify it here. When our author talks of " the affectation of the Pléiade," again, he begs a question which I do not grant. He makes much of the " devitalisation " of poetry, but Corneille was not " devitalised," nor Dryden, nor Filicaja. Their vitality was drawn into a different channel. I beg pardon for these carping remarks, which are not intended to hint depreciation of Mr. Robertson's work, but to sweep away obstacles to our complete enjoyment of it. The opening chapter on the controversy with the French critics which led to the creation of the Arcadian Academy is not the most convincing in the book, because the author is trammelled by the thousand and one threads of conflicting opinion which beset his footsteps. The best way to study his treatise is to grant him his premises, and to admit without further discussion that he is justified in announcing as a " discovery " that the credit of evolving a romantic type of æsthetic is due to certain Italians.

From the end of this first chapter the book is made up, to within a hundred pages of the close, of short monographs on the leaders of this Italian movement. There are seven of them, and they and their views are analysed in seven consecutive chapters. This is the body of the book, and its most valuable, because most original, contribution to knowledge. I wish—but that no doubt is idle weakness—that Professor Robertson could have brought himself to tell us more about the life and habits of these critics. I should find it a relief to turn from their Aristotelianism to their tricks and their manners. I am sure they did not all flourish under the sceptre of Pulchinello for nothing. But we must contemplate without frivolity their speculations as to the abstract conception of beauty.

The Arcadian Academy was founded in 1690. It was formed under the patronage of Queen Christina of Sweden, and its explicit purpose was to " renew the sweet studies and innocent customs which the ancient Arcadians cultivated." At a picnic party in the Prati di Castello, one of the most exquisite retreats which Rome offered to her lovers, verses were being recited, when one of the party cried out, " Behold! Arcadia reborn amongst us!" Thereupon, in the midst of infinite enthusiasm, fourteen " shepherds " founded an Academy; it was established in the gardens of the Franciscans on Monte Gianicoli; Crescimbeni was elected president and Gravina drew up the rules, the latter a brilliant lawyer, the former a heavy but well-informed historian of literature. Of Crescimbeni the professor has not much to say, but Gravina is the subject of a particularly interesting chapter. He is endeared to Professor Robertson by the fact that he repudiated the claims of France to lay down the law as to beauty and majesty and dramatic propriety :—

" Gravina was the first thinker in Europe to proclaim in unmistakable terms that " back to the Greeks " doctrine which was to provide the watchword for the later classical æsthetics of the eighteenth century; the first to repudiate the false Aristotelianism which had substituted the letter of Aristotle for the spirit; he was also the first to employ consciously and deliberately Descartes's critical scepticism as a basis for literary æsthetics."

It is plain that Gravina's is a figure well worthy to be drawn out of obscurity. He was, Professor Robertson firmly indicates, the most gifted of all the Arcadian group whose views on æsthetic occupy this volume. Gian Vincenzo Gravina was born in 1664 at a small town in Calabria; this was Rogiano, officially rebaptised Rogiano-Gravina in his honour on the second centenary of his birth. Here is a case of a prophet who has found honour in his own country; but Italians are so graceful! I am afraid it will be long before Maidstone is officially called Maidstone-Hazlitt, or Ottery-Saint-Mary Ottery-Coleridge. Gravina proceeded to Naples to study jurisprudence, which at first " repelled " him; he conquered this nausea and became one of the leading lawyers of Europe. Though law was his wife, literature was his business, and he began to appeal against the degenerate taste of his day, egged on to protest (it would seem) by the eccentric and flashing Queen of Sweden.

The new views were first put forward in a *ragionamento* on a pastoral play, the " Endimione "; Professor Robertson might have noted as a coincidence that the rules of the school of Marinists were also first advanced in a treatise on a single work, in Chapelain's dreary analysis of the " Adone." In 1712 Gravina, who had hitherto appeared solely as a critic, challenged the animadversions of his enemies, who inhabited " a veritable wasps' nest," by publishing five tragedies. Professor Robertson has nothing good to say of these, although Gravina himself admired them very much. He returned to criticism, and discovered a genius, Metastasio. This is the account the Professor gives of this incident :—

" Gravina happened to be passing through the Piazza di San Silvestro in Rome, and was attracted by a crowd of

An Apologist for Arcadia

people near a goldsmith's shop; they were listening to a little boy of twelve, who was improvising verses with the most extraordinary glibness. Gravina was much struck by his gifts, and offered him money, which was indignantly refused. But Gravina was not to be baulked; he found that the boy was the son of Felice Trapassi, druggist and macaroni-seller in the Via dei Cappellari, and returned a few days later with the offer to educate him. He wanted to make an orator and jurist of him, not, as his peculiar talent suggested, a poet. Thus Bonaventura Trapassi, who was later to be known to the world as Pietro Metastasio, became Gravina's adopted son."

This is like the story of how Matthew Prior was found by Lord Dorset reading Horace behind the bar of a tavern in Westminster. Gravina did not live to enjoy the fame of his protégé, for he died in the arms of Metastasio on the 6th of January, 1718.

Perhaps the most interesting of Professor Robertson's chapters is that devoted to Antonio Conti, because of that critic's relations with England, where he paid long visits on several occasions. Conti is the source of the wonderful word " Sasper," by which he introduced Shakespeare to his countrymen. Although he studied the English poets and translated them abundantly, he seems to have been incapable of spelling English words. He called Dryden " Draide," and Kensington " Chinsington." He never got any nearer to Shakespeare than " Sasper," which form, oddly enough, was adopted by other Italian writers, and even by the German Bodmer. Yet Conti was the friend of Sir Isaac Newton and a Fellow of the Royal Society, although we are told that he only talked French in London. He seems to have been acquainted with the Duke of Buckinghamshire, whom Professor Robertson calls the Duke of Buckingham, thus seeming to confuse him with the author of "The Rehearsal." The Duke of Buckinghamshire, who was a prolific writer in prose and verse, is a terror to cataloguers, since, being originally Sheffield, he rose to his dukedom through an earldom of Mulgrave and a marquisate of Normanby, and wrote under all those titles in succession. The Duke's two surviving plays are tragedies of "Julius Cæsar" and "Marcus Brutus," in which he did not exactly (as Professor Robertson, following Conti, says) revise the masterpiece of "Sasper," but wrote a couple of short tragedies on the same subject in neo-classic style. I think it likely that Conti was told by the Duke that "Sasper" was, although barbarous, a poet of considerable merit, and the Italian may have read the Duke's prologue, in which he says :—

> Hope to mend Shakespeare? or to match his style?
> 'Tis such a jest, would make a Stoic smile!
> Too fond of fame, our Poet soars too high,
> Yet freely owns he wants the wings to fly,
> So sensible of his presumptuous thought.

Conti was probably less sensible, and doubtless considered the Duke of Buckinghamshire (who was no fool) a better poet than "Sasper." At all events, when he returned to Italy, Conti produced two tragedies, a "Cæsar" and a "Brutus." These I suspect were translations or paraphrases of the Duke's plays, and bore but slight relation to "Sasper." But how are we to find out, since no one but Professor Robertson has read Conti's tragedies, and since I suspect that he has not examined those of the Duke, which, however, are not contemptible?

THE PORTRAIT OF ZÉLIDE

THE PORTRAIT OF ZÉLIDE

THROUGH the welter of those uncalled-for " Reminiscences " and lumbering " Lives," which are the plague of our time, three or four young writers have lately distinguished themselves by producing historicobiographical studies, carefully conceived and gracefully executed. In the plunging mass of books, their volumes stand out small and bright and succinct. It has been a pleasure to me to welcome these particular authors on successive occasions, and I hope to welcome them again. I need not repeat their names, but it is gratifying to add to the little group that of Mr. Geoffrey Scott, which was unknown to me until I opened the title-page of " The Portrait of Zélide." He also testifies, by the delicacy of his irony, by the moderation of his range, by his refinement and reserve, against the wallowing monsters of the hour. He adds to the presumption that English prose, although so dreadfully given over to shapelessness and noise, is " not quite enslaved, nor wholly vile," but, like Albion, may yet recover dignity. If this is Mr. Scott's earliest publication, he is to be congratulated on the ripeness of his judgment, but whether it is or no, he cannot fail, in the future, to find us curious to watch his progress.

The subject which Mr. Scott has chosen is one which lends itself to the ironic method. He essays to paint the portrait of a woman who is often mentioned in the records of her time, but has seldom been expatiated on; a feminine link stretched through the eighteenth and nineteenth centuries, but between two sections of them, so incongruous that her individuality has been snapped by the strain. She unites Boswell and Frederick of Prussia with Madame de Staël and the Directory. But pre-eminently she is part of the life of Benjamin Constant, yet a part which has hitherto been slurred over by his biographers. Hitherto, whatever attention has been given to Zélide has been subsidiary, she has depended for attention on her companion of the moment. Mr. Geoffrey Scott detaches her and places her in the front line of the scene. She becomes in his hands an individual and not an attribute.

It is true that a local Swiss historian, M. Philippe Godet, published twenty years ago a " massive " work on her and her friends; when he did this, he had already spent twenty years in collating the records which are preserved at Neuchâtel. Mr. Scott loyally expresses his debt to M. Godet, whose volumes (of which I confess that, though much interested in Benjamin Constant, I never before heard), are " of primarily local interest " and " very difficult to obtain." They may be treated, therefore, less as a biography than as a mine of material, from which Mr. Scott has dug his ore and refined it. Let us not pretend to have read M. Godet, or to wish to read him.

The " portrait " by Mr. Scott is, of course, a literary one, but he illustrates it by two artistic records of remarkable excellence. Zélide was fortunate enough to be drawn by La Tour and modelled by Houdon. The pastel represents her at the age of 26, and the bust at that of 31. It is natural to study these works of art before we read about the adventures of the lady. They are evidently admirable likenesses, and they present a face which, *pace* Mr. Scott and Zélide herself, I find typically Dutch. Isabella van Sersoskerken van Tuyll was, indeed, as Batavian by birth, in 1740, as it was possible to be, and though she disliked her own country and repudiated her own language for French, she retained, I think (Mr. Scott does not?), a strong tincture of

The Portrait of Zélide 95

Holland to the last. There is a sanguine and vivacious type of Dutchwoman, and she was an example of it. She belonged to one of the oldest Dutch families, and her childhood was divided between a moated castle at Zuylen and a gloomy house in Utrecht.

Perhaps Mr. Scott a little exaggerates the oppression of Zélide's childhood. The characters in the great classical novel of the eighteenth century, " Sara Burgerhart," were exactly her contemporaries, and lived a similar life without recrimination. (By the way, the first French translation of " Sara Burgerhart " was made by " Madame de St. Hyacinthe de Charrière born Van Tuyll van Sersoskerken." Who was this? I do not find that Mr. Scott throws any light on the question, but it would be amusing to trace a connection [1] between our Zélide and the two illustrious ladies who wrote, with the customary eye on Richardson, the best Dutch novel of the century.) Part of Zélide's restlessness, no doubt, came not from any restraint in her condition, but from her growing up just at the moment when the influence of French prose was invading and revolutionising social thought in Holland.

What indefatigable letter-writers there were a century and a-half ago ! Mr. Scott would have no tale to tell, no theory to expose, if his heroine and her platonic lovers had not indulged from the schoolroom to the grave in an orgy of correspondence. They all wrote daily, and often nightly, accounts of their own feelings, hopes, sentiments, aspirations, and intensities. Benjamin Constant tells Zélide that she has in his letters a true image of his mind, so that she may see " how everything alternates, meets, and mingles " in that mirrored repository of his soul. And what can Zélide do better than to return the compliment by giving him a

[1] It appears that this connection is certain. Zélide was the translator of " Sara Burgerhart," and I may boast of having made this minute discovery, which was not known to Mr. Geoffrey Scott, or even to M. Godet.

diagnosis of her own sensibility? They both wrote extremely well; they had carried the art of self-analysis to a state of perfection; and with a remarkable provision of wit they were singularly deprived of a sense of humour. The consequence was that they stored up for the curiosity of future students a sort of museum, in which dead feelings are preserved for ever in an atmosphere of camphor and dust.

These butterflies shine in Mr. Scott's cabinet with their bright wings expanded, and the pins are still running through them with which they stuck one another to the cardboard. The state of things is unparalleled. In the hush that preceded the Revolution, we seem to hear nothing but the goosequill-nib hurrying over sheets upon sheets of scented notepaper. The result does not appeal to everyone, but in the hands of a skilful annotator the portraiture it produces is fascinating.

The earliest of Zélide's frustrated lovers said that she could " warm the heart of a Laplander." The phrase goes to the core of the problem, since it introduces at the same time brilliance and chill, an Arctic brightness illusive and unstable, light without heat. Zélide was precociously learned and obstinately intellectual. From the time when, at 13, she is " determined to master Newton," to her old age when she worries her peasant maid into a study of Locke on " Human Understanding," her brain is never at rest. Mr. Scott thinks that she plunged into conic sections to drown the memory of her human disappointments, but it may just as well be argued that it was her mathematics which ruined her love affairs. She suffered from her own clairvoyance, and yet was desperately foolish; the source of her misfortunes was her exaggerated activity without any satisfying object. This, in her terrible clearness of vision, she saw, and yet could not avoid, and it is the very discrepancy between her theory and her practice which makes her interesting. She was a kind of Marie Bash-

The Portrait of Zélide

kirtseff, with less vanity and less executive power, but often singularly like. Zélide was excessively emotional, yet too fastidious to be satisfied. She said of herself, with her customary unflinching frankness, that she could not be happy with or without love.

Her troubled life was, accordingly, haunted by the vain image of love, yet never absorbed into it. All her suitors drew back: Hermanches, Bellegarde, Boswell, Lord Wemyss, the nameless Genevan lover, even Benjamin Constant, buzzed round the Lapland flame without finding any heat in it. It dazzled and attracted them, until, one and all, they found that it did not scorch their wings. It is quite plain that although there was so much talk of loving, not one of them was really thrilled by Zélide, and it is very doubtful whether she herself was ever genuinely moved. She was in love with love, but when the man presented himself, there was always the transparent chill between them, the repelling Lapland glitter. This, at least, is how I read the story, so tactfully and amusingly told by Mr. Geoffrey Scott.

Her relations with her adorers were consistently odd. Her first admirer, Hermanches de Rebecque, a Swiss Don Juan who was Voltaire's friend, saw her when she was a young girl at a ball in The Hague. They could not marry, they could not even meet, for Hermanches had a wife, and Zuylen was full of dragons. So they corresponded, in an ardent exchange of love-letters, for twelve long years! Why did they do it? What satisfaction could a man of the world, "comptant sur les doigts les femmes qui l'ont trop aimé," find in ceaseless exchange of long love-letters with a Dutch girl he never saw? The only possible answer is that her intellectual provocations excited a temperament which demanded, from her in particular, no other indulgence.

But even Hermanches considered this intrigue unsatisfactory, and he endeavoured to promote the marriage of

H

Zélide to his best friend, the Marquis de Bellegarde. The Marquis, who was thoroughly unintellectual, never felt himself comfortable with Zélide; the conic sections seemed to be always peeping out of her pocket. Yet he was content to marry her, and all the nobility of Holland, with the King of Prussia thrown in, combined to encourage the match. I am cynical enough to believe that, as Bellegarde did not like Zélide, there was an understanding that, after the marriage, Hermanches should see as much of the Marquise as he wished to. The extraordinary wooing went on for four years, Zélide offering no opposition; at the end of that time, in a final interview, Bellegarde confessed, with uncouth embarrassment, that he really could not.

And then the irrepressible James Boswell appeared on the scene, having left Dr. Johnson on the beach at Harwich, " rolling his majestic frame in the usual manner," and Mlle. de Tuyll was quite ready, or almost ready, to take up the surprising position of mistress at Auchinlech. Mr. Tinker has lately unfolded in full the amazing story, how Boswell thought he would, and consulted Voltaire, and then thought he wouldn't, and consulted Rousseau, and how Europe held its breath, and how after a long interval the lady received an epistle of seventeen pages laying it down decisively that Boswell's " wife must have a character directly opposite to my dear Zélide." Mlle. de Tuyll thereupon gave up the hope of passion, and married her brother's virtuous elderly tutor, M. de Charrière, and was respectably wretched for the rest of her life. But not unmoved.

Unhappy, "lost to the world, like a bright pebble on the floor of the Lake of Neuchâtel," Zélide languished for long years, but was fished up at last by one of the most remarkable men of the age, by no less a person than Benjanim Constant. He was nearly 20 (not 17, as he says in " Adolphe ") when he met the middle-aged lady of Colom-

The Portrait of Zélide

bier, whom he describes in his famous novel as " mécontente et retirée, n'ayant que son esprit pour ressource, et analysant tout avec son esprit." They fell into one another's arms, and Constant became a fixture in the house of the Charrières. The lovers, if lovers they can be called, spent the day in ceaseless conversation, and withdrew at cockcrow only to pour out the immense letters which Professor Rudler has published.

Their relations and the character of that correspondence are minutely examined by Mr. Scott, who rises to his very best when he describes how Benjamin was torn reluctantly out of the Lapland arms of Zélide into the ampler and fiercer embrace of Mme. de Staël. The ageing châtelaine of Colombier had no chance against the impetuosity of the fatal Ellénore. It was the vain struggle of eighteenth-century sensibility with nineteenth-century passion, and the conclusion was foregone. The whole story is extremely interesting, not merely for its own sake, but for the light it throws on the development of Benjamin Constant, to whose wonderful " Adolphe " it presents a sort of sentimental introduction.

NATURE IN POETRY

NATURE IN POETRY

THE exertions of two enthusiasts, Mr. Edmund Blunden and Mr. Alan Porter, were successful four years ago in reviving an interest in a poet who had been almost forgotten for nearly a century. This was John Clare, a Northamptonshire peasant, who was born in 1793, in the generation of Shelley and Keats. Clare attracted the momentary attention of his immediate contemporaries mainly because of his humble origin and rustic habits. The eighteenth century, in its decline, patronised poets who were ploughmen and milkmaids, cobblers and sailors before the mast. The sentiment was quite Rousseauish, and the interest rather social than æsthetic. Southey compiled a volume of these " uneducated bards," who were praised not so much for doing their poetry well as for doing it at all. In the patronage they received there was something of the attention given to a learned pig at a fair.

Clare was helped to print a volume of " Poems Descriptive of Rural Life and Scenery," in 1820. He was a very handsome man, with an aristocratic countenance, as we may see in the excellent portraits, sculpted or painted, which are reproduced in the new volume. It has been suggested that the blood of a noble family ran in his veins, and that the patronage he met with was concealed relationship. Whatever its source might be, it soon dried up. Clare was not a man who could easily be helped, and he fell into complete neglect and extreme destitution. In 1841 Clare was received into the Northampton County Asylum, where he died in 1864. Something of the detail of his sad story has been long given to the world. We are to hear it corrected and enlarged, for Mr. Blunden says that " the full Biography is yet to come."

The poems, here somewhat ineptly named " Madrigals," were collected by Mr. Blunden out of an immense mass of fragmentary MSS. preserved in the Peterborough Museum. If I read the preface correctly, all these poems were written during the twenty-three years which Clare spent in the lunatic asylum, where verse-writing was his incessant occupation. The 1920 volume presented the first harvest reaped by Messrs. Blunden and Porter in this neglected field, and the volume of 1924 is an aftermath. Let me hasten to say that the wealth betrayed by such a double selection is remarkable, since the second selection contains scarcely a single piece which is not worthy of preservation.

The double publication has greatly augmented the importance of Clare as a figure on our crowded Parnassus, and has made it certain that he can never again be overlooked, as he was between 1820 and 1920. He will take his place as one of the authentic English poets, and the only danger now to be apprehended is that he will be exalted unwisely. It is a natural weakness in those who have had the good fortune to find hidden treasure to exaggerate the value of what has so romantically been unearthed. The poetry of Clare is charming, his approach to Nature genuine and sincere, but when the claim is put forward that he was a great artist, for the sake of his own reputation we must be on our guard. When a responsible reviewer declares that Clare's faculty was " far purer than Wordsworth's," and " purer even than Shakespeare's," it is time to weigh our standards of merit.

Although Clare is his discovery, Mr. Blunden is not betrayed into this riot of hyperbole. He does not rank Clare above Wordsworth and Shakespeare as a poet of Nature. His definition of the theme is not injured by depreciation of other writers to the advantage of his Northamptonshire labourer, and yet it calls for a certain further discrimination. Mr. Blunden says :—

" The characteristics of Clare's Poetry are an unparalleled intimacy with the English countryside : a rare power of transfusing himself into the life of everything beneath the sky, save certain ardours and purposes of men; a natural ease of diction, well suited to hold the mirror up to Nature; a sense of the God in the Fly and the Cataract; a haunting sense of an Ethereal Love, Woman *in excelsis*, and, as the charm for his casual hearer, a delicate and elemental music."

This is well said—although I am afraid I cannot follow the fling about God and the Fly and the Cataract—and I think that each clause is *nearly* true, calculated, that is, to prepare the reader for what he will find in Clare, without mentioning what he will not find. Let us now take an example from the poet himself, the very characteristic sonnet called " The Foddering Boy," and see how far it justifies Mr. Blunden's definition :—

> The foddering boy along the crumping snows
>   With straw-band-belted legs and folded arm
> Hastens, and on the blast that keenly blows
>   Oft turns for breath, and beats his fingers warm,
> And shakes the lodging snows from off his clothes,
>   Buttoning his doublet closer from the storm
> And slouching his brown beaver o'er his nose—
> Then faces it again, and seeks the stack
>   Within its circling fence where hungry lows
> Expecting cattle, making many a track
>   About the snow, impatient for the sound
> When in huge forkfulls trailing at his back
>   He litters the sweet hay about the ground
> And brawls to call the staring cattle round.

Here, to a wonderful degree, we find the " unparalleled intimacy with the country-side," and an exactitude of observation which nowadays we call " photographic," but where is the " transfusion " which Mr. Blunden promised us? Every detail which photography can seize is precisely rendered, but all is exterior; there is not a phrase that shows the poet " transfusing " himself into the life of the Foddering Boy. Clare's is sheer descriptive poetry, painted with a wonderful delicacy and conscientiousness, but all from the outside. He concentrates his attention on the stray path rambling through the furze, on the patter of squirrels over the green moss, on the shaggy marten startling the great brown hornèd owl, and always has at his command the just phrase, the faultless vision, the economy and daring of epithet. His notes of birds and flowers are those of a naturalist, and it is, perhaps, ungracious to remark that this was a fashion of his time, as we may still see in such pieces as the botanical sonnets of Charlotte Smith. Clare does the pictorial and half-scientific business much better, of course, than Charlotte Smith did it, but surely we are far indeed in his water-colour drawings from the exaltation of " Tintern Abbey," from the human poignancy of " A Poet's Epitaph "? Clare hung over " the meanest flower that blows " with the rapture of a miniaturist, but it never gave him " thoughts that do often lie too deep for tears."

In the generation which preceded Clare's, Canning had pointed out that observation without reflection is of secondary value in imaginative literature. This is a remark which is too often forgotten in the criticism of descriptive poetry. To bring vividly before us the " oval leaves " of waterweed in the deep dyke among the rushes, to note the " marble " clouds of spring, to paint the wet blackbird cowering down on the whitethorn bush, requires a rare and beautiful talent which the Northamptonshire labourer possessed in a very remarkable degree. No one must dream of denying or belittling so precious a gift. But

Nature in Poetry

to excel in such clear painting is to be William Hunt or de Wint, not Titian or Velasquez. It is to be a Little Master of high accomplishment, but not a Great Master in Poetry. What is lacking is the intellectual element, the "organic sensibility" which Wordsworth demanded, and which he himself enjoyed in a superlative fullness. It is, to quote another Great Master, to be able to create out of the phenomena of Nature "forms more real than living man." This Clare could not do. He saw the tattered gold of the ragwort with perfect sincerity, and he makes us see it, but the sight suggests nothing to him beyond its own fresh beauty. It does not induce in him a train of thoughts, as the sight of the celandine did in Wordsworth. The admirers of Clare lay great stress on the stanza in which he describes the primrose

> With its little brimming eye,
> And its yellow rims so pale,
> And its crimp and curdled leaf—
> Who can pass its beauties by?

The accuracy of the picture is wonderful, but it is too much like a coloured plate in a botanical treatise. Here is nothing that transcends unreflecting observation, nothing that speaks to the spirit of Man. Indeed, without carping, we are bound to admit that here one is speaking to whom a primrose on a river's bank was just a primrose, and "nothing more." But the highest poetry requires more. So, too, let any unprejudiced lover of verse compare Clare's ode to the Skylark (p. 53) with either Shelley's or Wordsworth's, and he must confess that the Northamptonshire stanzas, charming as they are, belong to a lower order of inspiration.

It was the misfortune of Clare that, with unsurpassed exactitude of vision and delicate skill in stating fact, he was devoid of all reflective power. I am surprised that Mr. Blunden, whose introduction displays candour as well as sympathy, does not admit this defect. Clare had no thoughts. He wandered through the country, storing up images and sounds, but he wove his reproductions of these upon no intellectual basis. His was a camera, not a mind; and while we must admit that he showed a praiseworthy reserve in not pretending to find any philosophical relation between his negatives and the human spirit, still, the fact cannot be ignored that the philosophy was absent.

Connected with the absence of thought is the imperfection of form, which Mr. Blunden acknowledges, but is a little too indulgently disposed to slur over. He attributes it, perhaps justly, to Clare's lack of primary education, yet it seems more likely, in one who had read all the best English verse, to have been an inherent defect. Clare had a bad ear; he was satisfied to rhyme " alone " with " return," " crow " with " haw," and " season " with " peas in." His metrical structure is often loose, and his grammar not above reproach. Yet on these technical trifles I would not insist.

Let it not be thought that though I hint a fault I hesitate dislike. On the contrary, the verses of Clare give me great pleasure, and those not least which are contained in this collection of " Madrigals." His poetry is English in the extreme; not a phrase, not an epithet takes us out of our country, and hardly out of Clare's own county. As the habits of local life become modified by time, his record of Northamptonshire ways and scenes will increase in value. His " word-painting," to use a Victorian phrase now much fallen into disfavour, will keep alive his simple lyrics, and will remind successive generations how

> The little violets blue and white,
> Refreshed with dews of sable night,
> Come shining in the morning-light
> In thorn-enclosèd grounds;

Nature in Poetry

> And whether winds be cold or chill,
> When their rich smells delight instil,
> The young lamb blaas beside the hill
> And young spring happy sounds.

The collection before me has been produced with great beauty by the Beaumont Press; and, although Mr. Blunden modestly speaks of it as provisional, it will certainly be prized by all discerning book-collectors.

MAKING OUR FLESH CREEP

MAKING OUR FLESH CREEP

ONE night in June, 1764, Horace Walpole, lying in the Great North Bedchamber of Strawberry Hill, was the willing victim of a nightmare. He dreamed that he was in an ancient castle, and that, as he looked up the great staircase, he saw a gigantic hand in armour resting on the uppermost banister. The vision haunted him during the day, and in the evening he sat down and began to write, " without knowing in the least what " he " intended to say or relate." He was bored with politics, as we have often been, and he was very glad to think of anything else than elections. He would write a Gothic story, with a giant hand in armour as one of the properties.

He became engrossed in his tale, and he worked steadily at it for two months; the result was the famous " Castle of Otranto," of which Messrs. Constable have now published a sumptuous reprint, edited with devoted care by Mr. Montague Summers. Walpole was in his forty-seventh year, and his lethargy as a luxurious dilettante had been broken up by an increasing zeal for that pet toy, his private printing-press. He had begun to feel literary ambition stir in his ingenuous bosom. He was not sure, however, that his romance was likely to be welcome, so he did not order it to be set up at Strawberry Hill, but gave it to a London publisher, who brought it out, in conditions of whimsical pseudonymity, at Christmas, 1764.

The story enjoyed an instant and surprising success. Quite a considerable number of distinguished persons were afraid to go to bed after reading it. It raised that comfortable sensation of goose-flesh which is the charm of ghost-stories and reports of murders. When I read it now again I confess that I find it difficult to understand how it can have frightened anybody, or how any educated reader can have been taken in by the statement that it was translated from the Italian of 1529 as written by a Canon Onuphrio Muralto of the Church of St. Nicholas at Otranto. But the eighteenth century was extraordinarily gullible, and it swallowed the hoax so guilelessly that Horace Walpole, who wanted the credit of the thing, was obliged, in a second edition, to admit that Muralto was a fraud, and that its author had never been nearer Otranto than Twickenham.

The book survived in spite of this, and was eagerly read and slavishly imitated, while the peculiar interest of it is that it inaugurated a whole school of romances, culminating in those of Mrs. Radcliffe, who had more than a touch of genius, and in those of " Monk Lewis," who had just a touch. Half a century after the production of " The Castle of Otranto " the fashion for " horrid " Gothic stories received a severe wound in the inimitable pages of " Northanger Abbey," where Catherine Morland drew up, at the recommendation of " that sweet girl, Miss Andrews," a list of twelve new novels all about skeletons and mysterious horrors. But the taste for such things lingered on, and is not dead yet. Horace Walpole is responsible for it, and it is one of his claims to immortality.

Taken merely as a tale, however, " The Castle of Otranto " is a poor affair. The artlessness of it is amazing. It runs on like a romance which some girl makes up, night after night, for the amusement of children before they go to sleep, aimlessly inventing incidents that have no relation, and which lead to nothing. Most people know that, in the opening pages of it, a gigantic helmet, " a hundred times more large than any casque ever made for human being," crashes down out of the sky into the courtyard of the castle

Making our Flesh Creep   115

and "dashes to pieces" the heir to the duchy of Otranto. But few readers seem to have noticed that the author makes no further use of this phenomenon. It is never explained, it has no place in the evolution of the story, it is scarcely ever mentioned again. The same is true of the enormous arm and hand in armour, which are duly introduced later on. What these are, or why they appear, or what they have to do with the plot, Walpole forgets to mention. They are brought in wantonly, just to make our flesh creep. The author had not the skill to weave them into the woof of his narrative. For the famous picture, which, with no apparent purpose, gratuitously descends out of its panel and treads the floor, I can see no excuse at all; it seems to me an incident as silly as it is preposterous. Mr. Summers, led away perhaps by editorial enthusiasm, declares that anyone who objects to it is "singularly wanting in imagination and fancy." I must bow the head; I have always feared that I was wanting in imagination and fancy, but now I know it.

Oddly enough, it is the rapturous editor himself who weakens Walpole's claim to complete originality by bringing forward two curious instances of priority. He draws our attention to the fact that in 1762 Richard Hurd had published "Letters on Chivalry and Romance," from which Mr. Summers quotes some striking passages. Hurd was a very clever man, with ideas much in advance of his age, and his books, forgotten now, exercised a wide influence. We may be perfectly certain the Walpole read the "Letters," and that he responded to Hurd's appeal for a revival of feudal romance. When the critic recommends the cultivation of chivalrous superstition, because "the more solemn fancies of witchcraft and incantation were above measure striking and terrible," we hear the very accents of the second preface to "The Castle of Otranto."

But even more pertinent is the discovery by Mr. Montague

Summers (who appears to have read every book that ever was written!) that a " horrid " romance existed in English earlier than Walpole's. He has found that in 1762—which seems to be the significant date—a certain Dr. Leland published a romance called " Longsword." Even Mr. Summers admits that this work is " poorly executed," but it is adorned by a frontispiece which " depicts the exterior of a Gothic fane, where a Religious assists a Knight." Nothing could sound more Otrantoish than that, and evidently Walpole had a feeble precursor in Leland, whose novel, nevertheless, I am not tempted to peruse, any more than I am a bevy of later " horrid " tales of which Mr. Summers gives an exhaustive list. I am, however, faintly inquisitive about " Monks of Madrid," written by George Moore—in 1802! Here is a snare for bibliophils.

If it were not for the preface to the second edition, " The Castle of Otranto " would hardly deserve the honours of elaborate revival. That preface is an elegant and serious piece of writing, and shows that Walpole had a definite design before him—namely, " to blend the two kinds of romance, the ancient and the modern." There had recently been a remarkable revival of fictitious narrative, especially in the very fine contemporary and realistic novels of Richardson and Fielding. Smollett, too, had defined the novel as " a large diffused picture, comprehending the characters of life." Walpole, with his peculiar fondness for what was mysterious and supernatural, applauded but faintly these triumphs of his realistic contemporaries, but yet wished to combine " the boundless realms of invention " with a reasonable probability.

In his second preface he makes a series of sensible suggestions as to the way in which this should be done, and he very courageously asserts that he himself has done it in " The Castle of Otranto." But no careful reader of that romance can dare to agree with him. There never was a story in which probability was more cavalierly neglected. The best pages in the second preface are those dedicated to an admirable criticism of Voltaire, but Walpole seems to have no suspicion of the gulf which divides his own sloppy narrative from the delicate precision and faultless art of " Candide " or " L'Ingénu."

The reputation of " The Castle of Otranto," indeed, is an instance of the successful way in which an author can throw dust into the eyes of his readers. Walpole was an extremely clever man, and when he announced with the utmost assurance that he had reconciled the two kinds of fiction, and presented his story of the wicked Manfred and the innocent Isabella as evidence of the fact, the world took him at his word. Mr. Summers seems to do so still. But if we read " The Castle of Otranto " carefully we must see that there was in it no real blending of the fabulous and the probable.

Anything less " probable " than the plot of this vague and silly tale can hardly be imagined. There is a tyrannical duke, Manfred, who has invited a princess, Isabella, to travel from Vicenza to marry his son Conrad, the unfortunate youth who is presently squashed by the enormous helmet. She duly comes, quite alone, apparently without even a maid, and is pursued by the attentions of the bereaved but amorous parent. A mysterious Knight, who presently turns up from Vicenza, is, on the other hand, accompanied by several hundred men-at-arms, who are all put up for the night in the Castle, but who are never mentioned again. A peasant boy pushes in to look at the corpse of Conrad, and gets into such frequent trouble with the Duke that he is constantly being ordered off to execution, but survives, to learn, near the close of the tale and to his own great surprise, that he is really a long-lost Prince of Sicily.

A match is hastily being arranged, without any apparent

reason, between two of the characters, when attention is drawn to the fact that three drops of blood have fallen from the nose of the marble statue of a certain deceased Alfonso. " Probability," indeed ! The plot is a tissue of incoherence, poured out in engaging fluency, with frequent looseness of style and grammar, but in very high spirits. The only touches of " reality " are in the sub-comic characters of the servants. Matilda's chattering maid, Bianca, lightens with her conversation several dull passages in the lumbering tale.

Horace Walpole was even less successful in his second and final attempt to make our blood run cold. It does not appear to be known why, in 1768, he plunged for the first and last time into blank-verse tragedy. Walpole had, however, been taking a great interest in tragic drama, perhaps roused to it by Mme. du Deffand, who extolled the French. In a letter to her, which Mr. Summers does not quote, Walpole gives her his opinion of British tragedy during the preceding century :—

" It turned to tuneful nonsense in ' The Mourning Bride ' ; grew stark mad in Lee ; whose cloak, a little the worse for wear, fell on Young ; yet in both was still a poet's cloak. It recovered its senses in Hughes and Fenton, who were afraid it should relapse, and accordingly kept it down, with a timid, but amiable hand—and then it languished."

Walpole composed " The Mysterious Mother " in the hope of rousing it again, but once more his theory was superior to his practice. He complacently described his piece as made up of crimes, repentance, and horror ; but we do not know whether it made Mme. du Deffand shudder. Some people admired it, and Lady Diana Beauclerk made seven designs in " soot-water " to illustrate it, but Mrs. Clive could not be persuaded to act the principal part, nor would Garrick present it. Byron, however, himself a bad tragedian, thought it a work " of the highest order."

It is plain that Horace Walpole, whose powers in another field were magnificent, was not an adept in imaginative writing. " The Castle of Otranto " and " The Mysterious Mother " are failures, in consequence of his lack of moral seriousness and of technical skill. But the effort which he made is notable, and must be respected. He saw that the age he lived in was prosaic, and he strove to awaken it to wonder, as did his contemporaries " Ossian " and Chatterton. Walpole, in particular, perceived that entertainment was to be found in terror, in physical and ethical horror; he proclaimed the delight that refreshes the human spirit in being shocked. This is not a very worshipful quality in mankind, perhaps, but it exists, and it had been overlaid with deposits of common-sense. It is Walpole's credit that he provoked the poets and novelists to frighten us.

THE CONFESSIONS OF A
JUSTIFIED SINNER

THE CONFESSIONS OF A JUSTIFIED SINNER

EVERY dog should have his day, and I am little concerned to grudge the "Justified Sinner" his handsome reappearance in the hundredth year of his existence. But I find it difficult to share Mr. Welby's view of the superlative merit of a book which has been much discussed but never before entirely approved of. When it first appeared, in 1824, it was received very coldly and suspiciously, but it presently found admirers, and has never completely lacked them. Those, however, who have occupied themselves with it have always done so cautiously. They have admitted its incoherence, but have insisted on its vigour and intensity; they have apologised for its faults of construction.

Mr. Welby, for whose soundness of judgment I have much respect, goes further, and says that "the art of it is marvellous." He takes the erring Ettrick Shepherd under his full protection, and, indeed, if I may be pardoned the expression, he goes the whole Hogg. He has the courage to venture on perilous comparisons, and I shrink a little when I read that "Poe never invented anything with so much spiritual significance, Defoe never did anything with more convincing particularity." These are brave assertions; and the re-reading of this strange and horrible tale has not quite converted me to Mr. Welby's faith. But that "The Confessions of a Justified Sinner" is an extraordinary book I am more than ever willing to admit.

James Hogg, the putative creator of "The Justified Sinner" (for it is not quite certain how much of it is his) is chiefly, but, we are told, inaccurately, known by the picture of him as the Ettrick Shepherd in the "Noctes Ambrosianæ." He was a plebeian hanger-on in the circle of Sir Walter Scott, to whom his behaviour was by turns fulsome and impertinent. His social charm may be inferred from the fact that he was known among the intimates as "the Great Boar of the Forest," but he was tolerated, and even indulged, in consideration of his convivial arts and his undeniable literary talent. Nicknames stick, and Hogg has descended with his ticket as "the most creative of our uneducated poets." I do not know exactly what is meant by this, which would seem to exclude Burns and Keats. At all events, Hogg, who was born in the Vale of Ettrick in 1770, had been a domestic servant and then a shepherd, but always a voracious reader, before he was employed by Scott to collect old ballads for the "Border Minstrelsy."

After failing as a sheep-farmer in one of the misty Hebrides, Hogg proceeded to Edinburgh early in the century and "commenced author." He kept it up through thirty years of miscellaneous, and, to say the truth, not always very brilliant, writing in prose and verse; the vital residue of which is really the beautiful dim fairy-poem of "Bonnie Kilmeny" and the strange romance before us to-day. His most famous lyric, "Bird of the wilderness, blithsome and cumberless," has dropped out of the anthologies, and will not be put in again, nor his sentimental "When the Kye Comes Hame." It is an instance of the mutability of taste that a century ago grave critics considered that "few poets impress us so much with the idea of direct inspiration as Hogg." Even Mr. Welby would hardly say that now. But he wrote "Bonnie Kilmeny," and is credited with "The Confessions of a Justified Sinner," so that if Time has pared much away, something is left.

The grim story is a product of the Ettrick Shepherd's later years; it was published anonymously in 1824. Lockhart, who knew him well, said that " Hogg's notions of literary honesty were always exceedingly loose." Perhaps the boldest proposal on record is Hogg's suggestion that his own autobiography should be signed as the work of Sir Walter Scott after the death of Scott. He playfully insinuated that the same great man wrote Lockhart's books. He was capable of very irritating suggestions, and if his own authorship of " The Justified Sinner " has been called in question, Hogg has himself to thank. That work made an unlucky start, since the title of it disappointed the extremely religious reader, who bought it in hopes of a regale, and who was disgusted to find it a satire on his faith; while the heterodox were bored with such minute descriptions of Calvinistic practices.

Mr. Welby, whose preface might well be longer, and who takes for granted more knowledge of the facts than is quite reasonable, dwells upon the " inner meaning " of the tale. It may be that he is right, and that Hogg had a symbolic purpose; but we must remember that he was not a very subtle person, and that " spiritual significance " was not much in his line. I cannot say that I see in " The Justified Sinner " anything more recondite than a satire on the extravagant zeal of the Scottish Covenanters, taking the form of a Hoffmanesque romance. What was the temper of the Edinburgh wits of his day in regard to the national forms of religion may be easily seen from a perusal of their " Noctes " and their " Recreations." Hogg shared the general dislike of an excessive Puritanism, and his familiarity with country parishes in the Lowlands had supplied him with experience. Moreover, he places his frenzied narrative in the opening years of the eighteenth century, when almost anything might be believed about the savage adherents to the Sanquhar Declaration.

In Hogg's story, however, the Covenanters do not appear as martyrs, but as dangerous and unscrupulous malcontents, barely restrained from open violence by the law. A gay country gentleman, George Colwan, laird of Dalchastel and Balgrennan, marries a Glasgow heiress with a fortune. The marriage is unhappy from the first. The laird, " a droll, careless chap," is frustrated in his every wish by his lady, who is the most severe and gloomy of bigots. Mrs. Colwan gives birth to a son, who grows up generous, enlightened, and as handsome as the day, but she passes under the influence of a fanatical minister, Mr. Wringhim, with whom she takes perpetual counsel, against the wish of that Amorite, Hittite, and Girgashite, her profane husband. She becomes the mother of a second son, who bears the most regrettable likeness to Mr. Wringhim, a resemblance which grows upon body and mind until the boy is almost a copy of that formidable pastor, and is equally mean, ugly, and fanatical.

We must now explain that the story is, very inconveniently, told in two parallel parts. We have, first, the relation of an unnamed " Editor," whose sympathies are very plainly on the side of the elder son and his liberal ideas; and, secondly, the narrative (lapsing, thirdly, into the journal) of the younger son, who defends his extravagant faith unflinchingly. This arrangement is very inartistic, and leads the author into considerable confusion of detail, but allows of powerful and even thrilling episodes, which are often very well told. Indeed, the value of the book depends not on its plot, which is clumsy and unconvincing, but on a certain shuddering impetus with which certain scenes are breathlessly delineated. There is something of Salvator Rosa in the brush-work of the Ettrick Shepherd.

The contest between what are here styled the Court and the Country parties inspires the latter with incredible ferocity. The zeal of the Covenanters is directed, not against the unconverted worldling, but against the broad-minded ministers of religion. We are invited to inspect a crisis in the Scottish Church, where "the true Gospel preachers joined all on one side, and the upholders of pure morality and a blameless life on the other." It is the old antithesis between Faith and Works pushed to its wildest extremity. The doctrine of the Rev. Mr. Wringhim is that the elect are infallible, and the Scripture promises made to them binding in all situations and relations. Those who are "justified" cannot do wrong, and may safely commit what the world calls crimes; those who are not elect, however virtuous and godly they may appear to be, cannot do right. The Calvinist is made to define his own position in these terms :—

"I could not but despise in my heart the man who laid such a stress upon morals, leaving grace out of the question; and I viewed it as a deplorable instance of human depravity and self-conceit. . . . I had an inward thirst and longing to distinguish myself in the great cause of religion, and I thought . . . how I would astonish mankind, and confound their self-wisdom and their esteemed morality—blow up the idea of any dependence on good works, and *morality*, forsooth."

These views are instilled by Mr. Wringhim into the feebler mind of Robert Colwan, until he becomes inspired with a fanaticism even fiercer than that of his teacher. In the earlier portion of the narrative we are rather abruptly introduced to the loathing, purely theological in its nature, which the younger Colwan brother entertains for the elder, a sentiment that culminates in a peculiarly craven murder. But we need the second part to throw light on the development of Robert's madness.

There is here some confusion of thought on the author's part. He seems to represent Robert as insane, which Mr. Wringhim never is. But he also seems to regard him as responsible for his actions. The lad becomes extremely intimate with a mysterious young man, called the Prince, whom the reader immediately perceives to be the Devil, though this is never suspected by Robert. The Prince, who abounds in language of the strictest Calvinistic orthodoxy, ceaselessly suggests to his victim that the Lord desires to see the moderate clergy removed from society. Robert begins the good work by hiding in a wood and shooting an estimable and benevolent minister, the Rev. Mr. Blanchard, as he strolls by. No suspicion falls on Robert, and the Prince then urges him to carry out the same good work on the person of his brother George.

We must now return to the first part of the narrative, where are described the persecutions with which the zealot pursues his innocent and amiable relative. These culminate in a sort of riot, which Robert contrives to rouse in the streets of Edinburgh. This is perhaps the best episode in the book, told with very great vivacity and passion. Less fortunate is a scene where Robert unsuccessfully attempts to push George over a precipice near Arthur's Seat. Here, as elsewhere in the book, the feebleness of evidence given by Robert's victims is a fault in the story, which would be constantly coming to an end if the ordinary laws of legal practice prevailed. It is true that Robert invariably acts under the protection of what used in Evangelical circles to be called " the Personal Devil."

It is, I suppose, on the evasions by which Robert Colwan, till near the end, escapes punishment for his monstrous crimes, that Mr. Welby founds his comparison of Hogg with Poe, but I think the parallel one very disadvantageous to the author of " The Justified Sinner." In all Poe's best works of this nature, terror is evoked by the combination of mysterious and horrible circumstances, which, however, are invariably traced to a consistent and credible source. " The Murders in the Rue Morgue," and its still more masterly sequel, " Marie Roget," continue to exercise their potency over the reader because of the unflinching severity of their logic. Hogg, on the contrary, helps himself out of every difficulty by unsolicited aids of coincidence, ambiguity, and a reckless introduction of the supernatural. What his own view of Robert Colwan is we are left questioning. At one time his creator treats him as a hypocrite, again as a lunatic, again as a helpless victim vainly struggling against diabolical suggestion. There is no cohesion in the author's conception of a character which, just because of its appalling isolation from common human action, should have been zealously defined.

But there are many readers who are not affected by inconsistency of handling, and are indifferent to logic if a tale amuses them. They may still find entertainment in the imbroglio of the unfortunate Colwan family, many of whose remarkable adventures are told with great vigour and picturesqueness. More critical students will take pleasure in observing the peculiarities of the Rev. Mr. Wringhim, whose is the most lively figure in the book. It is a pity that Hogg so early lost interest in Wringhim, who has a reality lacking to the maniac Robert. Wringhim is the typical Scottish Tartuffe of the Dark Ages, with his " spine-breaking reflections," with his unflinching sacrifice of human pity to fanatical passion, with his spurts of derisive exultation at the sorrows of all who are not " elect," and with his unconscious but complete obliquity of moral vision. The picture was angrily resented by the descendants of the Covenanters. Hogg might have replied in the words of Molière, " les hypocrites se sont effarouchés,

K

et ont trouvé étrange que j'eusse la hardiesse de jouer leurs grimaces." But to publish " The Confessions of a Justified Sinner " in 1824 was not so courageous an act as to print " L'Imposteur " in 1669; and the Ettrick Shepherd was certainly not Molière.

A DOG WITH A BAD NAME

A DOG WITH A BAD NAME

THE shadows were beginning to close around the Ancien Régime when, in 1782, a long romance, strictly anonymous, appeared in the bookshops of Paris. It was called "Les Liaisons Dangereuses," and in its outward form, as well as somewhat in its inward essence, it was modelled upon Richardson's "Clarissa," French admiration of which, in Provost's translation, had grown, as M. Texte says, to infatuation. But from the first the new novel created a scandal, and its name has grown to be a by-word for literary infamy. It bore a motto from Rousseau's "Nouvelle Héloïse"—"I have observed the manners of my time, and I have published these letters," so that the legend speedily sprang up that they were genuine documents.

When it became known that the author was a certain Choderlos de Laclos, a captain of artillery attached to the Duke of Orléans, it was confidently whispered that these were letters from living persons which he had stolen when he was in garrison at Grénoble. There was no truth in this; the book was entirely a work of imagination, but it was closely studied from life, and it awakened not less resentment than curiosity. Both have continued almost to this day, and "Les Liaisons Dangereuses" has been treated as a shameful book, outside the pale of literature and unworthy of critical attention. Very little has been written about it in France, and practically nothing in English, although it has been abundantly read and reprinted. It has been a pariah to the critics. When Mr. Saintsbury wrote his excellent volumes on the French Novel, he did not mention "Les Liaisons Dangereuses," and he was naïvely reproached with having "forgotten" it. Mr. Saintsbury never "forgets" anything, but he did not choose to remember it.

Such is the remarkable work of fiction which an accomplished scholar has now ventured to introduce for the first time to English readers. Mr. Aldington, to whom we already owe an excellent translation of Cyrano de Bergerac (the original, not Rostand's renovation), has given close attention to Choderlos de Laclos' plain and nervous language, and he has prefixed to his translation a well-considered biography. We have here at last a Laclos, not exactly whitewashed, but explained and made credible. The monster of legend is slain, which is a very different thing from saying that "Les Liaisons Dangereuses" is what ladies call "nice."

It remains a hideous picture of treachery, intrigue, and dishonour, but there are two explanations on which it is proper to insist. One is that the legend of the obscenity of the book is absolutely baseless; the language is perfectly decent throughout. The other is the belief that "Les Liaisons Dangereuses" is an incentive to vice; the exact opposite is true—the novel is a satire, cynical and humiliating indeed, but unflinchingly severe, on the prevalent laxity of manners. Those who have asserted the contrary cannot have read it to the last bitter pages. Richardson was indulgent to Lovelace in the final duel; but Laclos hunts down Valmont and Madame de Merteuil with a savagery that scandalises even Mr. Aldington. Peccant beauty can deserve no worse chastisement than to languish after small-pox with a damaged complexion and the loss of one eye.

It is easy to disdain the novel of gallantry and sentiment which flourished in France through the middle of the eighteenth century, but as an episode in the development

A Dog with a Bad Name

of literature it is absurd to ignore it. From Marivaux to Restif we have a body of fiction which cannot be said to insist upon attention, but to invite and to reward it. These novelists, especially the earlier ones, reduced the passion of love to a pastime, of which they undertook to teach the rules and chronicle the records. Love with Crébillon, and even with Marivaux, is a matter in which the head takes the place of the heart. No less dignified a contemporary than Buffon declared that "il n'y a pas de bon dans l'amour que de physique," and in the baser sort of novelists this was expanded with unbridled licence. But in the better writers it was draped in urbanity of manners, in the elegance of frivolity, in the subtlety of the art of conversation. The subject-matter of each successive novel was the more and more searching anatomy of the female heart, and this reached its highest (and lowest) expression in the works of the younger Crébillon, to whom—at least to his most famous novel—Mr. Aldington is, I think, too indulgent.

Surely "Le Sopha" displays little "verve in satire," and is deformed by a good deal of baseness and dullness. There was merit in Crébillon, but it is not patent in his heavier writings, which are alembicated as well as corrupt. It is found in his dialogues, which are often singularly graceful. A contemporary, in the true language of the Regency, said that Crébillon spread the colours of the rainbow over a canvas of cobweb. This is partly true of such a story as "Le Hasard au Coin du Feu," with its erotic aphorisms and universal frivolous scepticism. Laclos, coming much later, had evidently studied Crébillon and Marivaux, but there is little of the cobweb and the rainbow in his grim and hateful irony, while he had more command over the instrument of prose than Crébillon, whose language is often less skilful than his thought. Laclos could always say exactly what he wished, and exercised his privilege.

The social woman of the Regency liked to be thought modest, emotional, and simple. She was in reality extremely complicated, cynically shameless, and as cold as a stone to anything but sensual pleasure. Those elements were analysed by all the novelists, but most searchingly by Laclos. In consequence, he was banned by feminine readers because of his clairvoyance, while men were equally disconcerted by his anatomy of their pretence to honour, passion, and fidelity. The ingenuity of the mode in which the inquiry is carried out is the best excuse for the somewhat perverse pleasure which we receive from the most graceful of these novels to-day. It is a purely intellectual enjoyment to follow the subtle and delicate counter-action of two caprices in these pagan stories. It is analogous to the satisfaction which the eye receives from a painting by Boucher or Fragonard. But in "Les Liaisons Dangereuses" there is nothing of Fragonard, except the fine drawing of character. The dreaminess of Marivaux, the rose-colour and silver tissue which took the crudity away from incontinence in Crébillon, have vanished in Laclos. Rousseau has risen above the horizon, the Revolution is at hand, and it is time that "cette coquetterie minaudière" shall cease. But Laclos is still bound to the conventions of the age in which he was young, and he approaches his tragic theme in the lightest attire. He trips towards the guillotine as though dressed for a *fête champêtre*.

The reading of these novels of the alcove is not to be recommended to any persons who do not possess what the Plymouth Brother called " a strong spiritual digestion." But it is undeniable that such elect readers may find in the best of them a legitimate intellectual entertainment. Thirty years ago, when I was enjoying interminable discussions with Coventry Patmore, I ventured to lend him Crébillon's " Le Hasard au Coin du Feu." It was a rash act, but Patmore was at once a saint and a psychologist.

He was also, more than any other man whom I have known, independent of all intellectual prejudice. He read the "libertine" dialogue with care, and he returned it to me with the remarkable judgment that it was capable of "a mystical and Catholic" interpretation, and had reminded him of some passages in St. John of the Cross. This criticism may sound odd, but it is at least not commonplace. It is useful as a reminder that all the appeals which these novels make to us to-day must be purely intellectual. They are mere bubbles of foam blown from the wave whence Venus rose, if we regard them otherwise than as exercises in emotional ingenuity. But the day of reckoning approaches, and even the *petits maîtres* grow serious; Choderlos de Laclos, though his cynicism seems at first to connive at corruption, becomes at last the most indignant of Timons.

The plot of " Les Liaisons Dangereuses " is very simple, and is economically conducted. Nothing is wasted on philosophical inquiries or on descriptions of scenery; in this respect the form of the book is a great improvement on that of " La Nouvelle Héloïse," and goes back to Richardson, Laclos's real model. The personages are few and well defined. They are all members of high Parisian society under Louis XV., all wealthy, unoccupied, and witty. There is a sensitive young grass-widow, Mme. de Tourvel; and a young girl, Cécile de Volanges, who has just returned home from the convent-school to her mother, Mme. de Volanges. There is a mild young gentleman, the Chevalier Danceny, who falls in love with Cécile; and there is an aged lady, the Marquise de Rosemonde, at whose château in the country half of the action takes place.

All these people are virtuous, and their virtue is very sympathetically revealed, but there are two serpents in this paradise, two inconscionable miscreants, the Marquise de Merteuil and the Vicomte de Valmont, who are set on the ruin of everybody, and succeed to the full in all their desperate schemes of seduction. The hypocrisy and villainy of this precious pair have given "Les Liaisons Dangereuses" the bad name from which it suffers, but it should be acknowledged that complete retribution comes in the end. Madame de Tourvel dies of a broken heart in a convent, and little Cécile is ruined, but Danceny kills Valmont in a duel, and the Merteuil is shamed and disfigured. It was early said, and has been constantly repeated since, that Choderlos de Laclos admired the impudence and Don Juanism of his hero, and in point of fact drew Valmont with complacency as a portrait of himself. Mr. Aldington exposes this myth with vigour, and proves its absurdity. He has devoted so much more research than I have to the life and writings of Choderlos de Laclos that I hesitate to make a suggestion which he will perhaps repudiate. Nevertheless, I submit to him, as the model for Valmont, a name which has never, I think, been advanced. It is that of perhaps the most abandoned scoundrel in the history of literature, the novelist of "Angola," the Chevalier de La Morlière. This man, who was twenty years Laclos's senior, was, like him, an officer serving in the garrison of Grénoble, a city which he filled with the ill-fame of his scandalous adventures. When Laclos was in Grénoble from 1769 to 1775, the escapades of the *mousquetaire de Sa Majesté* were still the talk of that town. La Morlière was the type of the ingenious and unscrupulous Don Juan, "plus connu par ses escroqueries et son impudence que par ses ouvrages," of which latter "Angora," a would-be Eastern tale in the manner of Crébillon, is, however, still readable. A confession attributed to La Morlière gives a view of his character which, in the light of the facts, is almost flattering :—

"Il ne faut point me demander comment, d'alcôve en alcôve, j'arrivai à cette dépravation qui était alors générale.

Je recevais l'exemple de haut et j'acceptais comme un vernis ce qui était une gangrène."

But what Morlière and the other libertine novelists of the Regency accepted as a polished adornment become mere horror in the harsh satire of Laclos. He was himself no saint, but had not sunk, and never did sink, to infamy like his hero. Morlière notoriously did; and I suggest that he was probably the model for Valmont.

Those who have condemned " Les Liaisons Dangereuses " as a didactically immoral book have not read it with patience and insight. If they had pushed on to Letter 86, they would have found the hypocrisy of Valmont nakedly exposed, while the infamy of Mme. de Merteuil early becomes too repulsive to be credible. Indeed, the weak point in the construction of the story is the necessity by which the arch-conspirators are forced to write to one another in terms the frankness of which is unnatural. It is absolutely incredible that a very clever woman of the world, anxious to preserve her position in society, should place herself in the power of a man like Valmont, of whose radical perfidy she was aware. She would *think* such malignant things, and perhaps *say* them, but never by any possibility *write* them. Possibly Choderlos de Laclos would have done better to choose a narrative form, but he was infatuated with the " Nouvelle Héloïse " and " Clarissa." (Valmont has the assurance to compare himself with St. Preux !) The letters in " Les Liaisons Dangereuses " are not so convincing as those in " Clarissa "; Richardson was the more sagacious master of the two. It is curious that the innocent correspondents—Cécile, Mme. de Tourvel, even Danceny—express themselves far more naturally than the wicked ones. This may surprisingly be laid to Laclos's credit, that he was more eloquent in the cause of virtue than in that of vice.

The question whether "Les Liaisons" is, or is not, a disgraceful publication remains unsettled. Mr. Aldington defends it with ingenuity and learning in his excellent introduction, and says that "a timid and prudish criticism" has hitherto withheld from Laclos the enthusiasm he deserves. I confess that I cannot mount with Mr. Aldington to these heights of rapture. I recognise in Choderlos de Laclos a concentrated vigour of purpose and a remarkable skill in satirical suggestion. The way in which he turns inside out the excessive delicacy of his age is amusing. But I find him dry, harsh, violent, without imaginative horizon. As to the supposed immorality of his novel, that is hardly to be mentioned in the twentieth century, which has produced books far more indecent than any in the eighteenth. An age which has tolerated the brutality of "La Garçonne" and the foul chaos of "Ulysses" must not make itself ridiculous by throwing stones at "Les Liaisons Dangereuses."

THE FABLE OF THE BEES

THE FABLE OF THE BEES

If the eighteenth century in literature was a Cinderella to the nineteenth, it threatens to become a Fairy Princess to the twentieth. We are now far enough away from it to be able to enjoy its picturesqueness, its vividness, and its variety. Excellent editions of its prose and verse appear in quick succession. It is now the turn of Bernard Mandeville, the Dutch physician who came over about 1698, learned English, and published a book which set all the divines and philosophers by the ears. The early decades of the century were distinguished by several intellectual scandals, and not the least noisy amongst these was the impertinent thesis that private vices are public benefits. The author of this notorious book was the black sheep of his time, and no one until now has thought of editing his works, although in his own age, as Mr. Kaye shows, they enjoyed an almost unparalleled circulation. Mandeville took himself seriously, and declared that the critics attacked his theory without reading his book. But as a fact it was immensely read, and a work which such men as William Law, Berkeley, Adam Smith, and "Capability" Brown thought worth refuting had no cause to complain of neglect. But "The Fable of the Bees" found no distinguished supporter, except very vaguely David Hume, and from the first it was considered disreputable. I do not think that it has been reprinted, until now, since 1806.

If Mandeville has waited long for an advocate, he has not waited in vain. Mr. F. B. Kaye has spent many years—he does not say how many—in the most thorough investigation of everything connected with the Dutch doctor, and his edition is a marvel of exhaustive erudition. It would be difficult to recall a case of an editor who had expended more pains on his subject. Not merely is the bibliography amazingly minute and (I imagine) accurate, but nothing is spared which can elucidate, however remotely, the history and purport of the book. It sounds ungracious to say it, but the work is almost *over-done*. Not merely is every drop squeezed out of the fruit of the orange, but every particle of essence out of the rind. There is nothing left, unless fresh biographical material should turn up, for any future editor to do. Nobody can hope to extend Mr. Kaye's explorations or throw fresh light upon the workings of the mind of Mandeville.

The only refuge for a critic is to challenge the editor's conclusions, expanded in a very full philosophical commentary. This anyone may do who chooses, though it is dangerous, because Mr. Kaye has considered every possible objection, and faces such wise men as Bishop Berkeley and Sir Leslie Stephen like a lion in the path of pyrrhonism. There is, however, one small question, one still whisper of doubt, which may possibly be raised. Was the notorious paradox of Mandeville quite worthy of all this apparatus? Mr. Kaye vigorously asserts that it was, and lest he should be baffled on the philosophic side, makes a bold attack on the æsthetic. He claims for Mandeville a place abreast of the most eminent prose-writers of the illustrious Age of Anne. He speaks of him, a foreign master of English style, as we speak to-day of Conrad. I shall return to this contention. In the meantime, who was Mandeville?

Thanks to Mr. Kaye's tireless investigations, this question is easily answered. He belonged to an old Dutch family of energetic professional distinction. His father was an eminent doctor of Rotterdam, where (and not at

Dort, as the text-books repeat) Bernard de Mandeville was born in November, 1670. He was educated at Leyden, where, at the age of fifteen, he pronounced what is pleasantly termed an *oratiuncula*, which, we are told, was witty in itself and foreshadowed the medical man. He took his degree of M.D. at Leyden when he was twenty, and began to practise as a physician. He made his special object the relief of "stomachic ferment," an agitating complaint which is too often treated with derision. He grew restless, and made the tour of Europe, coming at last to London, in which, as he tells us himself, he "happen'd to take great delight." He was, I think, well adapted to appreciate the liberty and oddity of English life, and we find him always writing of London as familiarly as though he had been born within sound of Bow Bells. He arrived, so far as we can judge, in 1698; the next year he married an English girl, and settled down as a doctor to modify the flatulence of, it would appear, a rather humble class of Londoners.

From this point onward, until he died in 1733, Mandeville disappears as a person. There is practically nothing whatever recorded about him, except, at rare intervals, the publication of his extravagantly popular works. He is scarcely mentioned by the memoir-writers; there exist no trustworthy reports of his appearance, of his manners, or of his adventures. Even Mr. Kaye, to his only too apparent disappointment, can find nothing at all.

There is one matter on which Mr. Kaye might have been more explicit, and that is Dr. Mandeville's professional status in London from 1698 onwards. Why did the Royal College of Physicians take no notice of him, and why (I have just looked to see) does his name never occur in its "Roll"? This is very curious, since Mandeville, as we now know, arrived with a reputable degree from Leyden, and belonged to a family illustrious in the medical profession

L

through four generations. He must have come over with good introductions, and it was the habit of the College to welcome foreign doctors who settled in London. In 1699, Dr. Abraham Cyprianus came over from Utrecht to practise here, and was almost immediately received as a Licentiate of the Royal College. It was the usual thing; why was Mandeville never thus recognised? Sir John Hawkins said that Mandeville " lived in obscure lodgings in London " and was " never able to acquire much practice." Hawkins, " one of the most unamiable liars who ever lived," may not be a trustworthy witness, but in this he probably reveals the truth.

Mr. Kaye extracts from Mandeville's dialogues what he takes to be revelations of the writer's condition and habits; the argument is ingenious, but must not be too confidently leant upon. It is impossible to avoid the final impression that Mandeville was neither in manners nor language very refined—he " mistook low humour and drollery for fine wit "—and that his practice was chiefly among the shopkeepers and publicans of his neighbourhood. Mr. Kaye is a little too anxious to make him out a gentleman.

A very remarkable feature of the literary career of Bernard Mandeville is the silence in which his theories were originally received, in contrast with the vociferous opposition which they suddenly encountered when they had already been nearly twenty years before the public. Mr. Kaye's minute bibliography reveals this odd fact, which I had never before seen commented upon. The author's original thesis, that what we consider moral frailties may be turned to the advantage of civil society, was originally sketched in an octosyllabic poem, called " The Grumbling Heir," in the manner of Swift, published in 1705. This was an allegorical fable, showing how a society of bees throve on dishonesty and selfishness, and sank to penury when Jove, by reforming them, deprived them of their competitive

The Fable of the Bees

vices. Nobody seems to have taken any notice of this piece, and it was not until 1714 that the author expanded it in prose, in what Mr. Kaye calls the "brilliant and devastating paradox" of his famous book.

But what Mr. Kaye does not explain is the fact that, even then, no human being is known to have been devastated by "The Fable of the Bees" until the second edition was issued late in 1723, when there rose a positive uproar about it. Totally ignored for nineteen years, the theory that private vices were public benefits suddenly became the most absorbing subject in every pulpit, pamphlet, and coffee-house. Meanwhile, the author had published various works, and particularly a treatise on those inconvenient ventosities on which he was an authority, but without attracting any attention. But in 1723 he suddenly had the good fortune to become the most attacked author about town. The Grand Jury of Middlesex presented "The Fable of the Bees" as a public nuisance, having a direct tendency to the subversion of all religion and civil government. Whether this was the cause or the result of the outburst of indignation is uncertain, but it was a splendid advertisement for Mandeville. Everybody wants to buy a book which has been burned by the common hangman, and apparently no serious effort was made to stop the sale of the "Fable," which became prodigious.

It is only fair to take Mandeville's own account of what it was he intended to convey in the book which caused so terrible a scandal. He wished, in the first place, to protest against the optimism of the age, which found its most eloquent expression in the "Characteristics" of Shaftesbury. He denied that the virtues of men, their friendly qualities and kind affections, were the foundation of society, but asserted, on the other hand, that, if these were too much encouraged, a softness and inefficiency would invade civil life. In the second place, as a corollary to the former, he daringly protested that the true source of all prosperity, all art and science, all vigour of government, was the prevalence of evil, so that " the moment evil ceases, society must be spoiled, if not totally destroyed." Mandeville, at the same time, declared himself no enemy to virtue, and was far from encouraging vice, but he thought that although theoretically it would be delightful to get rid of evil passions, it was practically impossible, as these, mainly in their competitive forms, were the forces which gave vitality to social order. If we were all perfectly good and unselfish, the world would sink into lethargy. We are kept alive by having to struggle with the individualities of others, and this struggle, although vicious in itself, creates advantages to the State, since—

"those who can enlarge their view, and will give themselves Leisure of gazing on the Prospect of concatenated Events, may in a hundred Places see Good spring up and pullulate from Evil, as naturally as Chickens do from eggs."

The great mistake which the indignant opponents of Mandeville made was to take him too seriously. Perhaps Mr. Kaye does so also. The fabulist was a man of no great delicacy, but amply provided with wit, and he was bent upon startling the moralists of the age out of their propriety. He was more anxious to amuse his readers than to convince them. I do not suppose that he believed that anyone would be persuaded by his paradoxes that avarice and prodigality must lead to public profit, or that reason is nothing more than the tool of men's passions. He used irony, the most dangerous of weapons, and his vivacity was taken for dogmatic impertinence. The real merit of Mandeville consists in his holding the doll up by the legs and letting the sawdust trickle away. He presents the illusions of convention turned inside out, and while

The Fable of the Bees 149

Pope and Shaftesbury were declaring that "Whatever is, is right," Mandeville was shrieking that whatever is, is wrong. His attitude in the Augustan Age is best exemplified by a parallel with that of Mr. Bernard Shaw, which, however, must not be pushed too far. Mandeville was led by his irony, and perhaps encouraged by his temperament, to take a vulgar and even a degrading view of human nature. Leslie Stephen, who was the only critic of the nineteenth century who took the trouble to read Mandeville with care, put a summary into his mouth, " You are all Yahoos, and I am a Yahoo; and so—let us eat, drink, and be merry." When everybody is equally depraved, no one can afford to throw stones.

Law and Berkeley fought against wickedness; Shaftesbury glozed it over; Mandeville accepted it and gloried in it. But their conflicting arguments have ceased to offer us any particular excitement, since the world of thought has shifted its point of view. These old casuists have to depend less on their ideas than on their style; we care little for what they said, but much for how they said it. Nothing about Mandeville's theories is likely ever to be more amply discussed or luminously stated than by Mr. Kaye in the introduction to the new edition. He defines the mood of Mandeville as "rigorism," and he returns to this phrase incessantly. I am not quite pleased, because " rigorism " is a quality clearly defined in Catholic theology, in a sense which differs from Mr. Kaye's; I like words to retain their meaning. The real charm of " The Fable of the Bees "—and it has a certain pungent charm —resides not in its didactic, but its illustrative passages, which are often extremely curious and vivid.

Mr. Kaye, who is a thorough-going enthusiast for his anarchical hero, praises the style of Mandeville in extravagant language. He prefers it to that of Addison, with which, however, it has no relation. The authors with whom Mandeville may reasonably be compared are Swift, and still more, as it seems to me, Arbuthnot. It is surely obvious that the author of " The Fable of the Bees " had read " Law is a Bottomless Pit." In neither the one nor the other writer is there a trace of the beautiful serenity and mellifluous dignity which raise Addison to the summit of prose-writing in the Age of Anne. Mandeville has plenty of Dutch mother-wit and Cockney observation, but he remains resolutely at a low level of sentiment, and though his rough, coarse phrases may, as Dr. Johnson said of them, open our views into real life, they ought not to be praised, as Mr. Kaye praises them, without reserve. Let my last word, however, be unqualified admiration for the zeal and competency with which that gentleman has carried out a formidable task.

THE DIARY OF A COUNTRY CLERGYMAN

THE DIARY OF A COUNTRY CLERGYMAN

If we go back far enough, the most trivial record of events takes a quaint colour which attracts the eye, but the editors of such miscellanies must be careful as they approach our own times. The success of Farington's "Diary" is likely to prove an irresistible temptation to those who find bundles of old papers in country garrets. I say this, offering no reproach to Mr. John Beresford, who has expended great industry and care in dressing up for us the confessions of a certain Reverend Mr. Woodforde, made to his diary between 1758 and 1781, but merely as a gentle warning. Mr. Woodforde, to tell the truth, is only just far enough removed from us, and only just amusing enough to be worthy of preservation on so broad a scale, and when Mr. Beresford says that he hopes to print the whole of the Diary, and that it will not be found possible to contain it in less than "a dozen stout volumes," I shrink a little, and ask myself, Will the amiable subject stand such extended treatment? I am afraid not.

Fanny Burney sternly says of the conversation of Woodforde's contemporary, Miss Gomme, that it was "lost and stagnant, like a poor little round old-fashioned garden-pond." Mr. Woodforde is not "lost," since Mr. Beresford has so admirably found him, but I confess that I feel him to be occasionally "stagnant." Even Mr. Beresford will admit that his life was a little round pond, whose duckweed was seldom ruffled by a breeze. Let us not be ungrateful;

there are engaging things in Woodforde's "Diary"—fish under the water, forget-me-nots and pimpernels on the edge of the pool, but I cannot help thinking of Miss Gomme as I turn the pages.

James Woodforde was born at Ansford, in Somersetshire, in 1740. His father was rector of Ansford and vicar of Castle Cary, which ancient borough will not thank Mr. Beresford for calling it a "village." All the Woodfordes seem to have kept diaries, and some of these are still in existence; the family tendency was to examine its own reflection in the pool. They were excellent and respectable men, of gentlemanly manners and a traditional leaning to the Church of England. Mr. Beresford claims, with justice, that the Diary he prints gives a fair impression of the condition of the clergy, which he thinks better of than did Macaulay and Lecky. No doubt such novelists as Fielding chose low types of parson for their more or less satirical, but on the whole realistic, pictures. It does not seem to be known what proportion of the clergy in the eighteenth century had taken their degrees at Oxford or Cambridge. Those who had done so, perhaps a minority, would be the selected class, a sort of ecclesiastical aristocracy. The Woodfordes through four generations had belonged to this class; in their sense, the Oxford training was a necessity. James was educated at Winchester, as his father Samuel had been before him, and we must think of his vacations as harmlessly spent in the paternal rectory of Ansford, until he reached an age at which he could proceed to matriculate in the usual way. Even Mr. Beresford has not been able to find out anything more about his childhood and boyhood.

A serious (but not too serious) youth of eighteen, James Woodforde arrived at New College, Oxford, in October, 1758. Not too serious, since the first object mentioned in the Diary is a pair of curling tongs, for which he paid two shillings and eightpence. He was able to make a striking appearance in a " superfine " suit of blue, with two white waistcoats and a new wig; but on more modest occasions he wore a " bad " chocolate suit, since the youngest and brightest of us cannot be always shining. There is a conscientious record of the drinking of much port wine, sometimes in company with the young gentleman's papa. James went shooting and riding a great deal, and in intervals between hearing Dr. Blackstone lecture on the Constitution, and composing lamentations over Saul and Jonathan in sapphic metre, he attended bull-baitings and thrashed the sadler's apprentice " for making verses on me." (I wish Mr. Beresford could have printed these verses.) He gave parties in college, where his friends grew " devilish drunk indeed," and he declaimed in chapel, in Latin, on minute points of ecclesiastical casuistry.

It is curious how distinct an impression of an undergraduate's life in Oxford in those days we are able to gain from the very slight and disconnected entries in the Diary. The lads played " crickett " in Pool Meadow, this game being apparently a new thing in the University. They also took walks, of an ingenuous character, with shop-girls; James had such a friend, called Nancy Bignell, whom he commissioned to make him six white handkerchiefs. When they were made, he presented her and her sister, Betsy, with a silver thimble each; and that seems to have been the end of the affair.

Five years before Woodforde appeared at New College Gibbon had gone down from Magdalen. Perhaps there had been a slight improvement in the state of things at the University since the days when the Fellows' conversation, like that of Miss Gomme, " stagnated in a round of college business, Tory politics, personal anecdotes, and private scandal," but much in Woodforde's artless entries may remind the reader of Gibbon's diatribes. " Their dull and deep potations excused the brisk intemperance of youth," which was not quite as "brisk" as might be imagined, after a supper consisting of one rabbit between three, with quantities of claret, madeira, and port to wash it down. How the young gentlemen were able to study the first three books of Hutchinson's "Moral Philosophy" and decipher manuscripts of Archbishop Laud after such copious draughts of liquor cannot easily be understood by our feebler generation. There seems to have been very little discipline in the college, and Woodforde was not far from resembling the eminent youthful Oxonian who outraged every law of the University "without once hearing the voice of admonition, without once feeling the hand of control."

It may be held, on the other side, that at the present moment control is too insistent and admonition too vociferous at Oxford and Cambridge. But in Woodforde's, as in other records of the University life of the eighteenth century, we feel sure that much is omitted because it was taken for granted, and that for those who sincerely wished to become versed in the classics and in theology there were ample opportunities. Woodforde, although his ambitions were modest, was one of these sincere and conscientious spirits.

On July 21, 1761, he was made a Fellow of his college, and all through that hot evening he treated the company to wine and punch in the stuffy Common Room. A few days later he exchanged paper snuff-boxes with one Nancy Rooke, and presented a still vaguer "Jenny" with court plaister and an ivory thimble. He expended twopence on oysters, and was "extremely well" all day afterwards. He collected his friends around him, and made them "immensely drunk," and all went well until he was suddenly "dunn'd" for half a hogshead of port. He notes, with ingenuous melancholy, "It is not in my power to pay it at present." It was high time that he hurried home to Ansford, where he recovered peace of mind and purse. He went to the county gaol, with three other friends, to visit the prisoners. Woodforde was much struck with a young good-looking fellow who was to be presently hanged for highway robbery. The friends stood him port wine and tobacco, and the convict " drank with us his last bottle and smoked a pipe with us." They gave him, between them, the gift of two shillings, although it is not clear what good a florin could be to a man who was going to be hanged the next morning. Woodforde went back to college to take his degree, being now in his twenty-fourth year. He was entertained after the ceremony by twenty-seven persons in Common Room " with wine and punch all the evening." Here is the end of it :—

"I sat up till after twelve o'clock, and then went to bed, and at three in the morning had my outward doors broken open, my glass door broke, and pulled out of bed, and brought into the Bachelors' Common Room, where I was obliged to drink and smoke, but not without a good many words. Peckham broke my doors, being very drunk, although they were open, which I do not relish of Peckham much."

Small blame to the new B.A., since Peckham must have been very tiresome.

After five years at Oxford, Woodforde took the two curacies of Thurlexton and Babcary, six miles from his home in Somersetshire; a few weeks later he resigned Thurlexton. He carried out his duties conscientiously, read prayers, and preached, and gave the ringers a pail of cider for ringing him in, and brewed strong beer, and rode about his parish in place of Mr. Cheese, the non-resident rector, " a very good kind of man," who never came near the place. Brother comes to stay with the curate, and causes him anxiety. "John is very indifferent by his being too busy with girls." We are spared the particulars, but there seems to have been trouble at Babcary, where the moral tone was not all that the curate might have wished. James takes rather a tragic view of Brother John: "I am afraid he will be ever miserable, but God forbid!" James was never miserable, except when he was to dine off ham and fowls and the maid forgot to boil the ham. The chief intellectual entertainment seems to have been going into Castle Cary to see plays acted. This is an interesting point. Are Otway's "Orphan" or Addison's "Cato" ever performed in the Court House at Castle Cary to-day? I am afraid not. Mr. Beresford is none too tragical over the deplorable decay of country gaieties. We read of a masquerade ball at the inn at Ansford, where the neighbouring clergy turned up in large numbers and danced most of the evening. Almost every page describes what the parson ate and drank, and the details of the parish are very humdrum.

The only real event which ever chequered the smooth surface of Woodforde's life was his acceptance of the living of Weston Longeville, in Norfolk. In April, 1775, he took up his abode, the Bishop, "a short, fat man," having behaved "exceedingly handsome and free." Woodforde's description of Norwich reads oddly after a century and a half of devastating extension and destruction:—

"We took a walk over the city in the morning, and we both agreed that it is the finest city in England by far; in the centre of it is a high hill, and on that a prodigious large old castle, almost perfect, and forms a complete square; round it is a fine terrace walk which commands the whole city. There are in the city 36 noble churches, mostly built with flint, besides many meeting-houses of diverse sorts. A noble river runs almost through the centre of the city. The city walls are also very perfect, and all round the city but where the river is. On the hills round the city stand many windmills, about a dozen, to be seen from Castle Mount."

He went with a friend to Yarmouth, where, no doubt for the first time in his life, he saw the sea. He was unusually moved; " it is a sweet beach," he writes, and a shoal of porpoises sported in the German Ocean for his particular benefit. His area of interest now opened out considerably. He went up to London, and saw the King and Queen, and went several times to the play. He returned on a visit to Oxford, where the authorities " behaved very polite and exceedingly civil," and where he preached a Latin sermon before the Vice-Chancellor in St. Mary's; next day he took his bachelor degree in divinity. After paying a three months' visit to his old haunts in Somersetshire, he went back to Norfolk, and settled down for the rest of his life at Weston Longeville. Here I must leave him, being, I confess, a little tired of reading so much about pig's face and greens, legs of mutton roasted, and wine and punch " in plenty." Yet I feel I do injustice to the worthy, kindly man, who seems an exact model for Praed's " Vicar " :—

> His talk was like a stream, which runs
>   With rapid change from rocks to roses:
> It slipped from politics to puns,
>   It passed from Mahomet to Moses;
> Beginning with the laws which keep
>   The planets in their radiant courses,
> And ending with some precept deep
>   For dressing eels, or shoeing horses.

This is the Reverend James Woodforde in a nutshell.

ANDREW LANG

ANDREW LANG

A DISTRACTED generation seems to have forgotten the charm of Andrew Lang. I hope that the publication of a handsome body of his poetical works will revive the sense of what an enchanter he was. I welcome it with cordiality, but I shall be still further delighted if it is followed by a revival of the best parts of his prose, since it must be admitted that Lang was only in a secondary degree a poet, while as a prose writer he was capable of effects unsurpassed by any one of his generation.

To-day, however, it is his verse which must be considered, and it is not easy to speak of it in terms which preserve the exact balance of truth. The fact is that we lack the word which should describe the writing of scholarly, sincere, and graceful verse that seldom quite reaches the highest level, and yet demands to be treated with sympathy and respect. There is a story—I believe still unpublished —of Wordsworth's meeting Moore in the drawing-room of Leigh Hunt, and saying to him, " You have written a great deal of elegant verse, Mr. Moore, but we should scarcely call it poetry, should we? " To which Moore tactfully replied, " Oh! certainly not, Mr. Wordsworth, certainly not! " Wordsworth was a little inclined to think that no one would get into heaven but himself. Yet there was a difference between " Tintern Abbey " and " Lalla Rookh," and Moore was man of the world enough to bow and to admit it.

In endeavouring to place the work of Andrew Lang at its true value, the critic is aided by the conciliatory attitude of the poet himself. When he published his "Rhymes Old and New," in 1888, he wrote: " I may as well repeat in prose what I have already said in verse : the Grass of Parnassus, the pretty autumn flower, grows in the marshes at the foot of the Muses Hill and other hills, not at the top, by any means." His reiterated allusions to " the unpermitted bay " and to " the peaks forbidden " make it very pathetic for us to realise how clear-sighted he became. In his boyhood he nourished the ardent hope that he might rise to the topmost rank. He was encouraged to believe himself the next Tennyson, the future Arnold; he was to be Théophile Gautier transferred to the graver British scene. Lang achieved much in his laborious crowded life, but he did not quite become the leading poet of his age. He did, however, become, in some wise, the characteristic poetic writer of a highly cultivated, disinterested, and gracious generation, and he will always be interesting as the typical figure of the " eighties." After the successive explosions of genius in Meredith and Swinburne, reverberations through the whole Victorian cavern, there came a lull, a period of partial silence, in which the voices of much less excited singers were heard whispering together about ballades and pantoums, and " the rules of verse."

If justice is to be done to Lang, he must not be measured by the great, resonant singers, but by the artists who did their recuperative work, usefully, too, though not so vociferously, after the tumult had died down. Andrew Lang, who, but for a defect (presently to be mentioned) would have been a consummate artist, took a prominent part in this task of " tidying-up " the slopes of Parnassus. Mrs. Lang tells us in her preface that her husband " was always ready to laugh at his own productions." That is quite true—with the reservation that he was human enough to dislike very much that anyone else should laugh at them. It showed his modesty and good taste; at the same time, the trait is not characteristic of the sublimest order of bards. Can anyone conceive Milton or Dante ready to laugh at his own productions?

Mrs. Lang, who deserves high praise for the judgment and courage of her selection, has not attempted to place her husband's poems before us in biographical or bibliographical order. She has, no doubt purposely, omitted all dates, and has refrained from any indication of previous arrangement. She has grouped the pieces together under a variety of headings, such as "Oxford and St. Andrews," "Scotland," "Loyal Lyrics," and the like. This order is very much to be commended, since a mere reprint of Andrew Lang's miscellaneous lyrics, in the successive volumes which he published in the course of his long life, would have produced a sense of inextricable confusion. He had a hundred interests, and they inspired his rhymes in turn, no one subject occupying his mind to the exclusion of the others, but each incessantly recurring. Mrs. Lang, therefore, has done his memory a benefit in discovering a pattern in this maze, and in giving her husband's poetical work a sequence which he never had the leisure or the inclination to demand for it. At the same time, it may be permissible, on historic grounds, to recall biographical conditions which Mrs. Lang has thought it best, for the moment, to ignore. Her collection presents to us, in excellent shape, the best results of her husband's work in poetry. It throws no light at all on the development of his genius.

Very little has been made public as yet about the career of Andrew Lang, who died twelve years ago, just too late to be included in the latest Supplement of the Dictionary of National Biography. He came up to Oxford from St. Andrews, he entered Balliol, where Jowett predicted for him the highest honours in literature, and he secured a fellowship at Merton. I am very glad that Mrs. Lang opens her collection with the beautiful verses, written (I think) at Oxford in 1865, and recalling the early days of which we are always hoping to hear something more definite :—

> St. Andrew by the northern sea,
> A haunted town it is to me !
> A little city, worn and gray,
>   The gray North Ocean girds it round;
> And o'er the rocks and o'er the bay,
>   The long sea-rollers surge and sound;
> And still the thin and biting spray
>   Drives down the melancholy street,
> And still endure, and still decay,
>   Towers that the salt winds vainly beat.
> Ghost-like and shadowy they stand
> Dim-mirrored in the wet sea-sand.

It was a very happy thought to begin the "Poetical Works" with these lines. They come as near as the sensitive mind of the poet ever came to a confession of what " the college of the scarlet gown " in the " haunted town " of St. Andrews meant to him. It was his place of spiritual pilgrimage to the end of his years.

Oxford came next, with its scholastic enchantments and its memories of old friends, but Oxford was never so dear to Lang as was the " little city, grey and sere," at the storm-swept extremity of Fife. He never spoke much about St. Andrews, but it was always present to his memory, and he loved it better than any other place on earth. As St. Andrews and Balliol had made him, he appeared at last, in 1872, with a slim volume, bound in ivory-coloured cloth, called " Ballads and Lyrics of Old France," in his hand. Tennyson and Morris were silent; Browning was proceeding to the extremity of caprice in " Pacchiarotto "; and Swinburne was beginning to repeat his effects.

There seemed to be room for a new poet. Lang presently

arrived from Oxford armed in a panoply of graces, and full of ambition to take his place in the forefront of the writers of his time. He had mastered, what few Englishmen fifty years ago knew or cared about, the romantic literature of France, and his earliest publication was in the main a paraphrase of selections from it. Here were the masters of the Pléiade, and, above all others, Ronsard. Lang hoped to be the Ronsard of a new English Renaissance. His translations showed, if they showed nothing else, a sympathy interpreted by the most delicate skill. Who, through the four centuries which intervened, had understood the spirit of Rémy Belleau so perfectly as the young Oxford don who wrote :—

> April, pride of murmuring
> Winds of spring,
> That, beneath the winnowed air,
> Trap with subtle nets and sweet
> Flora's feet,
> Flora's feet, the fleet and fair?

Why, after so propitious a start, made, too, at the relatively mature age of twenty-eight, Andrew Lang did not immediately proceed to original composition, I do not know. He appeared in London, in 1876, attended by a brilliant reputation, and he plunged into journalism. He continued his study of the Greeks, and he translated Theocritus and Homer. His fame as a prose-writer of extraordinary delicacy and wit was founded on his articles, mainly anonymous; he revolutionised the " high-brow " section of a daily newspaper. But his friends and admirers asked for more tangible evidence of his originality, and I do not know why he delayed in giving it.

At length, in 1880, appeared the " Ballades in Blue China," which now occupy the close of Mrs. Lang's first volume. They created a sensation which may be compared, and must indeed be compared, with the success of Théodore de Banville's " Odes Funambulesques." Lang had studied the form and language of Banville very closely; he had taken the " Petit Traité " as his text-book; he had transferred to his own blood the heady wine of the " Trente-six Ballades Joyeuses " of 1872. The little book, in its white parchment cover stamped with a studious Chinese monk in blue, from the reign of the Emperor Hwang, was a novelty in form as well as in substance to English readers.

Moreover, this measured, accomplished verse, dancing in fetters, corresponded with the fashion of the moment. Swinburne was trying to curb his redundancy by composing rondeaux. Austin Dobson, with a firmer hand and a more concentrated taste than Lang, was putting some of his most exquisite creations into the severe " French forms." All the young poets were writing chants-royals and villanelles. Most of Lang's ballades were playful and fantastic; occasionally, in a serious mood, he proved what could be done in a higher strain. His " Ballade of Sleep " is one of the gems of the nineteenth century; the exquisite " Ballade of True Wisdom " shows how perfect sincerity can be linked with perfect workmanship.

But all that he had hitherto published was brief, and, in Goethe's sense, occasional. The word went round among Lang's friends that he was at work on a long poem in six books, on the life and adventures of " Helen of Troy." This was to crown his labours and fix his ambition for once and all. In 1882 it appeared, a romantic Homeric epic in *rime royal*, accompanied by an essay in prose on the history and literature of the theme. Despite the eagerness with which it had been awaited, or perhaps even because of the exaggerated hopes which it had excited, the reception of " Helen of Troy " was cold in the extreme.

The author's disappointment was acute, and the consequence was that, until the end of his life, although he continued to rhyme with voluble assiduity, he never again took pains to make his poetry first-rate. Over "Helen of Troy" he had expended, perhaps, too much pains. It was almost more a study in archæology than a poem, so closely did the author hug the shores of tradition, so shy was he of steering out into the sea of imagination. "Helen of Troy" was treated, as it was bound to be treated, with respect, but it was not read. It will be found here, occupying nearly the whole of Mrs. Lang's fourth volume, and the curious reader may ask himself to-day whether it is possible to enjoy to-day what could not be liked forty years ago :—

> O'er Helen's shrine the grass is growing green,
>   In desolate Therapnæ; none the less
> Her sweet face now unworshipp'd and unseen
>   Abides the symbol of all loveliness,
>   Of Beauty ever stainless in the stress
> Of warring lusts and fears; and still divine,
>   Still ready with immortal peace to bless
> Them that with pure hearts worship at her shrine.

The reason why Lang, with so great a devotion to the art of poetry, and so remarkable a skill in versification, did not achieve more uncontested success in the exercise of it, may be sought in his temperament. Like Gray, it may be said of him that "he never spoke out." He shrank from a close examination of life, and from passion as from a devouring flame. He seemed to take refuge in literature from any such disillusion as too close a scrutiny of experience would have brought with it. Hence, he was tempted by his amazing facility of expression to gloze over emotions and to suppress facts that were inconvenient. The texture of his poetry was thus made smooth and flexible, but at the cost of richness. The student who is interested in such tasks may compare any canto of "Helen of Troy" with the "Eros and Psyche" of Mr. Robert Bridges. At first sight the similarity of style and form is remarkable, but the reader soon observes that the Poet Laureate has greatly the advantage in audacity and colour. He loads his palette and insults tradition, where Lang is assiduous to preserve tradition and maintain the just archaic tone.

In fine, I think that Lang should be regarded as a lyrist of artifice, to whom the visible and toiling world was a mystery over the surface of which he hung in a trance of curiosity, without attempting to penetrate it, and for whom everything human was a subject of lightly flying, flashing verse, half humorous, half melancholy. If we consider him too gravely, we lose him altogether.

ARTHUR O'SHAUGHNESSY

ARTHUR O'SHAUGHNESSY

IN the late 'sixties and early 'seventies the offices of the British Museum were a nest of singing birds, as Dr. Johnson more fantastically said of Pembroke College. Coventry Patmore, whose centenary we are just now celebrating, when not engaged on cataloguing the folios of the Fathers, was proclaiming " The Victories of Love." Richard Garnett, withdrawn for an hour out of the dust and strain of answering queries from his throne in the midst of the Reading-room, was inditing idylls and epigrams. There was occasionally visible, in the recesses of the library, that extraordinary, that unique figure, Théophile Marzials, whose features I must one of these days revive for the entertainment of my readers.

But not less characteristic than any of these was to be found, in the very bowels of the building, the elegant and melodious Arthur O'Shaughnessy, in an odour of spirits of wine, preserving in many a small and cunning phial rare fishes as graceful and pallid as himself. He was a sort of mystery, revealed twice a day. In the morning, a smart, swift figure in a long frock-coat, with romantic eyes and bushy whiskers, he would be seen entering the monument and descending into its depths, to be observed no more till he as swiftly rose and left it late in the afternoon. I do not forget the somewhat sceptical thrill I received, late in 1869, on being told that our official ichthyologist was "writing poetry." Would it be about fishes? No, not a gurnard nor a flounder was mentioned in " An Epic of Women," which appeared, not without creating a considerable sensation, in the early spring of 1870.

The passage of more than half a century is very trying to any reputation, but it surprises me that Mr. W. A. Percy, an American who has edited the handsome selection before me, should have found it difficult to obtain O'Shaughnessy's works, or should be able to take credit to himself for " the pious task " of making them " accessible to readers of English poetry." If this were needful, as I must suppose it was, Mr. Percy deserves the thanks of what I am afraid is a forgetful generation. O'Shaughnessy was solitary, a cryptic being; he died when he was young, and it seemed to be nobody's business to preserve his memory. It lies embalmed in nothing but his sad, emotional verse, like one of his own lepidosirens in a vase of spirits of wine. He has had fervent admirers—in particular, F. T. Palgrave (whose praise was even injudicious); and an American lady, Mrs. Moulton, who published a eulogy in 1894.

He appears in the anthologies, from which he will never be dislodged. But his four books have not been reprinted, and I do not question that they are now, as Mr. Percy testifies, difficult to purchase. This latest worshipper, indeed, seems to find the shrine absolutely deserted, and he frankly admits that he knows nothing about the history of the poet between his birth in 1844 and his death in 1881. I know a good deal more than that, although there is much about Arthur O'Shaughnessy, the most blameless of gentle spirits, which no one knows, and which it is needless that anyone should know. But something may, after all these years, be indicated to prevent his continuing to be, what he seems to have become, the veriest ghost among men of letters.

On January 20, 1873 (I am particular about this date), I, being then a transcriber in the Department of Printed Books, descended for a chat to the bald home of ichthyology. To my surprise, I found the poet, who had brushed his phials aside, with his head on his folded arms upon his table. He raised his face to me in tears, and when I inquired what was the matter, he replied by a question, "Have you not seen the newspaper? Lord Lytton is dead!" When I hinted my surprise at his emotion, he added, "No one will ever know what he was to me!" Arthur O'Shaughnessy's name (if that was his name) is not mentioned in the official Life of Sir Edward Bulwer Lytton, who nevertheless occupied a protective position towards the poet throughout his career. When Arthur was seventeen he received through Lytton an appointment in the British Museum, and at nineteen was promoted, in spite of the protests of professional zoologists, to the post he held until his death.

He was little adapted for such technical work at first; indeed, it used to be said that, having been the victim of an accident, he fitted the tail of one broken fish to the head of another so deftly that a German savant was deceived, and wrote a sensational memoir of a wholly new species. Whenever there was trouble of this kind, Bulwer Lytton saw his protégé safely through, and O'Shaughnessy, who was handy and intelligent, presently mastered his business, but his heart was never in his gallipots. His heart was on his sleeve, and the only matters which really interested him were verse and the passion of love, after which he thirsted as harts do after water-brooks. In an autobiographic sketch, he displayed the bent of his nature: "Sympathy after sympathy reawakens warmth, heat, passion, returning in soft tides to revivify my inmost being," and this was the whole of the inner life of a delicate and sentimental soul, strangely isolated from domestic happiness, not supported by ambition or humour, yet walking through life cheerfully, elegantly, amiably, searching for Love, and finding it, in the old phrase, an inhabitant of the rocks.

The reception of O'Shaughnessy's first book of poems was cordial, particularly among the younger poets. It gained him immediate hospitality from Rossetti, who was the god of the hour, and cordial notice from Swinburne. The critics were kind, and I cannot help recalling, after more than fifty years, the great pleasure given to him by the long review in the *Sunday Times*, written (I do not doubt) by Joseph Knight. The public was not very receptive in those days, and had been gorged by the Pre-Raphaelites; but a great many army-officers bought "An Epic of Women," deceived, it was said, by the apparent gallantry of the title. Two years later, O'Shaughnessy published "Lays of France," paraphrases of five of the verse-romances of the French poetess of the twelfth century, known as Marie de France. This was a happy idea, for Marie is of all mediæval writers the most like O'Shaughnessy himself, with her artful ease of narrative and her lax, melodious amorosity. The best of Marie's lays is "Eliduc," and this seems to me the best of O'Shaughnessy's also—tender, sad-coloured, and long-winded. In 1874 he published "Music and Moonlight," which contains some of his best lyrics, and a good deal that was hardly worth preservation. He experienced complicated bereavement; he married in the very odour of Pre-Raphaelitism, but lost his wife and both his infant children, and relapsed into solitude again. In the mid-winter of 1881 he rode outside an omnibus without overcoat or umbrella, caught a cold on his lungs, and died—so it was reported—in the hands of a Mrs. Gamp. After his death a friend collected a volume of "Songs of a Worker," from which the buoyancy of his early writing had evaporated, leaving little that can be read with pleasure. His lyric vein had been thin, and was soon exhausted.

There was small communication between literary Paris and London in the days immediately preceding the war of

1870. Arthur O'Shaughnessy used to go over to France for his holidays, and he was the first to bring us back authentic news of the Parnassians. He was presented to Victor Hugo and to Leconte de Lisle, but he was more comfortable with his own coevals, and he regaled us with anecdotes of Baudelaire told him by Coppée and Catulle Mendès. These were influences on his own poetry—a certain French character in which was eyed suspiciously by the British public of 1871. O'Shaughnessy was accused of being a purveyor of what Tennyson, in a silly phrase, had attacked as "poisonous honey brought from France." Journalists inveighed against what they called "Art pour Art"— believing that to be a French expression. O'Shaughnessy suffered from being supposed to be the apostle of this "Art pour Art."

He also suffered from the attitude of the major gods of the English poetical synod, who were not quite certain that their number was not complete before his arrival. But his most formidable opponent was his own extraordinary inequality of performance, and this he never mastered. Mr. Percy, who is an enthusiastic admirer, unwillingly admits that O'Shaughnessy's work is "by no means of uniform excellence." This is to put the truth very mildly, for it is safe to say that in three-fourths of the contents of his four books no merit whatever is to be found, except a sort of perfume individual to this poet, which tells the reader where he is, and encourages him to proceed.

No critical error leads to more futility of judgment than the dwelling in the first instance upon faults and failures. The point of departure should be admiration and appreciation, and when the merits of a writer are fixed we may consider his shortcomings. Every poet of consequence has written flat and awkward verses; some, like Wordsworth and Coleridge, have even abused their privilege in doing so. Yet no critic in his senses opens a study of those writers by an examination of " The Destiny of Nations " or " The Egyptian Maid "; he expatiates on " Kubla Khan " or " The Affliction of Margaret." In the case of no modern author is it more necessary to bear this principle in mind than in that of O'Shaughnessy, who needs to be protected against his own lack of self-criticism.

If we take his poetry at its best and analyse what distinguishes it from the work of other poets, we are struck by its lyrical art—soft, tremulous, and rich; this poet has the voice of the blackbird, not that of the nightingale or the lark. It is a flute-music, not strong in quality, nor wide in range, but of a piercing tenderness :—

> O ivory bird, that shakest thy wan plumes,
> And dost forget the sweetness of thy throat
> For a most strange and melancholy note—
> Thou wilt forsake the summer and the blooms
> And go to winter in a place remote !

There is never any searching after strange epithets or violent phrases, but the stream of verbal melody flows on without effort and without interruption to its appointed close. If the reader's ear is not attuned to enjoy the peculiar sound and perfume of this delicate sadness, argument is thrown away :

> There is an earthly glimmer in the Tomb :
>   And, healed in their own tears and with long sleep,
>   My eyes unclose and feel no need to weep;
> But, in the corner of the narrow room,
> Behold, Love's spirit standeth, with the bloom
>   That things made deathless by Death's self may keep.
>   O what a change ! for now his looks are deep,
> And a long patient smile he can assume :
> While Memory, in some soft monotone,
>   Is pouring like an oil into mine ear
>   The tale of a most short and hollow bliss,
> That I once throbbed indeed to call my own,
>   Holding it hardly between joy and fear—
>   And how that broke and how it came to this.

The poet is often more impassioned than here, as in the best known of his pieces, the wonderful "Fountain of Tears," and less resigned in his songs, such as "Has summer come without the rose" or "In all my singing and speaking," but the general content of the verse is limited to this simple order of emotions. It extends no further than the *desiderium*, the hopeless longing of the heart which has known what love is and has lost it, and finds nothing else worth living for. This involves, of course, a very limited outlook upon life, and one which to the ordinary man of energy seems futile and even reprehensible :—

> I made another garden, yea,
>   For my new love;
> I left the wild rose where it lay,
>   And set the new above.
> Why did the summer not begin?
>   Why did my heart not haste?
> My old love came and walked therein,
>   And laid the garden waste.

To the expression of this introspective melancholy O'Shaughnessy added a limpid beauty of light and colour, a subdued and partly tropical effulgence, which prevents the amorous monomania from becoming tiresome. This was a quality which he shared with none of his contemporaries. To give instances would be impossible here, since of all poets O'Shaughnessy is the most difficult to do justice to in a small space. His simplicity is diffuse, his effects belong to the whole poem and not to a line or to a couplet. One or two of his poems, and in particular the savage dream of were-wolves, called "Bisclaveret," suggest that O'Shaughnessy might have excelled in the presentation of spectral visions and violent action, but he was seldom content to wander far from the edge of the Fountain of Tears.

AUSTIN DOBSON

AUSTIN DOBSON

IN his sound and catholic "Popular History of English Poetry," recently published through Messrs. A. M. Philpot, Mr. Earle Welby says that "Dobson, despite his popularity, is undervalued." I believe this to be as true as it is paradoxical, and I would go so far as to modify the phrase by saying "because of his popularity." Since the original publication of Dobson's early poetry exactly half a century ago, the circulation of his verse has been wider than that of any other English verse-writer of his immediate generation, and since his death, on September 2, 1921, the reissue of his writings has continued. Notwithstanding that, or as I obstinately repeat because of that, his genius as a poet has never been whole-heartedly proclaimed, and he still lacks critical appreciation which is freely bestowed on bards much his inferiors in art and refinement.

The issue, for the first time, of a complete collection of Dobson's poems seems appropriate for a consideration of the problem why, being so generally enjoyed, he is not more vigorously praised. But, on closer inspection, we shall find that his is not a solitary case. The critics are suspicious of a talent which appeals to a wide audience. The extreme popularity of "The Angel in the House" long blinded the best judges to the merit of Coventry Patmore, and, were I not afraid of being invidious, I could point to cases much more recent in which the main argument against poets has been that their works have a ready sale. The notion that poetry is something secret, like the laws of the Rosicrucians, and can be recognised only by the elect, is a general opinion in the inner circle of connoisseurs; and there is something, no doubt, to be said for it. Popularity adds no value to the verse of an Eliza Cook or an Ella Wheeler Wilcox, and so far as it is founded on facile metre and shallow thought it is a beacon warning the serious reader away from the rocks. But the critic needs to discover two things—why the verse is popular and whether the poet's judgment coincides with that of the public.

Austin Dobson, who was by three years Swinburne's junior, began to write at a time when the public was both a little mystified and a little wearied by the violence of the new poetry. He started late, and he journeyed warily, not gaining confidence in the practice of his art until he passed his thirtieth year. Meanwhile, after being touched not at all to his disadvantage by the colour of the Pre-Raphaelites, he left their neighbourhood and attached himself to the band of easy rhymers who were numerous and fashionable in the 'seventies. But he served a far severer apprenticeship than they, and has his reward in being still remembered, while they are all forgotten.

> POPE taught him rhythm, PRIOR ease,
> PRAED buoyancy and banter;
> What modern bard would learn from these?
> Ah, *tempora mutantur*,

he wrote in 1900, looking back to his own sources. But in 1870 various "modern bards" were glancing at these models, and particularly at Praed. The amazing elasticity, the vaultings over metrical trapèzes, which attracted the young Dobson to the author of the "Letter of Advice," were powerful factors moulding his own early verse, and they prepared his popularity without aiding in the development of his genius.

On the verses which Dobson wrote between 1865 and 1875, the stamp of Praed becomes more evident the further the work recedes. Such pieces—and these are among the most durably "popular" that he ever wrote—as "A Gentleman of the Old School" and "Incognita," might have been written by Praed himself when he was not quite at the summit of his sparkling audacity. A later writer, born midway between Praed and Dobson, was to the latter rather a colleague than a master; this was Frederick Locker, a wit in verse of delicate neatness but rather limited scope. It must be admitted that Dobson was at a disadvantage in direct rivalry with Locker and Praed, and for a reason which may now be noted.

Austin Dobson was called, by the abuse of a phrase which never was French and will never be English, a writer of *vers de société*. If this annoying epithet means anything, it indicates a writer who, like the innumerable rhymers of the *ruelle* in seventeenth-century France, having hung about the social centre, was able to turn out verses directly referring to current persons and incidents. This was the advantage also of the English poets who preceded Dobson; Praed had danced with Araminta and received the whispered confidences of Medora Trevilian. When Locker mournfully demanded

> Where are the curls of Cantelupe,
> The laugh of Lady Di?

he mentioned real persons whom everyone had seen riding in the Row. But Dobson, whose life was uniform and sequestered to a remarkable degree, had no aptitude for fashionable converse, and in social respects was like a titmouse. He was completely conscious of this, and was vexed at the perpetual repetition of the "writer of *vers de société*" epithet, for which, however, as is only just to point out, his own title-page of 1873 had been responsible. He desired to substitute for *société* the phrase *lyra jocosa*, but his myriad admirers of "A Dead Letter" and "The

Child-Musician" would have none of this. Hence, before he could throw off the deluding influence of Praed and Locker, he was chained to an attribution which was proper to them but inappropriate to him. When he gained confidence in his own gifts, it was in the French and English romances of the eighteenth century, not in the observation of his own times, that he found his unique and proper sphere. To compare "The Ballad of Beau Brocade" or "The Ladies of St. James's" with "Dora versus Rose" is to realise what ingenuity Austin Dobson wasted in his early following of Praed.

Dobson's vogue with the admirers of his playful verse was already at its height when, refusing to accede to it, he set himself with intense application to the study of his art. It was about the year 1875, when he had passed the age of thirty-five, that he became profoundly moved, as so many poets of that generation were, by the "Petit Traité" of Théodore de Banville. No one learned so much as he from that extraordinary manual. We had the sonnet widely cultivated in England already; Austin Dobson proposed to introduce a variety of other "French forms"—the ballade, the rondeau, the chant royal, the villanelle. What attracted him to them was the discipline they demanded, the impossibility of cultivating them while yet remaining slipshod or irregular.

These "forms" are much despised to-day by writers who grudge the trouble of making their own verses scan, and who shrink from the labour of finding an intermediate rhyme. In Dobson's hands the ballade, elaborate and dignified, became an instrument of the highest art, and his examples of it are the best which any modern language has produced. A further impulse completed his apprenticeship. In 1877 Tennyson warned him against the dangers of facility, and recommended to him the terseness and fullness of Horace, proposing that Dobson should give close study to the workmanship of the "Odes." The mixture of pathos and jest in the great Latin miscellany instinctively attracted the young English poet, who took Tennyson's counsel to heart, and devoted some months to the minute analysis of the form of the "Odes." For the future, something definitely Horatian was added to his style, to its great advantage, although the muse of Austin Dobson was always more at home with Septimius and Posthumus than with Pyrrha and Lydia, of whose vagaries he was constitutionally a little shy.

Under the French and Latin influences of which I have just spoken, Austin Dobson achieved what, in my opinion, are his principal successes. It is a great convenience that in this new "complete" edition the date of composition of all the pieces has been recorded, especially since the editor has distributed the poems anew on a system of his own devising. When we examine the pages we find that this brief period from 1875 to 1880 is responsible for "The Idyll of the Carp" (Dobson's earliest experiment in lyrical dialogue), "Ars Victrix," the best rondeaux and ballades, and the inimitable "Beau Brocade." It also produced the set of minute lyrical dramas which he called "Proverbs in Porcelain." The reader who wishes to enjoy the genius of Austin Dobson at its highest point of perfection should study these miniature comedies, adding to them "Au Revoir," which the editor (for what reason I cannot conceive) has removed to another part of the book. There is nothing like them in English, and very little in French. They have a colour, a music, a tenderness which lift them far above the playful verse of the eighteenth century, the elegant and well-turned wit of writers like Chaulieu or of Grasset, although to this latter in his tales Dobson owed some allegiance.

It is not easy, without too copious quotation, to give examples of the art of "Proverbs in Porcelain," either when they are deliberately satirical, as "The Cap that Fits," almost boisterous in their humour, as "The Metamorphosis," or tender and even tear-compelling, as "Good-Night, Babette." Several of the little rhymed duologues bear a lyric in the heart of the conversation, and these songs, which include the facetious "When Jove, the Skies' Director," and the wistful "Once at the Angelus," are among Dobson's tiny masterpieces. After the period of which I have just spoken, he continued to write with perfection and delicacy, although not often with the same inspiration, but one quality never left him again, the determination to spare no pains, to devote unflinching hours to that *labor limae*, which seems to the amateur mere waste of time. I think it was Goethe who said that he enjoyed correcting his own poems as much as he did writing them. It was also Austin Dobson's favourite occupation.

I have hinted that in his most Horatian moods Dobson shrank from one phase of the Horatian experience. His type of womanhood was not Lyce or even Cynara, and he was content to find the feverish part of love disappearing as the odes of his favourite Latin master proceeded. The feminine ideal of Dobson is the fresh, innocent and unworldly, though by no means silly, maiden of seventeen. She appears before his window as out of one of Millais's drawings, in muslin and roses, with a garden hat and a book. She is ready for a little flirtation, but it must be carefully conducted, since she is excessively sensitive :—

> So I dare not woo you, Sweet,
> For a day,
> Lest I lose you in a flash,
> As I may;
> Did I tell you tender things,
> You would shake your sudden wings;—
> You would start from him who sings,
> And away !

Many of Dobson's early lyrics might have been written to illustrate scenes from the novels of Anthony Trollope, and they illustrate a like condition of cultivated middle-class society. At the present moment both seem old-fashioned, even dowdy, like the raiment of the inhabitants of Barset. But we must not ignore among the characteristics of Austin Dobson's prose and poetry the modesty of his outlook upon life. He shut his eyes to the violence of instinct and all the squalors of passion. In his otherwise almost faultless personal character, timidity was a feature which could not but be regretted. As he grew older his scruples grew upon him—his "apprehensions came in crowds," like those of Wordsworth's Margaret. He deprived himself of some of his beloved eighteenth-century authors because of the profane expressions they contained. He turned out of his library the poems of his favourite Théophile Gautier, because they harboured that harmless pleasantry, "Musée Secret." I do not pretend not to regret this prudery, which was a weakness that increased with advancing years. But I must bear witness that it was personal to the poet himself. No one was less pharisaical than he, no one ever was more careful not to press upon others what he accepted as a law to himself. Nor am I quite sure that the novelists of to-day, who worship the dirty devils of psycho-analysis, have anything much more attractive to offer us than the perhaps excessive stainlessness of the Victorian angels.

The careful preface to this "complete" edition is signed by the poet's son, Mr. Alban Dobson, whose judicious devotion to his father's memory is beyond praise. It is well to have a final *corpus* of the work of so meticulous a workman as this poet, who even in his eightieth year had not entirely lost his skill. At the same time, I must record the opinion that Austin Dobson's poetry will be valued mainly in selections. In these 481 pages there are some repetitions and even a certain monotony. We can trust Mr. Alban Dobson, who has already brought out one very charming anthology since his father's death, to bear in mind the limitations of human attention. That the best of the poems before me will ever be neglected I refuse to believe :—

> When the ways are heavy with mire and rut,
>   In November fogs, in December snows,
> When the North Wind howls, and the doors are shut,—
>   There is place and enough for the pains of prose;
>   But whenever a scent from the hawthorn blows,
> And the jasmine-stars at the casement climb,
>   And a Rosalind-face at the lattice shows,
> Then hey !—for the ripple of laughing rhyme !

and we may be glad to quit Austin Dobson with so optimistic a reflection.

W. D. HOWELLS

W. D. HOWELLS

FOR some reason, which I observe but fail to fathom, the indifference that always follows the excitement caused by the death of a prominent author is more acute in the case of the novelist than in any other. The poet or philosopher or historian, not having enjoyed the suffrages of a wide audience, suffers less than the story-teller, whose range is universal. The "best-seller" never recovers from the ordeal of Kensal Green, unless his work possesses extraordinary qualities of solid merit. He may live to be as old as he likes, and may still sell, but once let him die, and the cohort of his readers flees to the army of some surviving brother. It seems as though the ordinary reader of a novel must have a vague confidence that the tale he listens to is spun out of a living brain; the word from the tomb has no charm for him. Where, now, is Edna Lyall, and where is William Black? They have long been with the snows of yester-year.

The universal fate which attends all popular novelists, good or bad, fell almost immediately on the amiable and accomplished writer who was unquestionably the most famous American novelist of the end of last century and the beginning of this. Having brought to a close in 1920, at the age of eighty-three, a life full of honour and celebrity, William Dean Howells almost immediately sank into desuetude, and has ceased to be discussed or even read. His is a signal instance of the post-mortem ingratitude of the public.

Howells, however, was far too important a figure in the

literature of his country to suffer more than a temporary obscuration. He holds a very interesting place historically as the latest and the last-surviving member of the New England school which dominated American letters in the nineteenth century. During the thirty years which separated the passing of Lowell and his own decease, Howells was the most active and representative American man of letters. By his own lights, which were not quite our lights to-day, he guided critical taste, and supplied pure narrative entertainment through nearly half a century.

Such a man cannot disappear, though he may be eclipsed, and no doubt his talent will receive a justice denied to it to-day when his memory has passed further back into the general perspective. A beginning has been made by the solid and slightly ponderous monograph which lies before me to-day. Mr. Firkins, himself evidently an American, and presumably a New Englander, is well fitted to appreciate the national side of Howell's character, and although he has approached his subject with equal care and enthusiasm, he is not blind to its defects.

Of these, perhaps the most obvious is the excessive fecundity of the author. Howells wrote with indomitable pertinacity for more than fifty years, and the array of his works, his forty novels, his thirty plays, his innumerable tales and travels, his poems, his criticism, forms a bulk so formidable that no single reader could study him *in extenso*, and yet read anything else. I suspect that Mr. Firkins, painstaking and thorough though he is, has been foiled by some of the Miscellanies. It is a sinister fact that the Library Edition of Howells's Works, started in the heat of his popularity, after the issue of six volumes was presently " stopped or suspended," and is very unlikely to be resumed in these chillier days. Even Mr. Firkins, struggling between zeal and adversity, is obliged to admit that the vast bibliography he prints is "selective, not complete."

Excessive fluency, however, is not the only, nor the most evident, drawback which has alienated readers, and especially English readers, from the work of this able writer. It was the unhappy peculiarity of Howells to give way in two particulars to what can only be called a mis-judgment of the business of a writer. In the first place, he sacrificed everything to a theory of realism; in the second, he subordinated all principles of taste to an almost provincial anxiety to praise anything American *because* it was American.

To take the latter mistake before the former, it has regretfully to be said that Howells was a very bad critic, one of the worst. We might pass over this in silence, were it not for the unfortunate circumstance that he valued his own critical work very highly, thought it of national importance, and produced during his later years a vast quantity of it. He indulged in it a cluster of heresies, such as that it is snobbery to pretend to admire any literature except that of our own day; that American poetry is sufficient for all purposes, and that therefore no manly citizen needs visit "the mausoleum of the British poets"; that romance in any form is puerile and even immoral; that sex ought never to be emphasised; and that the American writer not only should satisfy, but does satisfy, every requirement of the American reader. Accordingly, if somebody from St. Louis writes "a real, downright American" book, even though it is a crude affair, that book must be praised to excess and preferred to the best product of an effete Europe. Mr. Firkins has had great difficulty with this aspect of his hero, which he is too honest to conceal, but which gives him evident pain.

The anti-romantic error was the other rock on which the barque of Howells struck. He was born into the generation which everywhere began to rebel against the excessive practice of romance. He was three years older than Zola, whose opinions were being disseminated in the newspapers when Howells first came up to Boston. He formed a strong opinion that in fiction nothing should be introduced that is not normal, probable, and superficial. His object, undoubtedly, was truth, and he said a great many pointed and wise things on the very difficult question of what is imaginative truth, particularly in his early volume of essays, called "Criticism and Fiction." But during the next thirty years, while he incessantly called attention to the subject in his practice and his theory, he became more and more the slave of his prejudices. He excused Hawthorne for his romance because he was an American, but he was pitiless to Scott and Thackeray, and, indeed, to all English novelists. He declared that Jane Austen was "the first and the last" of them to treat material with truthfulness.

This hatred of European romance became with him a mania, an obsession. He lifted his trumpet and blew out the glad tidings that an American lady called Sarah Orme Jewett was a far finer writer of short stories than Maupassant, in whom he quaintly detected traces of romanticism. But this was more than even Mr. Firkins can put up with.

When we come to examine in what this virtue of "realism" consisted, we are met with the strange discovery that what Howells really meant by it was a picture of the mere surface of life. He believed, we are told, "in the omnipresence of good," that is to say, he refused to observe any of the phenomena of evil. We are told by Mr. Firkins that Howells would not permit "the slightest relaxation in the demand for ethical tendency." In plainer words, he was the most rigorous of prudes. But how is a man to write severely "realistic" novels if he not merely does not call a spade a spade, but even denies that such an implement exists? This is how the subject-matter of the forty novels is described by Howells's devoted biographer:—

"Mr. Howells's taste has played the part of censor for his themes. In these forty volumes, adultery is never pictured; divorce once and sparingly ("A Modern Instance."); marriage discordant to the point of cleavage, only once and in the same novel with the divorce; crime only once with any fullness ("The Quality of Mercy"); politics never; religion passingly and superficially; science only in crepuscular psychology; mechanics, athletics, bodily exploits or collisions, very rarely."

The Gadfly in Shelley's drama sings:—

> All inn-doors and windows
> Were open to me :
> I saw all that sin does,
> Which lamps hardly see,

for the Gadfly is a genuine "realist." But Howells withdraws with a blush at the very notion of an open window. "The impudent lamps!" Howells would have nothing to do with them.

With all these drawbacks, what is it, then, that makes Howells a writer of permanent interest and charm? To discover this, we have briefly to recall his early career. He was born in 1837, the son of a bankrupt type-setter, in an Ohio village. He enjoyed no set education, having to earn his living as a printer's devil and then as a reporter from the age of twelve. For a little while he was a druggist's apprentice, like Ibsen, and meanwhile he was browsing on all the books he could borrow. He went to the State capital, Columbus, and became a journalist, and when he was twenty-three he made a brief holiday-visit to Boston, where he was kindly received by Lowell and Holmes; and to Concord, where Hawthorne wrote: "I find this young man worthy" on a card which introduced him to Emerson. The result was that a Consulate was offered him at Venice, and thither he went with his newly-married wife just before the outbreak of the Civil War. So, to his freshness, his rawness, his enthusiasm, his imperfect knowledge, Europe was suddenly revealed, and the result was what may be called his first book, "Venetian Life," published in 1866, and followed (I think, not as Mr. Firkins says in 1872, but) in 1867, by "Italian Journeys." These two collections of easy random impressions, although they are not in the form of fiction, bear in them the seed of Howells's earliest and best novels. They were followed by narratives—"A Foregone Conclusion," "Indian Summer," even "The Lady of the Aroostook" —in which the scene was prepared by the Italian experiences of the Consulship. All these books, the earliest in the overcrowded *corpus* of Howells's works, are full of delicate humour, refinement, and grace. His style, which was later to become at once lax and overburdened, is here elastic and even exquisite. In my judgment, Mr. Firkins, desirous to draw attention to the endless list of maturer books, does less than justice to these early stories of travel and the results of travel.

Then, in 1866, at the age of thirty, Howells, already considerably sobered, went back to America and settled in Cambridge. He was admitted to listen to the high converse of Longfellow and Lowell, and to take part, as he puts it, in "that life so refined, so intelligent, so gracefully simple" that he "doubted if the world could show its parallel." He was poor and active; with his eyes fixed on the beautiful Cambridge companionship, he rolled up his sleeves and began to write novels and edit magazines for a livelihood. The stories were now novels of New England life, more and more local, more and more democratic, less and less humorous and gay. The New

England conscience seized Howells in its grip; he cultivated an antipathy to tobacco " which steeled him for all time against the insinuations of the drug." " Of beer, also, he was apprehensive," Mr. Firkins gravely informs us, and " the tuition of his palate remained imperfect."

These reservations began to appear in the texture of his novels, but they were as nothing in comparison with his antipathy to any strong incursion of sex into fiction. Yet he still wrote with remarkable ease and elegance, he still noted the superficial characteristics of society with originality and acumen, and he still preserved the discipline of art. His novels until 1886 were excellent in form, " The Rise of Silas Lapham " being at once the most ambitious and the most characteristic of his writings. Had it been convenient or even possible for Howells to cease authorship at the approach of his fortieth year, it would be easier to enjoy his writings and more agreeable to appraise them than it is at present.

Space is utterly lacking here to define that robust determination and that generous self-sacrifice which made Howells gradually surrender the fine instincts of an artist in favour of an obstinate, and, as it may seem to us, provincial, concentration on the outside of the American cup and platter. Many elements combined, and to some of them Mr. Firkins, although admirably loyal and laborious, does not seem to be sensitive. I have here no opportunity of expatiating on Howells in person, as it was my happiness to know him long ago; he was the soul of generosity and sweetness, tremblingly alive, like an excited child, ardently devoted to literature as he understood it, wholly without guile. But on all this I must not dwell here, where I have to confine myself to a very brief general view of his writings, and in particular of the element in them which may hope to survive the winnowing of an altered wind of taste.

MRS. HUMPHRY WARD

MRS. HUMPHRY WARD

INEVITABLY, for an English public, the biography of a prominent public person appears as soon as the industry or the ability of the family permits the collection of documents. In the case of Mrs. Ward, the monument is exhibited early, less than two years after her decease. It has been executed by her daughter, and I cannot too promptly say how much the probity and the delicacy and the clear-sightedness with which the task has been performed strike me as I close the volume. There were so many traps laid for the indulgence of a daughter, so many opportunities for pardonable but unwise filial exaggeration, that I can but commend the tact of Mrs. George Trevelyan.

It is a duty as well as a pleasure to say this, because I cannot, with the best will in the world, wholly accept Mrs. George Trevelyan's estimate of her mother's literature, yet I might approve her less if I agreed with her more thoroughly. She has displayed a charming adroitness in manipulating what was rather monotonous as well as congested material. She has even lightened the density of her tale by little touches of liveliness which relieve the burden and the strain. To come to the issue at once, the weak point of Mrs. Ward as an imaginative writer was her terrible earnestness. She was full of the gold of enthusiasm and nobility, but something fatal in her temperament transmuted it to lead. Mrs. Trevelyan, who records so much, does not refer to Mr. Max Beerbohm's cartoon, in which Mary Augusta, aged about eight, looks up at her celebrated uncle and says, "Why, oh! why, Uncle Matt, will you not be always wholly serious?" The demonic Max cannot have known that, when Matthew Arnold published his exquisitely ironic preface to " Essays in Criticism," his precocious niece recorded that it had " the fault which the author professes to avoid, *that of being amusing* "! It was a fault that she at least escaped. Throughout her entire career Mrs. Ward was " wholly serious."

Mary Augusta was the eldest of the eight children of Thomas Arnold, an amiable and unfortunate gentleman who was always drifting, like a piece of seaweed at ebb and flow, from the Anglican to the Roman Church and back again. Her firmness of character was the hereditary consequence, if we can say so, of her father's irresolution. She was born in Van Diemen's Land, afterward called Tasmania, in 1851, and she was seven years old when she was brought to England to be plunged into " the Arnold environment." Mrs. Trevelyan treats the history and the atmosphere of that celebrated family with marked ability. It is pleasant to learn that Mary, now a boarder in Miss Anne Clough's admirable school at Ambleside, was " often naughty and wilful." She walked over the slopes of Wansdell in company with those monuments of virtuous irresolution, her father and Mr. Clough. I think, although neither she herself nor Mrs. Trevelyan would for a moment admit it, that she registered a vow that she would not resemble these martyrs of the dyspeptic conscience. If so, the pledge was kept; to the close of her strenuous and fatigued career, whatever Mary Ward was she was not irresolute. There is something inspiring and noble in the firmness with which she faced life, which presented itself to her in forms that were often attractive and alluring, but always perilous and at last fatal. The reader obtains a clearer impression of the evolution of

Mrs. Ward's character and the nature of her moral intrepidity from Mrs. Trevelyan than he does from the " Writer's Recollections " of 1918.

It must be frankly said that the latter effort at autobiography is one of the least felicitous of its author's productions. Mrs. Trevelyan somewhat strains the note of filial piety in her comments on " A Writer's Recollections." It was a book almost ostensibly performed as a pot-boiler, while Mrs. Ward was labouring with ill-health and depressed by her indefatigable activities during the war. It suffered from a certain pomposity and air of patronage which do her spirit an injustice. All readers who do not belong to the generation preceding her own, and these now are growing few, must turn from it to Mrs. Trevelyan's pages with relief. But I regret that she has passed too rapidly over the interesting early years, and especially the Oxford years, through fear of gleaning in a field which her mother had already harvested.

The record of girlhood is amusing and intelligible. The legend of faultless Arnold amenity, so irritating in some other memorials, is here agreeably shattered. " Polly is kind enough when she can patronise," mourned her afflicted father, who suffered, like the rest of her family, from " her domineering spirit." With untiring vigilance, with a lofty moral aim incessantly before her, Mrs. Ward tamed and guided this tendency to domineer, but it never expired. We read between the lines in her daughter's admirable study, and we see her persistent concinnity—to use a rare but useful word—fighting against all difficulties and inevitably getting the better of bad fortune. When we turn to contemplate her public work, our admiration of her steadiness of purpose is unbounded; she attacked the dragons with the helm of it firmly planted on her brows, and the sword of unwearied patience in her hand. Opinions will differ about the positive value of this persistence in intellectual matters. The relative value is unquestionable, for she was poor and yet determined to secure fame and influence. Few women have been more resolutely ambitious of pecuniary and social success, and still fewer have, during their lifetime, more signally and honourably attained it.

But the question will persist in recurring, Was the form which success took the form really appropriate to Mrs. Ward's unusual gifts? I am afraid I do not think that it was. She found her easiest path to fortune in writing novels. That she toiled up this road untiringly for forty years is a tribute to her power of concentration and to her violence of will. She was so immensely clever, so clear-brained, so finely equipped, so resolute and intelligent, that she wrote novels as, if she had chosen to do so, she could undoubtedly have painted landscapes or conducted a business. But it was done against the grain, until, after experiment upon experiment, she had learned every trick of the trade, and the effort, having become mechanical, appeared to be crowned with success.

The wisest of Mrs. Ward's early friends, and the one from whose affectionate candour she was most willing to receive advice, was Mandell Creighton, afterwards Bishop of London. When he read, in 1884, her first novel—"Miss Bretherton," a study of the career of Miss Mary Anderson—Creighton told her that she was writing "as a critic, not as a creator." This was a word of clairvoyance. That acutest, and yet kindest, of men saw that his ardent young friend was not pouring forth a narrative of human joys, sorrows, and perplexities, but throwing critical judgments into the form of a story. Mrs. Trevelyan delicately conjectures that "Mrs. Ward stored up this criticism for future use," but if so she certainly locked it up in a cupboard and lost the key, since all her efforts at fiction are of the class that Creighton deprecated. Her next novel, " Robert Elsmere," displayed her critical gift without one trace of the creative. Let Mrs. Trevelyan tell us the spirit in which her mother approached this celebrated romance :—

"She was fascinated by the intricacy and difficulty of the whole subject [of Christian origins], but more especially by such branches of it as the Synoptic Problem, or the relation of the Fourth Gospel to the rest; while the questions raised by the realisation that the Books of the New Testament were the products of an age steeped in miracle and wholly uncritical of the records of it, struck her as vital to the whole orthodox position."

A chain of valuable thoughts, no doubt; but how is a living, pulsing story of modern life to be based on the Synoptic Problem? Accordingly, with " a horrid feeling of tension and exhaustion," her long agony of meditation produced " Robert Elsmere," which so exactly reproduced the suppressed convictions of thousands of " honest doubters," that it became the " best-seller " of the season, and weaned Mr. Gladstone from his obsession about the Irish Church. All this may be very strange and unaccountable, but so far as Mrs. Ward herself was concerned, it proves her more finally than ever to be a critic, not a creator.

The critical talent, applied to fiction, carried Mrs. Ward on with a surprising effectiveness from her thirty-seventh to her forty-seventh year, and then it began to break down. The phenomena are curious, and worth observing. After the astonishing success of " Robert Elsmere," which was a tract for the use of specious unbelievers, she passed to " David Grieve," which was a novel indeed, but dull and artificial. Most people, faced by such a catastrophe as this, would have given up the chase. Mrs. Ward, with her astonishing force of character, merely set her teeth, and pursued it. She was determined, in spite of all her want of creative power, to create, and she produced " Marcella." If I had space at my command, I should like to show why " Marcella," written by the author of " David Grieve," was a miracle of will-power rewarded. It was composed in " a long struggle against sleeplessness, headache, and a bad bout of writer's cramp," but it showed no sign of these drawbacks. It was a triumphant piece of carpentry, well-designed, carefully proportioned and defiantly executed. A very large number of persons, especially in America, thought it interesting. Mrs. Ward went on, and she increased her audience, and she displayed more and more technical—but always critical— never creative—skill, until, in 1898, she achieved " Helbeck of Bannisdale."

This was her culminating book, so good in fact, that it might seem to a reader that Mrs. Ward was, by dint of determination, slipping into the ranks of the creators. But from this point on her powers declined. In " Eleanor " and " William Ashe " (1905) the click of the machine became audible, and after that there was practically an end. The novels of the last fifteen years are respectable, were never inspired, and are already forgotten. In the midst of all this, by a freak of which I cannot offer the least explanation, the story of " Bessie Costrell," which had real warmth, genuine psychology, and no rasp of the carpenter's adze, appeared as an unrelated portent. If it were necessary to present Mrs. Ward's talent in its most favourable form, this might be conveniently done by her two best books, " Bessie Costrell " and " Helbeck of Bannisdale."

Whatever could be attained by severity of self-discipline, applied to a mind of firm intelligence, was within the range of Mrs. Ward. Her writing, although without charm, was solid and correct. Her memory had been stringently trained, and stood her often in place of imagination. Her lack of humour betrayed her, as the years went on, to a sort of pontifical self-assurance, or, it may be more simply said, to a lack of sympathy with forms of thought and fancy which had not yet secured academic authority. It is a pity that circumstances forced her to adopt the facile art of fiction, towards which she had no real bent. Creighton judged accurately when he said that she was by nature a critic—a critic of the past, of the admitted and accepted. We may smile to note that the younger generations find no place in Mrs. Trevelyan's index; her distinguished mother was not much interested in intelligences later than those of Dr. Jowett and Mr. Gladstone. She could never have been an Anatole France or a Jules Lemaître, but one sees her as a possible Edmond Scherer.

Lest, however, the record of this strenuous career should seem to be not wholly harmonious, the reader will turn, past the rather dismal record of her novels, to the closing chapters of Mrs. Ward's life. Here we see her genuine greatness, revealed in a glow of patriotic self-sacrifice. If she was not a novelist of genius, she was a noble woman of action, and what she performed under terrible disadvantages of pain and fatigue will not cease to inspire admiration. Long before her strength began to fail, she had founded University Hall, she had started the Passmore Edwards Settlement, she had devoted herself to the care of the invalid children of the poor, she had opened the Evening Play Centres, and all this without, until 1917, the smallest help from the Government. Her violent and consistent opposition to Woman's Suffrage exemplified her courage and her conservatism. But it was at the outbreak of the war that her energy and her unselfishness asserted themselves to the full. The narrative of her

P

repeated journeys to America, France, and Italy, in the interests of the Allies, must be read with emotion so long as recollection of what this country went through in its unprecedented struggle is welcome to the attention of Englishmen. Whether Mary Augusta Ward has left a permanent impression on the literature of her country may fairly be questioned, but no honest man can doubt that she has bequeathed to us all an example of high faith and loyalty.

1923.

MR. SAINTSBURY

MR. SAINTSBURY

PERTINACIOUS readers of Mr. Saintsbury, and I am glad to think that they are many, will like to know, in the first instance, of what the collected edition of his Essays and Papers consists. It is naturally far from complete, since it contains hardly any of the French studies of which its author has published a profusion. It contains little which has not been reprinted before, except in its third volume, where will be found some unfamiliar things. Speaking broadly, the new edition is a reprint of three books, presumably out of print, which every student will be glad to recover. These are the " Essays in English Literature " of 1890, the " Miscellaneous Essays " of 1892, and the " Corrected Impressions " of 1895. This last, I may confess, is a particular favourite of mine. It has always seemed to me to represent Mr. Saintsbury at his best. He is nowhere more companionable, more easy of access; and nowhere more characteristic. It is obvious that the new volumes do not present to us a complete Saintsbury; far from it,—the biographer, the historian, the author of extended monographs is absent. But, at the same time, these essays are not in any degree what Mr. Saintsbury himself once denounced as " study-sweepings." They contain careful and deliberate sets of opinions which are none the less authoritative for being brief and for not being exhaustive.

The earliest of the chapters in the three stout volumes dates from nearly fifty years ago. The essays recede to a time when there was infinitely less written about literature than is published now, but when what was written was often of high value. It was the age of Matthew Arnold and Leslie Stephen; it was beginning to be the age of Swinburne and Pater. Mr. Saintsbury survives amongst us as a representative of that time, and of the French period of criticism from which, perhaps, he borrowed more than from his English precursors. He was, it is evident, much interested in the " critique romantique " of his early youth, and yet his own talent is as unlike that of Taine or of Paul de Saint Victor as it is that of the English writers I have mentioned. If a parallel can be found for him, it is perhaps Emile Montégut, whom, however, he has splendidly outrun in persistency. It has been of great advantage to Mr. Saintsbury's influence that he has lived so long, since the public has grown to accept points of view which were unfamiliar half a century ago. It has also become accustomed to Mr. Saintsbury's peculiarities of language, which long seemed to many readers a little disconcerting, but which are now taken as a matter of course.

The range of Mr. Saintsbury has been extremely wide, and it is hardly too much to say that there is no English author, of the least importance, flourishing between 1575 and 1875, on whom he has not expressed a definite judgment. Before the earlier of these dates in French literature he has been active, and his " History of Prosody " is sufficient to prove how familiar he is with mediæval and Middle English poetry from the origins to Spenser. Still, I think that there is no injustice in saying that his best-tilled field starts with Queen Elizabeth. In recent work, that is to say, in the prose and verse of the generations subsequent to his own, it is not unfair to suppose that his interest is modified by a certain impatience of untried methods and manners.

But what an amazing feat it had been to hold three

Mr. Saintsbury

centuries of literature at his fingers' ends, to be familiar with practically everything, and to forget nothing! For this is one of the principal achievements of Mr. Saintsbury, that he has arrived at a Pisgah-height from which he sees all authors and all books spread out around him, and can speak, at his leisure, of every one without prejudice, without exaggeration, and without lassitude. This breadth of vision is by no means a common quality, even among critics of a very high order. It was possessed by Sainte-Beuve, but hardly by anyone else. It was almost grotesquely absent in Matthew Arnold and in Hazlitt, to mention two of our very foremost writers. It was not possessed by Charles Lamb nor even desired by Andrew Lang. What is involved is an extraordinary tolerance, tempered by enthusiasm; a state of mind in which the most vivid elements in every contrasted production are the elements mainly insisted on and brought to light. Mr. Saintsbury has achieved, to a degree now best observed as we look back on his prolonged career, a unity of critical method which is scarcely to be paralleled.

One little drawback involved in this unity is that the practised reader comes to know, almost mechanically, what Mr. Saintsbury's judgment would be of any given manifestation. For instance, if a new canto of " The Faerie Queene " or of " Don Juan " were to be discovered, it would hardly be worth while to ask Mr. Saintsbury's opinion of it, because we should know beforehand.

The outstanding merit of the literary criticism which Mr. Saintsbury has been so widely disseminating during the last fifty years is based on that spirit of unity of which I have spoken. He has cultivated, with an admirable persistency, the comparative method in its widest sense. Many years ago, Mr. Saintsbury was engaged in a lively controversy with a prominent American writer who indulged in the patriotic fallacy of despising English authors.

From that dispute of thirty-five years ago, not reprinted in the present issue, I cannot resist the temptation to quote a lively passage, because it illuminates very pleasantly Mr. Saintsbury's own practice. He wrote :—

"I hope that we shall one day have a collection of Mr. Howells's critical *dicta* on novels and other things; that will be one of the most valuable, one of the most terrible of books, as showing what happens when a man speaks without knowledge. To read what Mr. Howells says of Thackeray is almost an illiberal education. The reason of the error is quite obvious. It is simply that the clever American does not know; he has not sufficient range of comparison. For my part, I should not dare to continue criticising so much as a circulating library novel, if I did not perpetually pay my respects to the classics of many literatures."

Mr. Saintsbury has never been inclined to encourage either the scientific or the metaphysical mode in criticism, although the former was widely advocated a quarter of a century ago, while the latter is much in evidence to-day. He has always held, and has often insisted, that with beauty science has absolutely nothing to do. If I am asked where the special critical aptitude of Mr. Saintsbury seems to me to lie, I am inclined to answer, in his attitude not as an analyst, or a preacher, or a controversialist, but as a judge. He does not shrink—he never has shrunk —from a strongly expressed personal opinion about any work of literary art presented to his notice. This is not habitual with many writers, who, often with considerable profit to their readers, deal agreeably with side-issues, and offer tentative conjectures. Very much of criticism nowadays is engaged in rubbing the sides of the stable-lantern till they gleam, while neglecting to light the wick. Mr.

Saintsbury, to a degree which exceeds that of all his compeers—and, indeed, by its readiness and confidence sometimes not a little exasperates them—concentrates his attention on illuminating the horse in his stall.

Now, to do this with success, very wide and sustained reading is necessary. There is a species of critic who takes the opposite line, and who, in his own sphere, is stimulating and fertile. My dear and ever-lamented friend, Walter Raleigh, was of the latter class. He began reading late in life, and he never approached omniscience. He trusted to his happy genius for direction and inspiration. But, for a critic of the class in which Mr. Saintsbury is supreme, vast, unwearied, and constantly repeated reading is essential, and is the secret of all authority.

No attempt to define the character of Mr. Saintsbury's work would be complete without a reference to his lack of prejudice. Hardly anyone approaches the study of books in a perfectly judicial spirit. There is almost always a trait of personal liking or disliking, which makes the critic unduly indulgent on one side, unduly harsh on the other. Political and, still more, religious antipathies enter into the consideration of pure literature, and warp the reviewer's honest judgment of the technical skill or success of the writing. I remember, in the days of my own ingenuous youth, being shocked by hearing D. G. Rossetti say of a certain collection of new poems which (he admitted) were not very good, that they must be praised in public because they were "on the right side," whatever that might mean. This is an error into which nobody has ever fallen less than Mr. Saintsbury, and it is curious in his case, because in his private capacity, as everyone knows, he holds opinions which are positive in the extreme. He is a Tory of the Tories, and uncompromising beyond the limits of practical politics. But face him with the literary product of a Socialist or an Atheist, and immediately all tincture of prejudice fades from him. He judges the work itself on its technical merits, with utmost impartiality.

An example has come to our hand in the essay on "Twenty Years of Political Satire," where the lampooning poets of the close of the eighteenth century, whose tenets and influence are abominable to the Conservative in Mr. Saintsbury, are impartially considered. Here more justice is done to the wit and agility of people like Peter Pindar and the authors of "The Rolliad" than has ever been done elsewhere. Mr. Saintsbury makes no secret of the amusement with which he has read these subversive and libertine satirists. But to see this quality at its very best, we may turn to the chapter called "Bolshevism in its Cradle," where the critic examines the writings of the unspeakable William Godwin, whose works advocated a complete reversal of all hitherto accepted principles of law, religion, and morals, in other words, of everything which Mr. Saintsbury holds dear. No exacerbated Communist, in full sympathy with Godwin's doctrines, could be more "fair" to the philosopher's writings, from the literary point of view, than is this Tory of the Tories.

The position of Mr. Saintsbury is one to be envied. He has, after a long and arduous effort, come to be regarded as a bulwark of authorship. No one living has done more than he to maintain the dignity of letters, and in particular to insist on the importance of criticism as an individual and creative branch of literature. His firmness has, in past years, occasionally seemed to those who differ from him to be arrogance, but no one was ever absurd enough to charge him with insincerity or subservience. May he long be preserved to preside in our court of literary appeal!

LAFCADIO HEARN

LAFCADIO HEARN

THAT there is something permanent in the fame of Lafcadio Hearn seems to be shown by the fact that, nineteen years after his death, two of his works are presented to the world simultaneously, in new forms, and from very different quarters. The volumes before me, " Pre-Raphaelite and other Poets," and " Youma," illustrate the two most important stages in the vagabond and unhappy career of this strange author, namely, his residence in the French West Indies and his professorship in Japan. There never was a man who was more a straw on the stream of the world than Hearn. He cannot be called cosmopolitan, because he never had a real home on earth. He was a wayfarer and a wanderer all his days, an unwilling exile from civilisation.

We may remind ourselves of the main incidents of his extraordinary life. He was the son of an Irish father and a Greek mother, and he owed his strange Christian name to the accident that he was born in the Ionian island of Leucadia or Lefcadia, in 1850. His mother, who had never learned a word of English, fled with a lover to Smyrna when the child was seven years old; she is not heard of again. His father marries once more, and he also disappears. After many vicissitudes, we find the infant Lafcadio with an aunt in Wales. He was sent to the Catholic school of Ushaw, where he lost the sight of one eye in an accident. The aunt vanishes, and then follows a time of prolonged mystery and misery. From 1866 to 1868 he was lost, like De Quincey a century earlier, or Francis Thompson in our own day, in the dark places of London.

What is known about the life of Lafcadio Hearn is mainly to be found in the biography published in 1906 by the most affectionate and patient of his friends, Miss Elizabeth Bisland. The biographer, touching with extreme tenderness upon the obscure passages in this sinister life, is unable to present Hearn to us in an amiable light, physically or morally. He was so short in stature as to be almost a dwarf, and was painfully conscious of his insignificance. There is a pathetic touch in one of his late letters, where he congratulates himself on being among the Japanese, who are a small race, so that his own mean figure is the less observed. But his countenance also was unpleasing, and the damaged eye a painful feature; in his portraits he is always photographed in profile, so as to show only the uninjured eye, which, however, is itself disagreeably prominent. We may bear in mind all this poverty and ugliness and distress, because of the marvellous resistance to it which the beautiful imagination of the man sustained through all his troubles.

His abject poverty in London was repeated, at the age of twenty, in New York. There was a gleam of light when he was apprenticed to a Syrian pedlar of looking-glasses in Cincinnati, but Hearn, who was inconceivably awkward, contrived to put his feet through one or more looking-glasses, and lost his job. He became a newspaper reporter in Cincinnati, and this was the beginning of his mental development. But, as Dr. Johnson has observed,

> Slow rises worth by poverty depress'd,

and Lafcadio Hearn was thirty-five before he began to make a mark in literature. Miss Bisland, discussing the cause of his long obscurity, puts much down to his "quivering sensibilities." He was incapable of preserving the friendship of anyone, for the very least friction roused him to "an anguish of resentment and bitterness," and he never mentioned again, or spoke to, the innocent offender. This was not a primrose path to social success. Meanwhile, however, Lafcadio Hearn was strenuously educating himself, and making a particular study of the French masters of romantic description. He had a violent antipathy to cold, and was driven to live in New Orleans by the need for warmth. By this time, his occasional writings had attracted attention, and he began to be known. In 1887 he gave up journalism altogether, and proceeded to Martinique, where he lived for three years. Here, as he said, he delightfully " dozed away in a land where the air is always warm, the sea always the colour of sapphire, the woods perpetually green as the plumage of a green parrot." He was happy at Grand Anse for the first time in his life.

It was in Martinique that he wrote some of his best books, and became the favourite author of a group of readers. The influence of Pierre Loti was strong upon him; perhaps it is not really inconsistent to add that he became, at this time, a disciple also of Henry James. He cultivated the best contemporary writers who responded to his particular aptitudes, and neglected those who did not. Even in later years, when he is in Japan, there is little or no trace of his taking an interest in any poetry or prose more than a hundred years old. He found the French West Indies a fruitful field for romantic research. The stories of M. Francis Jammes and Mme. Gérard d'Houville had not yet awakened an imaginative curiosity about life in the Antilles.

Martinique satiated the longings of poor Lafcadio, and he presently began to till the field he had found. I do not know what "Youma" is called in English, for I have not met with the original; but it seems to be skilfully translated by M. Marc Logé. "Youma" is a study of life in Martinique as it existed up to the revolution of the negroes in 1848. We are shown the routine of the patriarchal and picturesque existence of the creoles on the plantations, before the rebellion destroyed the artificial balance of the races, and led to complete emancipation. Everywhere around us we are conscious of the immense purple of the tropic ocean, ruffled by the trade winds. We stand under the shadow of palm-trees, or descend through fields of sugar-cane. The story is an idyll of the plantation, happy enough in its commencement, but closing in dreadful blazing tragedy. The reader will possibly prefer the descriptions of tropical scenery to the blameless adventures of the heroine, though these are not badly told.

The other volume on my table is representative of the phase in Lafcadio Hearn's career which is most familiar to the world, and has attracted to his name hundreds who without it would never have heard of him. He had returned to New York in 1889, but immediately fell into great distress, domestic, social, and monetary. To save the unlucky man from starvation, a plan was set on foot to send him to Japan to write a book. Here he found friends, and, in particular, Mr. Basil Chamberlain, through whose influence he was appointed a Middle-School teacher in the provincial town of Matsue, on the north-western coast of Japan.

Lafcadio Hearn now adopted Japanese citizenship, wore Japanese dress, and adopted the name of Yatumo Koizumi, in compliment to the lady, a member of the aristocratic family of Koizumi, whom, after some difficulty, he was allowed to marry. He dropped all his American habits and prejudices; he became more Oriental than the Japanese themselves, and yet he could never, I understand, completely master the Japanese language, although his life in the country extended over fourteen years. His wife, who ultimately learned English, and published some quaint recollections of him, confessed that " having been teased by the hard world, he often seemed to be indignant with the world."

His excessive touchiness caused him frequent inconvenience. After many ups and downs, he arrived at last at what seemed the firm position of Professor of English in the Imperial University of Tokio, where he began to deliver the lectures on poetry which became famous, and a selection from which forms the volume now before me. His life in Tokio, however, was a tragedy of miscomprehension; in the pathetic words of his wife, " he loved Japan with his whole heart, but his sincere love for Japan was not understood by Japanese." In 1903 he was expelled from his professorship, and although another chair was found for him in the University of Waseda, he was oppressed with melancholy at the hostility of his neighbours. It was his misfortune, poor man! to be unable to retain either affection or respect, although he was worthy of both. On September 26, 1904, after writing a long and vigorous letter to a Japanese captain, a letter printed by Miss Bisland, Lafcadio Hearn walked on the verandah of his house in the twilight, and suddenly sank down " as if the whole fabric of life had crumbled within "; he was dead.

The sets of lectures which Professor John Erskine has selected and published were delivered to the students at Tokio in the years between 1896 and 1902. It has to be borne in mind that they do not represent the written word of Hearn, nor were they subjected to any revision by him. He was in the habit of lecturing, slowly, in English, and there were about a dozen of his pupils who knew that language well enough to take down what he said. Their reports were preserved, and have been collected, the result being the pages now given to the public. This is a very odd, and we may think not very convenient mode of producing a book, but it probably does little injustice to the mind of Lafcadio Hearn. The lecturer took enormous pains with his work, and prepared himself for it with exhausting preliminary reading. Until he had passed the age of forty, Hearn seems to have enjoyed little opportunity for self-education, and in particular his knowledge of English literature was slight. For the service of his lectures, he read voraciously, and with an appetite unspoiled and unprejudiced. He was alone in a strange land, and he could enjoy no intercourse with those who exercised any authority in European taste. His opinions were formed in isolation, and they represent, to a very unusual degree, the impact of masterpieces on a mind unimpressed by previous cultivation. It is necessary to bear this in mind in reading the lectures, which otherwise will startle us by the emphasis with which they state views which have been long accepted, or propound experimental opinions which tradition is not ready to accept at all.

There is no metaphysical ingenuity and no great subtlety of thought in these lectures, which are marked by an almost naïve simplicity. We seem to be returning in them to the infancy of criticism, where everything is good or bad, beautiful or ugly. But this does not detract from their merit, which depends on their freshness, their artless enthusiasm, and also on the vigour with which impressions independently made on the enthusiasm of the lecturer are passed on to his audience. Moreover, when we examine these judgments carefully, we discover them to be more intelligently based, and more consistently guided by principle, than we at first thought them to be. We see poetry frankly described as Hearn saw it, and we are struck by the vigour of his analysis and the delicacy of his taste.

He was unconscious of, or indifferent to, the shibboleths of thirty years ago, and even now, although we have partly reverted to his views, he will not carry all readers with him. His tropical temperament, his thirst for warmth and colour and the flush of life, caused him to find a response in the poetry of D. G. Rossetti which some readers to-day may deem excessive. It may be that they are wrong and Hearn was right; Rossetti is shorn to-day of much of his legitimate prestige. Lafcadio Hearn admired Robert Buchanan, and his admiration was heretically based; but he admired Robert Bridges still more, for which much may be forgiven him. He was excellent,— if sometimes a little violent,—about Morris and Swinburne, and still more instructive about Browning. The lectures are illustrated by copious quotation. I cannot help wondering what the little yellow students made of " Dolores " and " Sister Helen," but I daresay they were pleased with " The Shaving of Shagpat."

SHELLEY'S WIDOW

SHELLEY'S WIDOW

AT this moment, when so much attention is being given to the adventures and characters of Byron and Shelley, it seems appropriate to turn to the pages in which the widow of the latter attempted, under feigned names, to paint the portraits of her husband and his friend. It is, of course, not unknown that Mary Wollstonecraft Shelley wrote a romance called " The Last Man," but the book was never reprinted, and has become very rare. Through the kindness of my friend, Mr. Thos. J. Wise, I am now in possession of a copy of this work, " The Last Man. By the Author of Frankenstein. 3 Vols. Henry Colburn. 1826," and I have been reading it with an interest which I would fain share with others.

That Mrs. Shelley's novel was anonymous, and its plot veiled by imaginary names and circumstances, has, I think, concealed the amount of biographical value which it contains. When she wrote it, the events of her husband's life and of Byron's were fresh in her memory, and she was incessantly occupied with them. In her solitary and melancholy condition, her thoughts were concentrated on what she had lived through in a few brilliant, feverish years, and her recollections were still intense. Neither the title-page of " The Last Man," nor its valuable introduction, bears any name or initials. Presumably the author was afraid that the anger of Sir Timothy Shelley would be roused if she made any personal revelations.

In the introduction, the unnamed author of " The Last Man " states, " I visited Naples in the year 1818." The

Shelleys, with Claire Clairemont and the child Allegra, left England in March of that year, and wandered for nearly nine months over the length and breadth of Italy. We may read the particulars of what they saw in Shelley's very remarkable series of letters to Peacock and Leigh Hunt. He described to the former his arrival at Naples in the first days of December, where the first circumstance which engaged his attention was the murder of a lad in broad daylight. In spite of this awkward greeting, the warm air of Naples did them all good. The author of " The Last Man " states in her preface, " On the 8th of December [1818], my companion and I crossed the Bay to visit the antiquities which are scattered on the shores of Baiæ." She continues :—

"We visited the so-called Elysian Fields and Avernus; and wandered through various ruined temples, baths, and classic spots; at length we entered the gloomy cavern of the Cumæan Sibyl. Our Lazzaroni bore flaming torches, which shone red, and almost dusky, in the murky subterranean passages. . . . We passed by a natural archway, leading to a second gallery, and enquired if we could not enter there also. The guides pointed to the reflection of their torches on the water that paved it, leaving us to form our own conclusion; but adding it was a pity, for it led to the Sibyl's Cave."

In Shelley's account of this excursion, he merely remarks that this Sibyl was not Virgil's Sibyl, and says no more, but manifestly Mary's imagination was inflamed by the mystery.

She explains that, pushing on from the outer gallery, they arrived at " a large, desert, dark cavern," which their guides declared was the Sibyl's Cave. The visitors were disappointed with it, but in the wall at the side they noticed a small opening, and Shelley determined, in spite of the vehement dissuasion of the lazzaroni, to explore this. Groping their way in, they found " a dim hypæthric cavern," which Shelley excitedly declared to be the real seat of the Sibyl. At the further end, the roof had partly fallen in ruins, and the open sky was above them. Leaves of trees were blown about the floor, and Shelley, taking up some of them, exclaimed : " *This* is the Sibyl's Cave; these are Sibylline leaves "; turning over what he had picked up, he pointed out to Mary marks on them which he declared to be written characters. He professed to recognise Chaldæan writing, and he excitedly pronounced the letters on the leaves to be as old as the Pyramids. This is a touch very characteristic of Shelley, and not, I think, preserved elsewhere. Mary says that during their stay at Naples they often returned to this cave, " sometimes alone, sometimes skimming the sunlit sea," whatever this alternative may involve. She represents the supposed hieroglyphics on the leaves to have greatly occupied the thoughts of " the selected and matchless companion of my toils," as she calls her husband, but there is nothing whatever about the Sibylline writing in any of Shelley's extant letters. Lapsing into Italian, she pathetically addresses the lost poet as *o mio nobil tesoro*. Finally, she collects a mass of the leaves, and takes them to their lodging to examine them at her leisure.

By a rather poor pretence, the novelist bids us believe that her romance was found inscribed upon the frail and attenuated foliage of the Sibyl's Cavern. By what art she interpreted the hieroglyphics, or whether Shelley, among his accomplishments, included a current acquaintance with the ancient Chaldee language, Mary does not explain. Her story is supposed to date from the year A.D. 2073, but her conception of the world three centuries ahead would not satisfy Mr. Wells and other revolutionary prophets, for she conceives no changes in the economic arrangements of society, while no daring mechanical inventions occur to her mind. The tale is the autobiography of a young man, closely connected with the English Court, whose father strangely resembles William Godwin, and whose mother, as seen through the eyes of a daughter, is as like Mary Wollstonecraft as one pea is like another.

The author has a sister, the unhappy Perdita, who is Claire Claremont to the life; " unloved and neglected, she repaid want of kindness with distrust and silence." The House of Windsor (this title has a successful touch of prophecy) abdicates the Crown " in compliance with the gentle force of the remonstrances " of the last King's subjects, and the heir-apparent, Adrian, becomes simply Earl of Windsor. He joins the narrator in the wild fells of Cumberland, and is portrayed as the "living spirit of genius and wit." He is, in fact, portrayed as Percy Bysshe Shelley in the light of love. The noble friends quit the mountains for London, and there discover the hero of the moment to be Lord Raymond, a youthful peer of dazzling genius, eminent beauty and prodigious fascination, who has thrown a spell over Europe. I betray no confidence when I reveal that Lord Raymond is Byron.

In the portrait of Lord Raymond in " The Last Man," there is even less attempt at concealment than in that of Earl Adrian. Here we have Byron's person, character, and history drawn by the practised hand of one who had known him long and carefully observed him. Raymond is a proud and violent aristocrat, the sole remnant of a noble but impoverished family, whose first wish is personal aggrandisement, and who, "willing to achieve honour, is yet a votary of pleasure." He has been crowned with glory, but has been checked by repulse from a source whence he least expected it; he has writhed under public insult, and is on the point of quitting England with a vow never to return. He wanders over Europe, and becomes an adventurer in the Greek wars. " He looked on the structure of society as but part of the machinery which supported the web on which his life was traced. The earth was spread out as a highway for him; the heavens built up as a canopy for him." I do not know how it is that Mary Shelley's description of Lord Raymond's personal appearance seems to have escaped the attention of Byron's biographers :—

" His physiognomy, which varied as he spoke, was beautiful in every change. The usual expression of his eyes was soft, though at times he could make them even glare with ferocity; his complexion was colourless; and every trait spoke predominant self-will. His smile was pleasing, though disdain too often curled his lips—lips which to female eyes were the very throne of love and beauty. His voice, usually gentle, often startled you by a sharp discordant note, which showed that his usual low tone was rather the work of study than nature. Thus full of contradictions, unbending yet haughty [sic], gentle yet fierce, tender and again neglectful, he by some strange art found easy entrance to the admiration and affection of women."

This analysis of Byron's charm, by a woman who studied him carefully, but was never in love with him, ought to modify the impression, nowadays so widely dispersed, that Byron was really not charming at all. " Unbending " is evidently a slip of Mary's pen for " supple " or " affable," since she constantly dwells on Lord Raymond's determination to seem amiable in spite of his excess of pride.

The contrast between the dispositions of Raymond and Adrian is highly wrought, and exposes, almost without an attempt at concealment, the notions Mary Shelley had formed with regard to Byron and her husband. It is needless to say that Adrian is painted in brighter colours than the haughty and sinister Raymond. But the portrait of the latter is not overcharged, and there are numerous passages which evidently reflect the care with which Mary Shelley had observed their splendid but embarrassing visitor. She notes the power which Byron had of assuming a gentleness he was far from feeling. Hard pushed in controversy, all sign of anger drops from Raymond; to the astonishment of those who expect a burst of passion, " his countenance becomes bland, his voice softly melodious, his manner soothing, his grace and sweetness like the mild breathing of a flute." There can be no doubt that Mary Shelley had often witnessed such an abrupt change in the manner of Byron, and had felt the strength which the power so to moderate his feelings gave him in argument. This was adaptability which the more earnest and less humorous Shelley could not pretend to possess.

The Claire Claremont incident is, of course, treated from a Godwin point of view; Raymond is the sad deceiver. There are confused echoes of the Lady Byron business, of which Mary Shelley probably knew very little. Shelley's misunderstandings with his father are echoed in the trouble which Adrian has with his "haughty and disappointed" mother, who has no sympathy with her son's erratic politics, nor shares his passionate confidence in the perfectibility of man. The story becomes rather wild. Adrian and the author of the romance live in Windsor Castle in great magnificence, and Raymond, who is recalled from Greece, is elected Lord Protector of Great Britain in spite of the intrigues of "his shuffling Grace of ———." Raymond, however, becomes the object of insult, and, too proud to rebut a scandal, he resigns the Protectorate, and shakes off the dust of England.

Now he becomes pure Byron again. His act creates "an unexampled sensation," which deepens when it becomes known that he is about to engage in an expedition for the liberation of Greece. (Although the date has now become about A.D. 2090, it seems that Greece still languishes under the tyranny of the Crescent.) And now the purpose of Mary Shelley becomes clear. She supposes that Byron, instead of dying ignominiously at Missolonghi, had become the Commander-in-Chief of the Greek Army. He would have been numbered among the leading citizens of Athens, and his name added to the list of Grecian heroes. Percy Shelley, not drowned at Lerici, would have found it impossible to refrain from joining his illustrious friend. She works out this ingenious scheme profusely. The Earl of Windsor becomes a volunteer under the command of Lord Raymond. That is to say, Shelley, accompanied by Mary and her children, and by Claire and her daughter, start for Athens, and are received with enthusiasm by a chorus of Hellene patriots.

But Byron has in the meantime been taken prisoner by the Turks in a bloody battle. He escapes, however, and all his heart is set on the conquest of Constantinople. Shelley swears that he will stand by his side, draw his sword in the Greek cause, and be hailed as co-victor before the altar of St. Sophia. The armies reach Constantinople to find the streets motionless; all the inhabitants have abruptly died of the plague. Byron stands before the city's vanquished walls and "dares not call himself a conqueror." From this point onwards, the romance merely deals with the spread of the pestilence, which extends over the whole world, and gradually destroys mankind. England is not spared, and the horrid scenes are described with not a little of the power displayed in Mary Shelley's better-known romances, "Frankenstein" and "Valperga." We reach at length the date A.D. 2100, "the last year of the world," when the hero, after inscribing his momentous tale on the leaves in the Sibyl's Cavern, discovers himself to be the only human being left alive on the face of the globe. He starts in a "worn skiff" for "the spicy groves of some odorous island in the far Indian Ocean," apparently without taking with him any stores or means of further sustenance.

THE SORROWS OF OVID

THE SORROWS OF OVID

THE ever-welcome Loeb Library, in a fresh batch of its delightful treasury of the Classics, includes a new version of the poems which Ovid wrote during his exile. The volume is edited by Professor Arthur Leslie Wheeler with every kind of apparatus which can aid, and yet not overburden, the lay student. The publications of this series, as is commonly pointed out, are intended not for schoolboys and not for professional scholars, but for the ordinary cultivated reader, whom they help to approach the famous writers of antiquity not as instruments of torture in the hands of a grammarian, but as living portions of literature. This method is nowhere more appropriate than in dealing with the most celebrated, and in several respects the most curious and even mysterious anecdote in the literary history of Rome, namely, the sudden and irrevocable exile of the last and most fashionable of the great Augustan poets. There does not exist another so striking instance of the impact of imperial despotism at the opening of the Christian era. The seventeenth century, in which genius so often found itself in opposition to authority, was never tired of pointing at

> Ovid to Pontus sent for too much wit

as an example of the danger of being clever. Fortunately, where so much is lost, enough remains to whet a curiosity which can never be fully gratified. The story is just enough preserved to excite perennial interest.

Let us examine the circumstances. Publius Ovidius

Naso was born at Sulmo, the lovely and lonely Sulmona of our day, forty-three years before the birth of Christ. His family was of equestrian rank, as the poet does not fail to record; in after years he rode in knightly dress before the approving eyes of Augustus. He lisped in numbers, and his earliest biographer relates that when his father was about to punish him for his incessant jingling, he cried out, " Spare me! and I will never spout another verse!" We have something like this in English history, for, when the parent of Isaac Watts, incensed at his son for rhyming on every possible occasion, was about to chastise him, did not the infant fall on his knees and cry :—

> Oh! father, do some pity take,
> And I will no more verses make?

The early career of Ovid is too well known to need repetition here. He studied rhetoric in Rome, and being eminently successful, proceeded to Athens to finish his education, as a youth from Oxford or Cambridge might go to-day to Paris. He travelled in Asia, he was admitted to the brilliant literary society of Augustan Rome, and, before his beard was grown, he was celebrated as the author of love-poetry of incomparable sweetness and seduction. He tells us of the great men with whom he mingled as an equal. He saw Virgil, that " blessed writer," *felix auctor*, and Tibullus, but he was too young to enjoy their friendship. On the other hand, he was intimate with Horace, perhaps with Propertius, and certainly with a host of others, then famous but now become to us the mere shadows of a shade, some of them known only because Ovid commends them.

Ovid outlived his great contemporaries, and at the death of Propertius found himself without a rival. He wrote with great fluency, and in a manner which reminds us of Prior or Voiture rather than of the severer masters. He does not seem to have penetrated the highest social circles, except on State occasions, but he was the darling of the ladies, the laureate of fashion, and above all the arbiter of love and amatory intrigue. He became—or remained—rich; he possessed a fine house in Rome and a country-seat in the island of Elba; and the crown was placed on his popularity by the publication, in the first year of our era, of the "Art of Love," a poem which codified the rules of amatory intrigue. There is reason to think that some scandal was caused by this work, which, however, contained nothing very terrible. Still, Ovid seems to have felt that now, in middle years, and married to a devoted wife, he ought to be more serious, and he published his "Fasti," a didactic poem on the calendar of the public year. He started a work of wide scope and universal interest, his famous "Metamorphoses." Ovid was now at the height of his fame and success, without a cloud on his horizon.

Suddenly the bolt fell. He was enjoying himself at Elba, in the year A.D. 8, when he received, together with the news of the death of his most powerful patron Messalla Corvinus, an Imperial edict banishing him for ever from Italy. He was to quit Rome for the uttermost parts of the Empire and never to come back. Professor Wheeler gives some particulars which define the punishment without explaining it. Ovid was not to be treated as an *exul*—that is to say, as an outlaw—but as *relegatus*—that is to say, one sent away as far as possible. An exul might go whither he would, so that he quitted Italy, a relegatus had to stay at whatever spot was mentioned in the edict. On the other hand, while all the property of an exul was confiscated, that of a relegatus could still be enjoyed by his family. An exul, moreover, might hold no communication with Rome, while a relegatus might correspond with his friends as much as he liked. This responds to Ovid's condition. His wife retained his fortune and establishment, and he was allowed to write and to receive letters. On the other hand, he must never stir from his place of exile. This was Tomi (or Tomis as Professor Wheeler will have us spell it), the present Kustendje, a Rumanian port on the Black Sea, at the end of what was later to be Trajan's Wall. There was a studied malignity in sending the delicate and elderly poet, most social and refined of human beings, to this horrible place, which lay on the very confines of the Roman world. Tomis was not even a colony; it possessed no Latin-speaking inhabitants; it was a lodge in a wilderness of Sarmatian savages.

What the excuse was for this cruel expulsion is a question which has tantalised opinion ever since the Renaissance. Our only means of answering it is to read with extreme care what Ovid himself says. His two volumes, the "Tristia" and the "Ex Ponto," tell a great deal, but not half enough. Unfortunately, the private letters in prose which he is known to have written from Tomis are not preserved. The poems, although they are very outspoken, have the disadvantage of being entirely apologetic. They were written in the hope that they would be shown to Augustus and would melt his heart, which they failed to do. Hence they do not specifically re-state anything which Augustus would naturally know. They are eager, pitiful, and humble, they reiterate the poet's remorseful acknowledgment of his sin, but they fail to define what that was. Ovid admits that the Emperor's stern act had two causes, and he speaks plainly about them. There had been on his part a *carmen* and an *error*. The "poem" is acknowledged to be "The Art of Love"; the "mistake" is left vague. But, in the first instance, a difficulty at once arises. If "The Art of Love" was considered so scandalous as to call for violent punishment, why had seven years been allowed to lapse since its publication? It had been immediately and permanently popular; Augustus must long have been perfectly well acquainted with it. Why did he suddenly, after

The Sorrows of Ovid

so great a lapse of time, decide that its author must be banished to the ends of the earth? This puzzled Ovid himself, and though he wisely submits to the Imperial will, he not without reason complains that " The Art of Love " contained nothing so subversive of morality as did the works of various other poets who were left unscathed. We can see the truth of this for ourselves. Catullus before him and Martial after him were far more indecent, to our modern ears at least, than Ovid, and nobody ever dreamed of banishing, or even blaming, them. Ovid submissively concedes that he was sent away because he was the Preceptor of Love, but he cannot have seriously believed this, nor need we. There must have been some unnamed cause for the anger of Augustus, and " The Art of Love " must have been the pretext for punishment. It seems, even as a pretext, a poor one.

We turn to the " error," and if we could but discover what this was, we should doubtless understand the whole cause of the exile of Ovid. We may take it that Augustus, though scandalised by " The Art of Love," was much more pained, and even enraged, by some definite, some culminating impertinence. The nearest that Ovid comes in the " Trista " to an explanation of his want of tact is a comparison of himself to Actæon, the huntsman who accidentally saw Diana bathing in a valley of Cithæron. Those who have divided, as we must do, the " error " from the " carmen," have conjectured that Ovid had committed an identical indiscretion. I hesitate to differ from general opinion on a matter so much discussed, but I cannot think of the poet dashing into Livia's bathroom, like a blundering plumber. Ovid was nothing if not allusive and rhetorical, and it seems to me that if he had literally seen Diana *sine veste*, the last thing he would dream of doing would be to remind Augustus of the particular offence. I would rather believe the " error " to have been a literary impertinence of some kind, probably an epigram. Ovid says, "Verse caused Cæsar to brand me"; the bolt fell straight from the palace on the Palatine, where, I think, a treacherous acquaintance had been reading to the Emperor a waggish copy of verses, in the worst taste, in which Livia Drusilla was involved. If that formidable woman was roused by an insult, the marvel is, as Ovid himself naïvely remarks, not that he was punished, but that his life was spared.

The poet hastened back to Rome in the hope of melting the heart of his Augustus, but Jupiter was inexorable. Nothing was to be done, but he must hurry off to the wild shores of Pontus. The last night at home was delirious. He gathered his slaves about him and embraced his family with tears; he gazed for the last time at his books, his beautiful collection of manuscript poems, bound in purple, with white ivory bosses on the binding; he handled them, smooth with pumice; he turned over, for the last time, their rubricated title-pages. His heart-broken wife (she was his third) entreated to be allowed to share his banishment, but he persuaded her to remain in Rome, so that she might work for his possible deliverance. Then, in sickening mental disturbance and extreme physical discomfort, he started on his endless exile. The voyage was a rough one, at all events by intervals, but I gather that Ovid must have been a fairly good sailor. At all events, he sat up on deck in the Ionian Ocean writing poetry, although the breaking waves sprayed his lips with their cold salt. He gives a detailed account of his voyage, and tells us where the ship called. He cannot have been very ill, because although " the narrowing Symplegades whitened the straits of Propontis with spray " he was hard at it, while the water splashed the paper and the foam dimmed his eyes. Not everyone, however gifted, would continue to write verses in a gale on the Hellespont.

But he was extremely unhappy, and his wretchedness

seemed almost unbearable when he landed at Tomis. The life there was terrible, in the midst of barbarians, with no interest of any kind to divert his mind from his misfortunes. Professor Wheeler remarks what a chance Ovid had of studying the geography and ethnology of Pontus, and of exploring the mountain region at the back. But this was the last project which would have occurred to the feeble and timid poet, spent by fifty years of Roman luxury. He says that Homer himself would not have been able to sing at Tomis, but Ovid did persevere, sustained by the yearning hope of recall. He sent his poems to his wife, envying them their happy fate of returning to Italy, of " gazing on Rome," as he puts it.

The inhabitants of Pontus were not unkind to him, but they could offer him no intellectual companionship and no cultivated sympathy. Moreover, they were always quarrelling with one another, Sarmatians with Getans. Ovid lived in constant fear of being accidentally assassinated during a scuffle; he felt somebody's sword for ever at his throat. His delicate constitution was harassed by the climate, which was so severe in winter that the long locks of the men of Tomis " tinkled with ice." His wine froze in its jar, and had to be served in solid fragments; it was so bad that the poet was forced to drink water, and this made him ill. " The water, you see, disagrees with me," he sang, like Louis Philippe in exile long afterwards. He lived to hear of the death of Augustus and of the accession of Tiberius, and again his hopes ran high. But a new generation had arisen, and Ovid was forgotten. At the age of sixty, after ten years of Pontic solitude, he died at Tomis, a fact the knowledge of which we owe to a person singularly unlike him in character and genius, St. Jerome.

A SURGEON'S RECOLLECTIONS

A SURGEON'S RECOLLECTIONS

IN the abnormal state into which the Great War has thrown the conscience of the world certain virtues have, for the moment, lost their predominant value. The sentiment of pity has been strained so violently and so long by recent events that it is like a cord which has exhausted its elasticity. "We are the children of earth's grey-grown age," and our generation has seen so many sorrows that we are in danger of becoming insensible to the pain of individuals. When our writers expatiate upon pity they are apt to present it in a distorted and even a grotesque form which robs it of its direct appeal to the emotions. A glance at an ordinary American comic newspaper tells us how violence of physical discomfort may be made to seem funny to people who have lost their sensitiveness, and who do not attempt to realise the horrors at which they giggle.

To bring back the public consciousness to a wholesome capacity for sympathy is no unworthy aim for any author, and perhaps it is necessary that he should be a member of the medical profession. The surgeon has more liberty than any other man to dwell with wholesomeness on pain, because he alone can assuage its worst manifestations. I can imagine few experiences more moving than those of the practitioner who, in advanced years, turns over the pages of his old case-books, and is confronted with the names, like ghosts, of the patients whom he dimly remembers, and whose trances of terror and agony have left faint or clear impressions upon the surface of his mind. He recollects, in some instances, nothing but the look, a tone in the voice, a feature in the frame. Then some peculiarity flashes across his memory, and he recalls a salient incident or even the outline of an experience.

Sir Frederick Treves is a practised writer upon many subjects, but he has never, I think, until now dived for treasure into the depths of his own professional memory.[1] For more than forty years he has been struggling against disease in several of its most dreadful forms, and he must have gained a singular knowledge of the capacity of the human being to endure. Goethe remarks somewhere—and every surgeon must assent to the statement—that a man or a woman can only bear a certain degree of pain, physical or moral. What exceeds that proportion merely tends to insensibility and indifference—*dolor decrescit*, as a Roman moralist says. It is the glory of recent surgery that it has, by a thousand arts and appliances, contrived to alleviate the excess of pain and preserve the sensibility of the patient.

The old notion that medical science was a mystery closed to the profane, and that a haughty demeanour was needed to keep the patient humble and subdued, lasted much longer than we often realise. The magnificent Dr. Akenside, when on his visiting days he advanced through St. Thomas's Hospital, was preceded by servitors who swept the patients away with brooms lest they should approach too near. The Memoirs of that amiable Quaker physician, Dr. Lettsom, show how brutal was the tone of the conventional surgeon or doctor in the eighteenth century. But many will be surprised to read Sir Frederick Treves's account of the state of the London Hospital less than fifty years ago. His picture of the Receiving Room in such an institution is amazing, especially to those of us who are old enough to have easily recollected it. So true is it that what

---

[1] This was written before the death of the eminent surgeon in December 1923.

A Surgeon's Recollections 253

has always been is easily supposed to be inevitable, and is very slow to awaken surprise or indignation ! The most striking and perhaps the most valuable of Sir Frederick Treves's chapters is that devoted to the case of the monster once universally known, but now entirely forgotten, as the Elephant Man. This unfortunate being was born about the year 1863, as is believed, at Leicester. He was so dreadfully malformed that it is difficult to know how he contrived to reach maturity. It appears from what could be collected about his past that his mother abandoned him when he was an infant, and that he found his way into the workhouse. Sir Frederick Treves's theory seems to be that the poor creature's appearance, which must from birth have been repulsive, greatly increased in hideousness as he grew up. He developed hip-disease, in addition to his other distresses, was removed to a hospital, and at last attracted the notice of some circus-keeper, who took him round the country on exhibition. " He passed from the workhouse to the hospital, from the hospital to the workhouse, then from this town to that town, or from one showman's caravan to another." Thus was passed his terrible youth, during the whole of which he never knew a home or any semblance of one. His conformation made him incapable of smiling, and the only smiles which reached him were those of ridicule and buffoonery.

I must not spoil Sir Frederick Treves's thrilling narrative by telling the series of accidents through which, when his miseries had actually reached the last stage of endurance, they were arrested and assuaged by the ministrations of the surgeon. The story is one which, if it were not intimately and minutely true, would be regarded as preposterously romantic, and Sir Frederick tells it to perfection. The story I will not repeat, but it calls for some reflections.

Robert Merrick, the unfortunate youth of twenty-one whom Sir Frederick Treves, by a marvellous series of coincidences, was able to succour at the worst crises of his distress, was absurdly called the Elephant Man, because of the abnormal shape and size of his head, and because of a protuberance which might be rudely taken for a trunk or for a tusk. In perfectly moderate language Sir Frederick Treves sketches for us the unparalleled deformity of this wretched being, whose last few years were spared any further degradation by the generosity of a troop of sympathisers. But from infancy up to the age when Sir Frederick accidentally discovered him in the back shop of a heartless showman, the life of Merrick had been a prolonged Calvary, and the cross he bore between his miserable shoulders had grown heavier and heavier, until, at the last desperate moment of his recovery, he was finally sinking under the weight of it. The story, admirably, though modestly, told by the great surgeon, is one of the most thrilling that could be designed, and fiction pales before it.

But what seems to me the most extraordinary fact about the Elephant Man was his moral temperament. He went through miseries which were not relaxed by day or by night, and yet the excess of his sorrows never destroyed or even impaired his sensibility. At the very worst, the disturbance of his inner being was not great. Here was a man whose contact with exterior things was horrible almost beyond parallel, and who, until he met Sir Frederick Treves, had never known respite from his constant humiliation and wretchedness, and who, without removal of his physical disability being possible, could yet become happy. In the dreadful story, nothing strikes me as more thrilling than that, in his last refuge at the London Hospital, he could say more than once " I am happy every hour of the day."

In what, then, does happiness consist? Plainly, the natural temperament of Robert Merrick was serene, amiable, and conciliatory. By a very natural instinct of pity, Sir Frederick, when he first concentrated his attention on the dreadful object in the vacant greengrocer's shop in the Mile End Road, believed, and hoped, that the poor monster was imbecile. He could not be, surely, conscious of his awful condition, nor observant of the dismal circumstances. The presumption was that the Elephant Man was what Trinculo, equally in error, took Caliban to be—" a very shallow monster, a very weak monster, a most credulous monster." But observation soon showed that this was not the case. Merrick was sensitive and intelligent beyond the average, and in that awful body there was encased a romantic soul tremulously conscious of his isolation.

The effect of his wretchedness was the opposite of what scorn and pain produced in the son of Sycorax. Not from the Elephant Man was heard a syllable of denunciation of those whose cruelties had made his childhood and youth a kind of hell. Caliban could scream :

All the infections that the sun sucks up
From bogs, fens, flats, on Prosper fall, and make him
By inch-meal a disease.

but no such revengeful curse ever proceeded from Robert Merrick. Shakespeare's delineation of the warped and corroded temper of his monster is doubtless absolutely correct, but the case of the Elephant Man surpasses it in wonder. Here we have a species of modern miracle, which, if it were not known to be true, would endanger credence. " As a specimen of humanity," says the observer to whom he owed all the felicity which was within his widest possibility, " as a specimen of humanity, Merrick was ignoble and repulsive ; but the spirit of Merrick, if it could be seen in the form of the living, would assume the figure of an upstanding and heroic man, smooth-browed and clean of limb, and with eyes that flashed undaunted courage."

This serenity and placable contentment are, to me, the most wonderful elements in a wonderful story, and I should like Sir Frederick Treves, who deals with the outer aspect of the poor Elephant Man, to tell us something more about the inner characteristics. Almost every part of Merrick's body—apparently with the sole exception of his left arm and hand, which were beautifully formed—was abnormal in development and extravagantly misshapen. What was the effect of this deformity on his nerves and his digestive system? This the great surgeon who analysed his case so carefully does not mention, although, no doubt, he possesses elaborate notes on the subject.

It seems difficult to believe that the exaggeration and contortion of the osseous and muscular forms should not disturb the inner working of the machine. As an ignorant layman, I should have supposed that the monstrosity would have led to a series of disorders such as Shakespeare clearly indicates in his study of Caliban. Like the famous character in " The Tempest," the voice of the Elephant Man was "as hobgoblin as his person," that faculty at least being affected by his afflictions. I am too little versed in teratology to know what is the effect on the nerves of such distortions, but that Merrick should have been capable of active and romantic happiness, and should have escaped all the revulsions of anger, reverberating on the physical well-being of his poor body, fills me with astonishment, and here I ask for a little more light from Sir Frederick Treves.

The Elephant Man detains me too long. The reader will do justice to the many other instances which Sir Frederick draws from his life's experience in his profession. Nearly three hundred years ago, his first biographer tells us that the illustrious Thomas Sydenham began, " before anyone else, to communicate to the World the useful Observations he made in the course of his Practice." It seems odd that such records should have been delayed so long, although medicine and surgery had been, in more or less fluctuating advance, pursued since the beginning of the world. I am convinced that the really learned, with the aid of a Loeb translation,

A Surgeon's Recollections 257

could produce instances from Hippocrates or Galen. The memories of Sir Frederick Treves are tenderer, and perhaps more practical. He teaches us lessons regarding human character, which are always entertaining, and sometimes sensational. His pages give a terrible impression of the monotony which is the bane of most lives not steeled against it by special preparation. " A Sea Lover " recounts how a mining engineer, whose youth and early manhood had been spent in the extreme of an African isolation, came back to England with the determination to live by the sea, and how, in fact, he died gazing at it.

In the course of a professional career the medical man, if he is worth his salt, gains an insight into human character which the most eminent dramatist might envy, and this is perhaps why doctors have been so cruelly maligned by Molière and by Mr. George Bernard Shaw. Physicians know too much and tell too little. Sir Frederick Treves has not been so deeply occupied in his labours of benevolence but that he has spared attention to the elemental passions and emotions of those who have sought his help in their desperate moments :—

" [The surgeon] notes how they act under strain and stress, under the threat of danger or when menaced by death. He observes their behaviour both during suffering and after relief from pain, the manner in which they bear losses and alarms, and how they express the consciousness of joy. These are the common emotional experiences of life, common alike to the caveman and the man of the twentieth century. Among the matters of interest in this purview is the comparative bearing of men and of women when subject to the hand of the surgeon. Which of the two makes the better patient is a question that cannot be answered in a word. Speaking generally, women bear pain better than men. They endure a long illness better, both physically

S

and morally. They are more patient and submissive, less defiant of fate, and, I think I may add, more logical."

In this connection, the amusing analysis of a woman's hysterical indulgence in " nerves " is an exception to the general method of the book, since it is put into her own mouth. It is not, perhaps, quite happy that, in this instance alone, the patient should speak for herself, since the hands are the hands of Esau, and the male voice of the sarcastic surgeon sounds through the sensitive female mask. This nameless lady complains of a thousand ailments, all of which are imaginary, and she is a nuisance to everyone with whom she comes in contact. At length she is suddenly and completely cured by a fright in connection with the genuinely serious and almost tragic adventure of a woman as wise and brave as she herself is weak and silly.

Sir Frederick Treves has no mercy for what our ancestors vaguely called " the spleen," and perhaps he is disinclined to recognise that where the patient laments the torment of a dozen complaints which do not really exist, she (or he) is really suffering from some thirteenth disorder of which no one suspects the presence. In " A Cure for Nerves " I am not so much astonished that the " cure " is sudden as that it is final and complete. That Sir Frederick Treves writes with picturesqueness and force is no surprise to those who are acquainted with his super-guide-books and other writings, but I think that this is the first time that he has taken us into his confidence about his famous professional adventures. That field must be hardly touched, and I hope that he will not fail to return to it.

1923

LOUIS COUPERUS
A TRIBUTE AND A MEMORY

LOUIS COUPERUS
A TRIBUTE AND A MEMORY

IN 1890, my friend Jan van der Poorten-Schwartz, who wrote excellent novels about Dutch life in English, sent me a story called " Noodlot " (" Destiny ") by a young Dutchman, who was displaying, as he thought, signal merit. Maarten Maartens, who adored our country to such an extent that he abandoned his native language to write exclusively in ours, was very anxious that literary relations should be formed between Holland and England. At that time I was editing for Mr. Heinemann a series which we called " The International Library," and we had already included in it Norwegian, Spanish, Russian, and Italian novels. The series ultimately extended much further, to the ends of Europe, and I think beyond them, but in 1890 we had as yet no Dutchman. Maarten Maartens, a sensitive prophet, was sure that the young Louis Couperus, for that was the name of the author of " Noodlot," was going to win a prominent place among his countrymen; what even he did not anticipate was that he would far outstrip all his rivals, and become the representative novelist of Holland.

I read " Noodlot," and liked it very much, and in 1891 it duly appeared (translated skilfully by Mrs. Clara Bell) inside the peach-pink covers of our " International Library." I prefixed a little sketch of what Dutch imaginative literature had been since its remarkable revival in 1880, and there, it gratifies me to believe, the name of Louis Couperus was first presented to the British public. We called the book " Footsteps of Fate," and it enjoyed a certain success, sufficient to encourage Mr. Grein, in the next year, to bring out an English version of Couperus's earlier novel, " Eline Vere." Shortly after this, it was the good fortune of the young Dutchman to find an assiduous and most competent translator in the late Mr. Teixeira de Mattos, who did not weary, to the end of his life, in making Couperus known in England.

Only six weeks before the lamented and unexpected death of the novelist, Holland was celebrating his sixtieth birthday with a zeal of which a faint echo was heard in most countries. Louis Marie Anne Couperus, the fourth son of Jan Ricus Couperus, and his wife Geertruida Johanna Reynst, was born in The Hague on June 10, 1863. When he was ten years old the whole family migrated to Java, and occupied a fine house in Batavia. I shall speak presently of what he said of Java when I saw him last, and of his nostalgia for the tropics, and of the influence on his genius of the remote Indian archipelago. He attributed to it a certain languor, which he never threw off in spite of his prodigious intellectual activity, and a certain solution of nervous force which we had to take his word for. At the age of fifteen, he was sent back to The Hague to complete his education, and I think that, at a very early time of life, he earned his livelihood by teaching, which he hated.

In 1884 and 1887 he published two little volumes of extremely modern verse, the second called by the pleasing title of " Orchids." These I have never seen, for Couperus told me not to look at them; he said they were " a mixture of Baudelaire and Rossetti, boiled in syrup." He was very ready with amusing self-depreciation of this kind, but I dare say, in this instance, he did his poems no injustice, for he was not a poet, but a great prose-writer learning his trade by experimenting in verse.

Then, in 1889, he had the good fortune to see his first

novel, "Eline Vere," accepted as a serial by the most influential Dutch literary journal of the day, "De Gids." This is a sort of "éducation sentimentale"; the growth of mind and character in the life of a young artist, Hugo Aylva, who is quite obviously a self-portrait of the author. There is not a little of what I suppose would be classed as orchidaceous in this book, where beauty for beauty's sake, the perfume of flowers, the hauteur of intellect, and the splendour of jewels take too prominent a place. There is one predominant "orchid," the heroine, Mathilde, who is really rather preposterous. There was a tendency to over-luscious melancholy and egotistical self-analysis in "Eline Vere" which the author was to outgrow without ever entirely abandoning.

In his next book, "Noodlot," there was a great advance both in common sense and in narrative skill. The main scene of this novel was laid in London—to be precise, indeed, in a lovely cottage in St. John's Wood. The subject, worked out with much skill, was that of a flourishing young Dutchman, Frank Westhove, settled at work in London, who has almost unconsciously become the oak supporting an idle ivy of a youth called Robert van Maeren, who lives upon his friend in complete parasitism. Frank falls in love with Eva Rhodes, the daughter of a baronet, and proposes to marry her; he is perfectly eligible, and the young people are devoted. But they have reckoned without the criminal selfishness of Van Maeren, who shrinks from no perfidy to escape being turned out into the world to work. He succeeds in dividing the lovers, but a horrid fate befalls him.

Next came, in 1892, "Extasy," a novel of violent tragedy, in which two souls who have worked one another up into a frenzy of mutual excitement fall apart after a short period of extravagant passion, and fail to recover their former rapture. Each story showed an advance in narrative power on its immediate predecessor, and Couperus now flung himself exclusively into the creation of character and incident. To this period belongs that very remarkable novel, " Van Oude Menschen " (" Old People and the Things that Pass "), which Teixeira de Mattos translated and Mr. Stephen McKenna introduced in 1919; it belonged, however, to a much earlier period, to (I think) 1902. Mr. McKenna believes that " Van Oude Menschen " is one of the six best world-novels of our age. I cannot give an opinion on this point, because I do not know what the other five are. The hero and heroine suffer remorse for a crime they committed in Java sixty years before, and their mental agonies are awful. I am not sure that I do not think there should be a close time for murderers, especially for exotic ones, but the situation, as Couperus depicts it, is very thrilling, and all the subsidiary characters are acutely delineated.

But a change came over the mind of Couperus. He thought that Dutch literature was overcrowded with bourgeois tragedies, and that he himself had been too passive under the influence of Flaubert. He began to revolt against social realism, and to lead a reaction in favour of individualism and romance. He had been preceded by a writer of great talent, Frederik van Eeden, whose mystical " Kleine Johannes " had enjoyed a deserved success. Couperus turned from realistic studies of common life to-day in The Hague, and particularly to a revival of the romance of antiquity. Life is short, and I have to confess that I have not had time to make myself acquainted with any of these later books, for an idea of which I have to lean upon the report of Drs. K. H. De Raaf and J. J. Griss, who, in their valuable history of Dutch literature, called " Zeven Eeuwen Spiegel,"[1] devote considerable attention to them. " Antiek Tourisme " (" A Tour in Antiquity "),

[1] Published by W. L. and J. Brusse, Rotterdam, 1920.

issued in 1912, must be a very odd book, and so must be
" De Boeken der Kleine Zielen " (" The Books of the Little
Souls "), a symbolic picture, placed in the world of ancient
Egypt, of the struggles and victories of a modern æsthete.
It is not necessary to read Dutch to enjoy all these stories,
since Mr. Teixeira de Mattos was an ideal translator. I
believe that he included in his series " Majesteit "
(" Majesty "), which is a very powerful and exciting account
of how an Emperor of the Lipari Isles was murdered by
anarchists.

Louis Couperus paid occasional visits to this country,
but they were brief, and he remained known to few Englishmen, although his acquaintance with our literature and even
our customs was considerable. His sympathy with
English habits of thought was genuine, but limited by his
wonder at our difference from other Europeans. I recollect
his expressing this sense of the isolation of England when he
came to see me first, in 1898. Courteous and a little timid,
Couperus produced little effect in a crowd; to know him
it was necessary to see him alone or in very congenial
company.

My happiest memory of him is the latest; and I think
as a picture of one so famous and so little known it may be
held to be not without interest. It was in the summer of
1921 that, during a flying visit to London, he came to see me
at my house one afternoon, where I happened to be alone.
I had not seen him for twenty-two years, and I found him
a good deal changed, and for the better. He looked more
prosperous, more elegant, and a great deal more healthy.
He was extremely amiable, even affectionate, and said he
never forgot that I was his earliest English admirer and
exponent. He was trim and well-groomed, with tufts of
grey whisker on each side of the pale oval of his face, to which
black-rimmed glasses gave a certain owl-like aspect. He
held his head a little on one side, with an almost languorous

smile, very engaging; and he talked excellent English in a soft, low voice. Nothing about him suggested the conventional idea of a Dutchman.

He told me of the immense success of his books in Holland, and of how kind his countrymen were to him, " now, at last! " But he added that he could not live in his " own dear country, because of the winds in Holland— they are so cold! " He was intensely, almost morbidly susceptible to temperature, and this delicacy he attributed to his childish years in the heat of Java; accordingly he now lived habitually in Italy, in Florence. He complained to me of a perpetual quiver of the nerves, a sort of shudder, but added : " It is of no consequence; it is a malady from my early youth." He told me that he was now (July, 1921) starting for a year and a-half in the Malay Archipelago, with his wife; they were going out in great luxury and state, and were to be received in Batavia with public honours. " It is perhaps a weakness, but I like all that! " he murmured, smiling. " But I will flee from Batavia as soon as I can. I must see the jungle; I must go up to the holy tablelands where the great ruined temples are; and I must see more than Java,—I must visit Palembang, and Borneo, perhaps, and the beautiful Spice Islands, as you call them. Hot forests and gentle savage orientals, away from this cold civilisation of the North. Mrs. Couperus says that we ought to have gone ten years ago, that it is too late, for I have fifty-eight years. But, no! I tell her that my heart is tropical, the Equator will make me young again! "

He spoke to me with freedom and without affectation about his novels, which were already very numerous, and were enjoying a cumulating success : " The old ones share the popularity of the new ones." He was not, however, satisfied with what he had published, and hoped that his romantic voyage through the islands of the East would start him on a new path, to better things. " When I have seen Java once more, I will write another novel all about the mysterious life there, and it shall be better,—it shall be my best!" He told me that he and Mr. Teixeira de Mattos had had trouble with the English booksellers. " They say I am improper! What do they mean by 'improper'? We Continentals find you so difficult to understand. I am a Latin of the Latins, you must know,"—and he laughed softly, bending his oval head still further on his shoulder, and drooping his eyelids,—" I must tell you that my mind is very un-moral! You are all so Puritan here, and I have such a sympathy with the *suburra*. The English publishers say this and that must be altered. Why should I be false? My heart is so tropic." He said that he had been very much attracted by the works of Mr. Stephen McKenna, who was his favourite among the young English writers. " To be consistently psychologue, oh! that is what a novelist should be. Here in England are you not a little too fond of adventure, not students enough of the soul? Perhaps!"

This visit, which I have allowed myself to recover, gave me great pleasure. It is not very often that people engaged in the same profession find an opportunity of exchanging genuine impressions. Couperus was affectionate and simple and at the same time startlingly penetrating. He had the air and some of the stigmata of genius. I parted from him on this last occasion with reluctance, and shall long remember how he left my house, lingeringly, smiling more than ever, and with soft protestations of esteem. I heard no further from him, nor do I know what were the results of his adventures in the Spice Islands. But I learn, with unaffected grief, that he died of blood-poisoning on the 16th of July, 1923. The literature of Europe is the poorer by it.

VAUBAN

VAUBAN

EVERYONE who loves France, and desires to comprehend the virtues and weaknesses of that noble nation, will do well to master the record of Vauban's career, which M. Daniel Halévy has set down with consummate art and discretion. Let us not object that our habits have not prepared us to follow with intelligence the history of the greatest of all military engineers. It is true that the curtains mentioned here have nothing to do with bedsteads, as Dr. Slop was long ago informed, but the reader will not have to order Corporal Trim to step home for Stevinus. The subject of bastions and half-moons need not be discussed in terms which would satisfy my Uncle Toby, and we are not called upon to "make fortifications for your Honour something like a tansy, with all their batteries, saps, ditches, and palisadoes." The lay reader may take it for granted that Sébastien de Vauban was the greatest architect of ravelins and citadels that the world has ever seen.

If that were all, we might leave his memory, very respectfully, to the technical student. But he was a man of extraordinary force and beauty of character, who struggled in hard times against a variety of difficulties, some of which, being moral and not physical, proved insurmountable. He typified the French temperament at its highest elevation, and he came at last into fatal collision with some of its worst faults. It is as an epitome of France that M. Daniel Halévy presents the great engineer to our notice.

The glory of Vauban in the seventeenth century was that he drew right across Europe, from the North Sea to the

Mediterranean, a frontier-wall of fortresses, a cuirass of stone, which protected his beloved country from all her envious rivals on the east. So many of his bastions have been swept away that the traveller may easily overlook the extent and the completeness of what Vauban accomplished. He found France exposed to every chance of insult; he left her protected, as a great fortified city might be, behind the most impregnable of walls. This is what makes the name of Vauban beloved in France, where the long open edge of the east is a perpetual menace.

What France has always needed, and what to-day she most desires, is security. Far above the wish for money, for the " reparations " of which we hear so much, is the insistence on being protected against the implacable and unscrupulous enemy behind the Rhine. Until the power for evil of that enemy is checkmated, the palpitation of France, the endless aching anxiety, can never cease. The man who first grappled with this terrible problem of achieving security for the French frontier, and who pursued his aim till it was finished, was a superb artist, no doubt, but he was first of all a far-sighted patriot. It is for this reason, and by the exercise of the tireless and disinterested energy of which M. Halévy gives so eloquent a record, that Vauban has won his place as one of the heroes of French history.

This is why, in 1808, Napoleon, desiring to inflame the national ardour of France, solemnly brought the heart of the great architect from his village church in Burgundy, and gave it sumptuous burial in the Invalides. This was a revival of Vauban's glory, after the unmerited disgrace of his old age. But we must turn to M. Halévy's documented page.

In a small country house at Bazoches, among the hills of the Morvan, was born, at the beginning of May, 1633, the third son of a country gentleman of reduced means. Sébastien Le Prestre Vauban, the companion of his brothers and the peasant boys around, instructed in the elements of knowledge by the village curé, did not leave his home till he was seventeen years of age. All we know of his start in active life is a phrase of his own, where he says that he entered the Army, in the regiment of Condé, in 1651, " having a fair tincture of mathematics and of fortifications, and drawing none so badly." He took service as what was called an engineer, a name involving modest duties, of which M. Halévy gives a detailed account.

His early career is obscure, but we find him attached to the famous Minister, Louvois, and gradually appreciated by that astute and sedulous servant of the State. We dimly perceive Vauban, under Louvois's orders, visiting the whole frontier of France, from Dunkirk to Antibes and back again, studying all the military posts, untiring in his fortifying plans. His chance did not come until 1669, when Louis XIV. declared war with Spain, and started to seize the cities of Spanish Flanders, with Vauban as his " engineer."

The nominal head of the fortifications had been Clerville, whose plans were lumbering and timid. The young King, who liked to have young men about him, rejected Clerville's plans, and turned to Vauban, who was thirty-five. Given a free hand, the bold Burgundian undertook to build a Flemish frontier for his Majesty, and so forge for France a buckler of stone.

During the next quarter of a century we see Vauban at work in ceaseless and exhausting service. He carried out the ambitious designs of Louis XIV., but not blindly. He had the superlative courage, fatal to his happiness at last, of opposing the Royal will when he thought it ill-advised. He perceived much more clearly than the King, or even than Louvois, that the fortune of France was then, as it is now, as it must always be, a terrestrial, not a maritime, affair. Vauban gave not a thought to the protection of the Atlantic

T

coast of France. He left that in the hands of Colbert's
" Marine du Roi," which made a terrible mess of it. Vauban
did not care; if Luxembourg was rebuilt and Douai
impregnable, what did it matter what happened to Brest?

The great thing was to strengthen the eastern frontier, to
add buttress to buttress, to hold the line from the North Sea
to the Alps, to conquer there or perish. Vauban has been
blamed because he turned away from this single aim to
help the King in his gargantuan effort to glorify Versailles
beyond the wildest dreams of Belshazzar. But those who
speak thus forget what the authority of the Crown was in
1680; it was absolute, and the greatest genius in the land
had no choice but to obey. Moreover, it is by no means
certain that Vauban did not, at first, before the ambition
of the King became so insensate, sympathise with the notion
of the magnificence of the palace. M. Daniel Halévy points
out with great judgment that we must not look for modern
prejudices in the character of such a man as Vauban. He
was a very pure type of the Frenchman of the seventeenth
century, with all the contemporary passion for *faste*, for
pomp and magnificence of style. What he had not got,
although it was the common error and defect of the leading
characters of his time, was the self-sufficiency, the blind
pride of the tyrant who will not brook interference with the
most intemperate of his projects.

Now, at the height of his effort for the protection of
France, the lamentable crisis comes. Vauban and Louis
XIV. fell out in 1687 over the question of the revocation of
the Edict of Nantes. The architect was a devout but not
a fanatical Catholic, and he viewed with alarm, which was
partly humane and partly political, the King's determination to root out of all the provinces of France every trace
of the reformed religion. Vauban dissented humanely,
because he was a man broad-minded and compassionate,
to whom persecution was in itself distasteful, but also

politically because he saw that this violent act would draw together into concerted resistance all the Protestant Powers of Europe, reviving their slackened zeal and renewing their mutual confidence.

Vauban opposed the Revocation not merely because it was cruel, but because it was stupid. What he saw that France was rousing was a unity of Protestantism, which would be a direct menace to peace, and France could no longer afford the luxury of war. It is at this moment that we begin to meet with a new Vauban, who is, no doubt, only the old one ripened by experience and circumstance. He becomes what Fontenelle—in that exquisite eulogy which is the despair of biographers, and which should be read by everyone who attempts the definition of character—what Fontenelle calls an " introducer of the truth." The idea is charming; in the magnificent Court of Louis XIV., where every other splendid quality found place, Vauban, as master of the ceremonies, presented Truth, a shy nymph whom no one before him had thought it needful to summon.

This time the King forgave him, and it is not quite certain whether his full plea for a gentler policy ever reached the Royal ear. The plenitude of Louis XIV.'s majesty, the tireless ambition which urged him forward, the unscrupulous self-confidence and arrogant force of the monarch, unbated now although his health and his temper were increasingly uncertain and his fear of death grown chronic—these are phenomena which astonish us afresh every time we approach the Sun-King from a different point of view. Vauban, with all the glory of his past, with all the lustre of his genius round him, was no more than a stable-boy if once he should dare to gainsay the Royal judgment. But, for the moment, there was no outburst. On the contrary, the King gave orders that not a shovelful of earth was to be moved in France without Vauban's permission. M. Halévy recounts the prodigies which the so-called " engineer " performed in ten professions; he was at the head of every branch of military service.

He groaned under the mountain of his duties; "they are more than I can perform," he wrote; "they embrace too many things for one man to execute with perfection; after forty years of intense application and wider experience than anyone ever had before me, I could not proceed were it not for the mercy of Him who hath saved me till now!" In answer, the implacable monarch sent him through the length and breadth of France on a mission of renewed intensity.

This perhaps is the moment to turn from M. Daniel Halévy, and remind ourselves of the picture of Vauban given by Saint Simon, who did not like, but could not help respecting him. Let me try to reproduce Saint Simon's loose, vivid incorrectitude :—

"Monsieur de Vauban was a man of ordinary stature, rather burly, very much the soldier in appearance, but at the same time with a look of being rustic and coarse, not to say brutal and ferocious. He was really the exact opposite of this; there never breathed a man more gentle, more sympathetic, more obliging, more respectful, more ready to do a thousand offices of politeness, and most niggardly in sparing the lives of his men. He had a way sometimes of taking whatever was offered him, but only that he might give the whole of it to others."

The humanity of Vauban was the feature in his character which led to his downfall. M. Halévy quotes a letter to Louvois in which the great engineer speaks of a wretched deserter whose fate excites his "compassion." Compassion! It was a word not used in the armies of Louis XIV., but it was characteristic of Vauban. Gradually the sufferings of the common people of France became so manifest to him that he could refrain no longer from speech. As a patriot, he could not allow his country to perish without making an effort to open the eyes of the old fanatical despot at Versailles. Perhaps M. Daniel Halévy should have spared a word to remind us that La Bruyère, ten years earlier, in his great chapter on " Des Biens de Fortune," had spoken out with regard to the condition of the peasant. But La Bruyère was not in a position, by the elegance of one anonymous essay, to bring about a political change. It was by the lips of the great Marshal of France that the earliest practical suggestion of reform was uttered. It was this noble voice which was first lifted in courageous appeal against the cruel subjection and torment of the poor.

A due consideration of the interests of his people was urged on the King by Vauban in 1698, in the midst of his vast labours and exhausting problems of strategy. He issued the famous pamphlet, " Le Dixme Royale," in which he implored Louis XIV. to restrain the waste of his Ministers, in other words of himself, by taking pity on "the most ruined and most wretched part of the realm," the overtaxed and patient lower class. He dared to inform the monarch that it is the poor who, " by their labour and their trade, enrich the King and all the State." In vibrating accents, such as never before were heard in France, the man who had preserved and protected the country for thirty years asked, as his reward, some pity for the poor. His plea was rejected with violence and arrogance, and he was never again the force behind the throne which he had been. The obstinacy of Louis XIV. drove the country onwards and downwards, and Vauban lived on, half in disgrace, to witness Ramillies and Turin.

In the midst of the wild riot of those last years we perceive the calm figure of the great Burgundian, still all rectitude, simplicity, and benevolence, but made powerless by the frenzy of obstinate anger which had taken possession of France. The chronicle of all this is given by M. Daniel Halévy in an admirable shape at once graceful and concise. This little monograph, in which all is told which can interest the reader, and nothing that can fatigue or distract him, might be studied with advantage by those English manufacturers of uncouth and desultory " lives," of which Mr. Asquith has lately been speaking with a ridicule which they well deserve.

ROMAN PICTURES

ROMAN PICTURES

AFTER giving us, with unbroken gravity, a study of childish impressions of a stately English demesne, Mr. Percy Lubbock now takes us to Rome in a spirit of exalted hilarity. If " Earlham " was concentrated and solemn, " Roman Pictures " is diffuse and entertaining, and offers, I think, the first instance of a deliberate desire to amuse on the part of this ingenious author. I have only one objection to bring against the book, and that is in regard to its name. " Roman Pictures " suggests one of those dreary portfolios of line-engravings which used to lumber the drawing-room tables of our grandmothers, with representations of the Pantheon restored and of the Corso seen by moonlight. We feared to turn the page lest we should confront a " Sunset from the Palatine."

I recall a terrible work of this species, called " Edifizj di Roma Antica," with fanciful reconstructions of the imperial buildings all done out of the author's head. Mr. Lubbock might have found almost any title more exhilarating than " Roman Pictures," which does not describe in the least what he gives, namely, sarcastic portraits in miniature of persons falsely styled Roman, exotic parasites none of them really representative of the Eternal City. No writer can be more unlike Mr. Lubbock than Thackeray, but the reader of the present volume is irresistibly reminded, by the form of it, of " The Book of Snobs."

There is a sort of parallel, too, in " The Yellowplush Memoirs," and we may compare Mr. Lubbock's Deering with the Hon. Algernon Deuceace; but perhaps I am now becoming too fantastic. What I would point out is that the "Roman Pictures" are not really pictures at all, but sketches, almost caricatures, of separate figures, each of them grotesque and exotic in relation with Rome itself. "Some Would-be Roman Snobs" would be my title, but I am sure Mr. Lubbock will reject it with indignation.

The story—for it is a kind of connected narrative—is supposed to be told by an ingenuous and cultivated English lad of twenty who has come alone to Rome to enjoy the antiquities and the associations. The month has been April, the weather divine, and the works of art have been completely rewarding, but over all things there falls satiety, and the pilgrim is conscious of a sudden sense of insufficiency in Baedeker. The red octavo tells much, but omits so much more.

The youth has been wandering in the steps of the guide-book, visiting here a mouldering church and there a cold statue, but what of it all is living? How much does he know of Rome who only knows the Rome of Baedeker? This is an inquiry which must often strike the traveller in fields that are superficially familiar, and over which a shining but unbroken surface glitters. Beneath that specious and dignified shell what marvels lurk hidden, what monsters, what avatars of past civilisation? Such thoughts descend upon our pilgrim as he loiters by the famous Fontana delle Tartarughe, that pretty fountain whose generous vase is upborne by extravagant young rascals, who fling about their limbs and sport with ascending tortoises as stiff as they themselves are supple. The pilgrim stands in the splash of the dripping water, and he feels that something has broken the great bubble of imagination in which he has for a month past been walking. He is conscious that while, in such a blessed infatuation, Rome has taken possession of him, he has not in the smallest degree taken possession of Rome. He is aware that a life pulses and buzzes around him of which he has not the slightest cognisance, and he longs to turn away from the monuments of the motionless past and share the inner bustle of the present. At this moment he turns, and behold, Deering at his side—" my precious Deering, of whose presence in Rome I had been quite unaware!"

Deering presents himself as Rome itself; he is that living Rome on whose surface the pilgrim merely floats like a leaf. He is so very Roman that he has almost abandoned the use of the English language; when their native speech is proposed as the medium of communication, Deering deprecates *ma come, ma come!* " It seemed he could hardly frame his lips to the uncouth noises of the northern Goth." This, one may remark, was excessive, since, as a matter of fact, the sound of English is said to be less " uncouth " in the ear of an Italian than that of any other foreign tongue. However this may be, the preciousness of Deering depends upon his being able to unveil the secrets of Rome to his fledgeling fellow-countryman, and this he prepares to do with the utmost magnanimity.

The first surprise which awaits the neophyte is to discover that the central post, the *omphalos*, of Rome is a certain café in the Via Nazionale, whither Deering presently conducts him, and where, according to the instructor, he will learn " to live the life of the place." Deering himself, having put on black clothes and a broad-brimmed hat, and having powdered his nose, believes himself to compete as a comrade with the young sculptors, poets, and journalists of the place. " There seems to be something of the Italian in me," he remarks, with a glance into the mirrors of the café, but no evidence is forthcoming that the Italians take him seriously, or indeed take him at all. His acquaintances are just English and American exiles like himself, and this, if I may be pardoned for giving away the secret of Mr. Percy Lubbock's satire, is the clue to its peculiar humour. We pass from scene to scene and from group to group, and each is just going to reveal to our pilgrim the inner secret of Rome.

Unfortunately this is never done, because, in spite of clothes and speech and food, and all the magic of environment, not one of the pretenders has, himself or herself, actually seized that secret, but remains to the end just an uprooted Anglo-Saxon floating on the surface, as any tourist may float, with nothing but Baedeker to cover his nakedness.

All this is gradually led up to; and I am conscience-smitten for spoiling the point of Mr. Lubbock's joke, yet I do not really spoil it, because it is his telling of the tale which is in fact so entertaining. The reader, like the young pilgrim himself, remains the dupe of the romantic fallacy that what Hawthorne merely guessed at and what wholly escaped Zola, is going to be divulged to him through Deering. The great splendid cage, under the vault of blue Italian sky, is going to be unlocked and the bird let out, the mystical, the immortal bird of many-coloured plumages whom the ages and the angels style " Rome."

Bannock is going to turn the key, but Bannock proves to be no more than a boisterous American baritone, with the voice of a bassoon, who has failed at the Italian Opera. He, though dingy and aggrieved, and rejected by the flower of Rome, knows nothing. The invitation, then, must come through Jaffrey, who dances at the Olympia Winter Garden, and who has a golden-haired Edna to share pink liquids with him while they rest their elbows on the marble-topped table in the Via Nazionale café. But in spite of all the local colouring, Edna turns out to be no more Roman than Jaff. The outpourings of both proclaim a common origin, not Monte Gianicolo, but Peckham Rye. Deering admits the deception, for Deering is of a world superior to Jaffrey and Bannock, and he attempts to redeem the momentary fiasco by reference to Cooksey. " Cooksey," he cries with enthusiasm, " will tell you—Cooksey calls all the Cardinals by their Christian names ! "

Cooksey, who has just been pursuing a monsignor down the nave of a church with a mop, seems promising indeed; by one so intimate with the Papacy the secrets of the Vatican will now surely be revealed. But no, even Cooksey, though ready to point out cardinals—and " rum old devils they are," too—proves totally unilluminating when it comes to detail. Still, Cooksey it is who takes the pilgrim to an audience at St. Peter's, during which, for a few moments, the genius of the place peeps (or flashes) out, only to be withdrawn. Then, an old scholar, working daily in the Vatican library, and a young seminarist, who uses thirty-five different kinds of scented soap and has a collection of secular poets all bound in apricot linen, offer their services in the great business of revealing Rome, but prove inadequate; and so we go on from illusion to illusion, and meet a decayed revolutionary, with his shabby but distinguished daughters; a tireless archæologist lecturing in and on the Forum; Fräulein Dahl, a matriarch of dim Teutonic tribes of tourists; several dingy Bohemians, one large female novelist, several honest Jesuits, and some dishonest painters, all devoted to Rome, all swimming or sinking in the shallow places of Roman society, but not one of them capable of penetrating the mystery. Rome remains inviolate; like the doctrine of the Rosicrucians, which, though a hundred thousand men should have looked upon it, yet continued to be untouched, imperturbable, out of sight, and unrevealed to the whole godless world for ever.

Probably it is my own fault, but I confess that I think Mr. Lubbock more successful with the opening, and again with the closing chapters of this amusing tale than with the middle of it. The beginning could hardly be better, so delicious is the richness of the setting, the slyness of the irony, the beauty of the studied sentences. The successive figures are drawn with extraordinary firmness and set against a sumptuous background. Then—unless my instinct is at fault—the narrative flags a little. Miss Gilpin and the Clarksons are somewhat dim and dull, Olga and Mimi positively almost tiresome.

The author wakes up again in the procession of Julia and her crew to the Professor's outdoor lecture in the Forum, and finally in the fine scene of the reception at the palace of the English-born Marchesa, whose last refinement of propinquity to Rome, without penetration of the innermost Roman sentiment, sets the seal upon the irony of the book. And then Deering, who put all these silhouettes in motion at the beginning, reappears on the last page " as much a stranger in the palace of the Dark Shops as the forlorn Marchesa herself "; and he and the pilgrim find themselves once more by morning light at the Fontana delle Tartarughe whence they started, and where the skipping boys of bronze are still tormenting the elusive tortoises. " Roman Pictures " (how I hate this title !) is a book of whimsical originality and exquisite workmanship, and worthy of one of the best prose-writers of our time.

THE NERVES OF FRANCE

THE NERVES OF FRANCE

THE old formula that to understand is to forgive is applicable not merely to the acts of private individuals, but of nations too. In order to be in a position to praise or blame the policy of a race, it is needful to comprehend a great many factors which escape the knowledge of the wisest of foreign observers. The great countries must inevitably remain in " isolation "—whether " splendid " or not must be a matter of opinion. During the last few months we have indulged in this country in a great deal of censure of French policy, or, at mildest, in a great deal of vague discussion. So far as that discussion or censure deals with the effect of foreign polity on our own internal welfare, by all means let it be pursued; but let us frankly admit that we are thinking about our own interests. Let us not sit in judgment on the psychology of our Allies without being quite sure that we know what it is.

For my own part, although I have studied the mind of France with infatuation for half a century, I confess that I do not know the secret. I seem to hold the key, but to fumble with the lock. If smart young political journalists, who go to Paris for ten days, and write a report of the situation to their newspaper coloured by the known prejudices of the proprietors of that paper, know more, it is that they are cleverer than I. To me the conscience of France is an enigma, perpetually attractive, perpetually illusive. But I am sure that the only way to enter even a little way into it is to endeavour to analyse some of its myriad forms. For that reason, and because I am tired of seeing sentiments attributed to the French which prove that the first letters of their moral alphabet have not been studied by the critic, I present to my readers to-day a novel that has just appeared, in which certain emotions and experiences that have had much to do with the Ruhr crisis are luminously developed. I do not know how " Les Défaitistes " will be received in Paris; I write before there has been time for a single French opinion to reach me. I think we often err by repeating the chatter of some café on the boulevards instead of forming an English judgment on the particular case.

The author of " Les Défaitistes," M. Louis Dumur, offers it as the third and, I think, final part of a work of which " Nach Paris " and " Le Boucher de Verdun " were the first and second. Those books were crowded, violent, and unbalanced; they were immensely read, furiously attacked, and enthusiastically admired. The new instalment is sure of being no less boisterously entertained; its courage will be called scandalous and its statements will be contradicted. I have nothing to do with all that. I am not setting forth a eulogy of " Les Défaitistes " nor an attack upon it. In these matters the attitude of a foreigner should be one of inquiry, not of praise or blame.

What we want to do is, if possible, to understand. The careful reading of this bewildering book, half history, half novel, with its passion and its confusion, its immense collection of facts and statements, its extraordinary mixture of fiction, some of it (I confess) too lurid for my taste, with audacious biography of public persons, some of them still living, cannot but help us to form an idea of at least a fragment of the great dumb purpose of the wounded French nation.

A peculiarity of the situation is that the author is a Genevese by birth and early education, and that his stories of Swiss life, such as " Le Centenaire de Jean Jacques

Rousseau" and " L'École de Dimanche" were delicate and extremely humorous. The war changed all that, and it seems to have deprived M. Dumur of humour as well as of delicacy. He is as unlike his former self as Zola is unlike Mrs. Gaskell.

But to the theme of " Les Défaitistes." In the two earlier sections of his war-work M. Dumur treated the scene in Germany and on the battlefields. In the present volume he confines himself, after a brief sojourn in Berne, to the heart of Paris. His subject is the danger to France and to society from the activities of those who were secretly opposed to the prosecution of the war. These belonged to widely different classes, ranging from the theoretical pacifists who loved their country but ranged themselves under Tolstoi's banner of non-resistance, to positive traitors and spies who were labouring underground to bring about the victory of Germany. The best elements of political and military life, the healthier and more virile part of the population, were never seduced by the former nor tainted with the latter. But the progress of the disease was neglected by the Government, and, as is matter of history, the extraordinary mischance which had placed Malvy at the Home Office, and kept him there until his existence became a crying scandal, encouraged the growth of defeatism. Tolerated by the masses, secretly encouraged at the Intérieur, internationalism, anti-patriotism, anarchy, and treason contrived to play into the hands of the agents of Germany to an extent which must always remain surprising to the historian. The purpose of M. Dumur's novel is to give a picture of the result of all this subterranean upheaval.

There is a certain interest in tracing the history of words in connection with their local sense, and it may therefore be well to note how and when the odd term *défaitisme*, certainly unknown to the Dictionary of the Academy and unhallowed by Littré, came into existence.

It appears that it was invented by the Russian publicist, Gregor Alexinsky, an ally of Kerensky, who disapproved of the Bolshevist policy. Alexinsky, in a pamphlet issued in French, attacked Trotsky for supposing the Tsar and capitalism to be the main evils, whereas the most formidable of all the foes of Russia was the military power of Germany. He charged the Bolshevists with being so blind in their fanaticism as actually to desire the defeat of their own country, and he called them *porajentsy*, translating this into French by a word which he invented, *défaitistes*, or persons not merely expecting, but desiring defeat.

The phrase was immediately taken up in Paris, and applied to such people on a wide range, from the magnificent M. Anatole France down to such ignoble creatures as Almereyda and Bolo. But this involved a serious confusion of thought, because the objects which inspired these different persons were entirely disparate. There were political, artistic, social, and sentimental causes at work, starting from sources which seemed to have no possible relation with one another. But they were gradually fused together into a more or less conscious effort to stem the torrent of active patriotism, to bind the hands and trip up the feet of those who were forced to accept the abnegations and the sorrows of war in order to put an end to the intolerable tyranny of German imperialism. There was, at first, nothing in common between such dreaming ideologues as M. Romain Rolland and the spies who were ultimately shot, but they, and all the others, of whatever complexion, who endeavoured to undermine the wall of French resistance, were really working together, whether they knew it or not, to bring about the bankruptcy of civilisation and deliver Europe in chains to the Hohenzollerns.

With their expert intelligence, the Germans perceived this much sooner than did the French. Towards the end

The Nerves of France

of 1914, roused from their complacency by the surprises of the battle of the Marne, the German authorities recognised that a subtler plan than had hitherto occurred to them must be executed in order to reduce the resistance of the Allies, which proved to be more serious than they had anticipated. Excellently informed by their agents of the various groups of thought in Paris, the Germans promptly determined to make use of the dissolvents which they detected to draw together the various bands of those who despaired of the Republic, and to apply them to Teutonic ends. They determined to employ their propaganda in terrifying the Parisian citizen with the bogey of financial ruin, to exaggerate the legend of German military omnipotence, to hint a doubt of the efficiency of the French preparations, to spread panic by dwelling on the uselessness of prolonging the war, to disseminate suspicion of the rectitude of Ministers, of the credit of generals, and in every way to break down the moral fortitude of France.

Above all, they attempted to dissolve the courage of those Frenchmen who were not actually fighting by exaggerating the power and malignity of Germany. Their agents were to hint how terrible would be the punishment of a people who resisted a Power which was divinely invested with the sovereignty of the world. Every month of vain resistance would but make more appalling the chastisement which would eventually fall upon the wretched nation which dared to defy the All-Highest. In spreading these ideas, which were like the germs of some exhausting disease, they availed themselves of the demoralisation produced, often in the most unintentional way, by the weakness and the timidity of the pacifists (or pacificists) of the intellectual order. So much it seems necessary to say in order to prepare the reader for M. Dumur's sensational narrative. He undertakes to tell us what the "defaitists" were doing from 1915 to 1917, and how Germany took advantage of their state of mind.

It will be asked how the novelist has been able to lead us through paths so tortuous and obscure. But much is explained by the fact that he has had the advantage of using the report drawn up by a repentant neutral agent in the German service. This agent, as we learn, is not anxious—very naturally—that his name should be published, but he is willing to admit that he is a Dane. Accordingly, the hero of the novel is a citizen of Denmark, by name Harald Arendsen, and we find him in Berne when the story opens. The aspect of the Swiss capital during the war is given with extraordinary vivacity, and we are enabled to understand what the compelling force of German culture and German organisation was able to exercise on the mind of a brilliant young Danish student who had been educated in Germany. It passes the skill of M. Dumur to make his hero sympathetic, and his adventures are not always easily credible, but that is beyond our purpose. The young Dane writes essays, in German, extolling the German cause with such rapture that he attracts the notice of the authorities, and is paid to go to Paris as a spy in their service.

The rest of the story is occupied with what he sees and hears rather than with what he does, for which we have mainly to take his own word. It is perhaps a weakness in the plot that, beyond spending a vast amount of German money, and caballing with other spies, it is not easy to perceive of what use he is to his masters. He is mixed up in a good many disgraceful intrigues, and at last he murders (in self-defence) a beautiful, wicked Frenchwoman of the direst spy species. He is not a nice young man, and I am not persuaded to admire him by his suddenly going over to the side of the Allies a few days before the Armistice.

To mingle fiction with fact, or rather to make fact palatable by trimming it with fiction, is always questionable. But what makes " Les Défaitistes " really important is not the adventures of its hero, nor its rather mechanical and preposterous love-passages. These are only set to garnish out the feast. The importance of the record rests on its revelations, which appear to be astonishingly accurate, whenever they deal with passages where evidence can be produced. I doubt whether any work calling itself fiction was ever more full of details purporting to be unbiassed recent history, and this is what makes " Les Défaitistes " interesting.

We heard something in England of the fate of the beautiful Dutch dancer who called herself Mata-Hari, but the exact details of her detection and her execution as a spy have perhaps never before been told so circumstantially. We have portraits of such passing figures of defeatism as Almereyda and the staff of *Le Bonnet Rouge*, while a certain English journalist cuts a very sorry figure in the tale. But the most overpowering and, unless the novelist is perfectly sure of his facts, the most audacious portrait is that of M. Caillaux, where the novelist appears to borrow successive confidential " interviews " implicitly from the *cahier* of his Danish friend. In brief, " Les Défaitistes " is a book on the authenticity of which an English reader may well decide to express no opinion, but he will be safe if he emphasises its fascinating and unusual interest.

1923.

AMERICAN FOLK-SONG

AMERICAN FOLK-SONG

UNTIL quite lately, the mention of an "American ballad" brought to the mind either a poem by some popular author, such as Longfellow or Whittier, or else an edition of European ballads prepared by the late Professor Child, of Harvard, or by his successor, Professor Kittredge. The study of aboriginal American folk-song is an entirely recent thing, and arose five or six years ago over collections of oral literature made in Kentucky and West Virginia. It was found that in the mountains of those States there survived traditional songs and stories in verse which came from the soil itself, and not from Europe. This discovery instantly attracted a great deal of attention, and since then folk-poems have been industriously collected throughout the central and western provinces. It is amazing how ample the harvest proved to be when once it had been decided that it was worthy to be garnered.

Among those who have distinguished themselves in this work, no one has done better than the lady who edits the collection now before me, Miss Louise Pound, Professor of English in the University of Nebraska. The selected pieces which she has here arranged are often pathetic or amusing in themselves, but they are particularly valuable to the student of comparative literature as throwing light on what is still, and probably always will be, a mystery, namely, the mode in which our own famous Border ballads came into existence. The reader must not approach Miss Pound's volume in search of poetry, for of this he will find little or nothing, but in hopes to learn what force it is which transmits, orally, from generation to generation rhymed versions of local incidents or popular traditions. It should be noted that no place is found here for sophisticated pieces of patriotism like "Yankee Doodle" and "John Brown's Body," but only for genuine ballads of an old simple kind, invented or adapted in remote American districts. These are of the same order,—although, of course, infinitely inferior to those in imaginative inspiration,—as the European masterpieces, "Childe Maurice" or "Little Musgrave." That the mountains of Kentucky and the swamps of Missouri have produced a multitude of such poems is as interesting as it is surprising.

These American ballads are, as Miss Pound is fond of repeating, in a state of flux. There is no standard form for any of them, and the singer or reciter is apt to take liberties with a text which is recited, but not written down. It will be interesting to note what will take place now that these pieces have been captured, circulated, and printed. Will they continue to be popular? Will the published form be accepted as correct? Will the ballad lose its charm for those who listened to it when it was orally romantic now that it is in everyone's hands, diffused and vulgar? Probably it will lose its charm, and the art or practice of making ballads may die in America as it has long since died in Europe.

All the more, then, we prize what the industry of collectors has gathered during the last five years, since it is improbable that a second harvest can be reaped. If the American ballad should pass away, with the Dodo and the Great Auk, we need not very bitterly deplore it, since its level of merit cannot be said to be high, and time is not likely to raise it. But it ranks among the legitimate curiosities of literature.

The American ballads are of several kinds. First of all, we meet with recent transformations of ancient poems, like "Lord Randal" and "Barbary Allen," which recur over and over again in European folk-song. In these there are alterations made to suit the different experience of the auditor. For instance, in the ballad of "The Two Sisters," as recited in North Carolina, the story follows closely on the lines of the famous English ballad, but the body of the murdered sister is perceived not by the son of the miller of Binnorie, but by a farmer's wife, who "was sitting on a rock, Tying and a-sewing of a black silk knot." It is odd how many of the romantic and aristocratic features of the originals have been preserved in some of these adapted ballads. They are, however, usually stripped of all poetical merit, and the decay of style is deplorable.

More interest attaches to the purely native ballads, which are devoted to incidents, often local in the first instance, which have arrested public curiosity. Whether the delicacy of the editor has Bowdlerised the text, or whether the ballad-minstrels of the Alleghanys are modest far beyond their kind in Europe, I know not, but register the fact that the reticence of these American ballads is extraordinary. That surly watch-dog of old times, the Reverend Cotton Mather, was indignant that amatory and ribald rhymes should be sung in the chaste streets of Boston. He could have objected to no single stanza in the whole of Professor Pound's collection. On the other hand, murder and robbery, crimes the humour of which, to judge by the funny journals of the United States, never comes amiss to an American audience, are amply represented.

The mode in which these ballads spring out of the heart of the community is mysterious. An incident of no great importance in itself derives, from some local condition, which is soon lost, an interest that responds to a set of rough verses. These a nameless bard sets to a popular air, or to music which he makes popular in connection with his words. Then, without premeditation, like a strong weed in a garden, there shoots up a ballad sung by hundreds of persons who have no possible connection with the facts which are commemorated. For instance, simultaneous and widely differing versions of a ballad describing how a young man was killed by a snake in the hay-field are reported from Montana, Missouri, Nebraska, and doubtless from other central States. In each case a local spot is described, and a local victim named. Here is the Nebraska version :—

>In Springfield Mountain there did dwell
>A lovely couple that I love so well.
>
>He went out in the meadow for to mow,
>When a garter-snake gathered him by the toe.
>
>He mowed just twice around the field
>When a rattle-snake gathered him by the heel.
>
>O he stepped back as he thought best
>Right into a yaller-jacket's nest.

(The neighbourhood was evidently " unhealthy " in the matter of vermin. But, to proceed :—)

>" O Billie dear, why did you go
>Out in the meadow for to mow ? "
>
>" O Mary dear, I thought you knowed
>' Twas your Pa's hay, and it had to be mowed."

That is all; and quite enough. Mary doubtless surrendered, without a murmur, to the agricultural fatality.

The Western ballads, though like the Central ones without a spark of poetry, are nevertheless full of character. The view of the cowboy adventure is not that made familiar to us in the stories of Bret Harte and other romantic novelists, save in one or two obviously artificial examples, such as " One night as I lay on the prairie." The genuine cowboy ballads do not conceal the hardships and the drudgery of the ranch. There is a good deal of spirit in " The Old Chisholm Trail," and people who thirst for local colour can imbibe deep draughts of it in literature of this kind :—

> My hoss throwed me off at the creek called Mud.
> My hoss throwed me off round the 2-U herd.
>
> Last time I saw him he was going cross the level
> A-kicking up his heels, and a-running like the devil.
>
> It's cloudy in the West, a-looking like rain,
> And my damned old slicker's in the wagon again.
>
> Crippled my hoss, I don't know how,
> Ropin' at the horns of a 2-U cow.

But the general tone is less boisterous, even a little depressed. The " tenderfoot," with all his disabilities and illusions, is the subject of a surprisingly large number of ballads. I cannot believe that any youth who heard " The Buffalo-Skinners " recited would willingly adopt so distressing an employment. I have the impression that some of these cowboy songs are of very recent date, and in " Starving to Death," a singularly pessimistic example, I fancy that I trace an echo of Mr. Rudyard Kipling.

The general tenour of these Western ditties seems to be that life on the prairie is so disgusting that a wise youth will stop in Missouri and get him a wife, " and live on corn dodgers the rest of his life," rather than face it. Cheyenne, which is, I think, in Colorado, is a centre of these cowboy ditties, with several of which the name of a certain Yank Hitson is connected, this being the only instance in which any suggestion is made of authorship or origin. The reader may trace a sort of echo, probably quite unconscious, of the stock-riding Australian ballads of Adam Lindsay Gordon in these cowboy pieces from the Far West, but the entire absence of the poetic element in the latter distinguishes them.

The realistic character of the indigenous American ballads is an interesting feature. In the Border and the Danish poems which best illustrate the Old World type the supernatural element is very often prominent. Thomas the Rhymer is carried off, as he lies under the Eildon Tree, by a bright lady in a gown of grass-green silk, who is the Faery Queen, and who keeps him in captivity in Elf-land for seven long years. Earl Mar's Daughter is wooed by a sprightly dove which turns into an enchanted prince. Kempion kisses a fiery dragon, and at the third embrace the horror is transformed into a lovely maiden. I find no trace of all this fantastic mediæval romance in the ballads of Kentucky and Virginia, but instead of it I meet with a rude humour, as in the story of Johnny Sands, whose wife ties his hands behind his back when he threatens to drown himself :—

> And now he's standing on the brink :
> She ran with all her force
> To push him in—he stepped aside,
> And she fell in, of course.
> Now splashing, dashing like a fish,
> " O save me, Johnny Sands ! "
> " I can't, my dear, though much I wish,
> For you have tied my hands."

This ballad, which seems to have been composed about eighty years ago, has " achieved enormous vogue," the editor tells us. It is, no doubt, a lively piece, but little of the perfume of " The Two Sisters of Binnorie," upon which it was possibly founded, seems to cling about it.

The ballad I have just mentioned, like many others in this collection, owed its " enormous vogue " to the fact that it was carried round the country by travelling troupes of reciters, called " entertainers " and, sometimes, " minstrels." There used to be itinerant bands who conveyed the popularity of such verses from township to township, and these were particularly prevalent fifty years ago. This mode of diffusion appears to have ceased, and no doubt with it the vitality of the topical ballad has declined. Professor Pound reports that, although the ballads are still occasionally heard in village parlours, they are no longer publicly sung to the accompaniment of the accordion or the mouth-organ, except in some mountainous districts of the South-east. Evidently the art, if it can in this pedestrian form be called an art, of ballad-writing and singing is rapidly falling into desuetude. None too soon, therefore, are efforts being made to rescue it from mere oral currency, since it has considerable historical importance, if little literary charm.

THE BROTHER OF THE BRONTËS

THE BROTHER OF THE BRONTËS

AN irresistible impulse urges an increasing number of clever people to pounce upon the verdicts of history and turn them inside out. The vices of our typical saints are exposed, and the virtues of our accepted criminals are insisted upon. Clio is shown to have been invariably mistaken, and we are left we know not where, in a state of bewildered confusion. Tiberius was a good, kind nobleman, who organised pleasant Sunday-school treats in his palace at Capreæa. Judas Iscariot was a far-sighted financial genius, misunderstood by his Communist colleagues. If Henry VIII. had a fault, it was a too-complacent indulgence towards his giddy wives, who for their part meant no harm. In the eyes of the biographical whitewasher nobody means any harm, except evil characters like Marcus Aurelius and Mrs. Elizabeth Fry.

This tendency to accept the topsy-turvy position, in which the critic attracts attention by standing on his head, has invaded the admired seclusion of Haworth Parsonage. For seventy years, the three wonderful Brontë sisters have been seen radiant against the background of a deplorable brother, " the dissolute and art-loving Branwell," as Sir Sidney Lee severely styles him. Suddenly, all that is changed, and we are called upon to believe that Branwell was not dissolute, and that he wrote his sisters' books. In fact, that he was the flower of the flock. But before we crown him, let us consider the evidence.

Patrick Branwell Brontë was born in 1817, being younger than Charlotte and older than Emily and Anne. He was first heard of in Mrs. Gaskell's " Life " of Charlotte, where he was dealt with faithfully, too faithfully, indeed, since the gifted biographess had to eat humble pie, and suppress some of her remarks in a second edition. Her judgment, however, was that, " to begin with," Branwell was " perhaps the greatest genius in this rare family." That meant that his natural talents, exhibited in early childhood, exceeded those of his sisters, but were soon obscured by opium, alcohol, and evil living generally. He became the bane of the Haworth family, and the black sheep of their circle.

It cannot be said that any of the early biographers gave any proof of their statement that Branwell was immensely gifted as a child. Gradually, it became known that he had pretensions to genius, but these have been very widely rejected. He does not seem, in his later befuddled years, to have made any claim to literary distinction, except what is brought out by the two works before me to-day. It has always appeared certain that he was a constant nuisance to his remarkable sisters, but it has never been admitted that he approached them in talent, and still less that he shared in their brilliant feats of composition. But now two persuasive voices are simultaneously raised, claiming for the unhappy Branwell a place in English literature which no one has seriously claimed for him before. Mr. Drinkwater prints his version of some of the Odes of Horace, and Miss Alice Law urges that he wrote " Wuthering Heights."

In this instance, I suspect Mr. Drinkwater of being what the Dorking lady called Andrew Lang, " no serious seeker after truth." His manifesto in favour of Branwell is ardent, but he seems conscious that it is paradoxical. Mr. Drinkwater has become possessed of the manuscript of a complete translation of Horace's First Book of Odes, made by Branwell Brontë in 1840. This document has formed a good excuse for Mr. Drinkwater to write an excellent critical preface on Translations from Horace in general and Conington's in particular. He also gives a very fair analysis of what is known of Branwell's career as an artist, if it can be called a career. He draws no more attention than it deserves to the strange but unique and invaluable portrait of Emily which is now one of the treasures of the National Portrait Gallery.

Mr. Drinkwater, however, goes too far when he says that this work is " one of the most beautiful things in the collection." However, I will not discuss art with him, but when he declares that in some of Branwell's " lovely renderings " of Horace " there is hardly a flaw from beginning to end," I turn with eagerness to the poems, and find this :—

> Who's the Maid thou'lt snatch, lamenting
> O'er her lover gone;
> Soft relenting—soon consenting
> To be Thine alone?
> Who shall be the bright-haired boy
> Waiting with the cup of joy,
> And, like his father, skilled to employ
> The arms to China known.

I am obstinate enough to prefer Conington, and even Sir Theodore Martin. But I admit frankly that Branwell often does much better than this, yet never so well as Mr. Drinkwater tries to persuade himself to think. As to Branwell's " poetic achievement " and " clear lyrical beauty," I think Mr. Drinkwater is laughing at us,—and knows it.

If Mr. Drinkwater is whimsical, Miss Law is in deadly earnest. She confesses, at the outset, that her feeling for Branwell " preponderates " over her " admiration for the genius of his sisters." She is prepared, if called upon, to sacrifice that genius on the altar of her impassioned admiration of Branwell, and to give Charlotte, Emily, and Anne a very subaltern rank in the family. There is an element of generosity in Miss Law's attitude which I should be the last to deny. It must be admitted that the eulogists of the sisters have overdone the obloquy which they have poured on " this lost and degraded man," as Sir Wemyss Reid called him. He is, to be sure, a poor scalded dog that has never had his day, and, from Mrs. Gaskell downwards, everybody has thrown half a brick at him.

There has been one exception. Mr. Leyland, who wrote a book about the Brontë family in 1886, mentions that about forty years before that date he met Branwell Brontë at Sowerby Bridge Station. On that occasion he " showed none of those traces of intemperance with which some writers have unjustly credited him." This interview coloured the rest of Mr. Leyland's life, until he became a sort of inspired protagonist for Branwell. Branwell had appeared to be quite sober that morning on the platform of the railway station where he was clerk, and therefore he was never drunk ! Such is the logic of the sentimental biographer in the face of evidence. Shortly after the interview with Mr. Leyland, the railway company dismissed Branwell Brontë for " irregularities." Perhaps the authorities saw him more often, and less favourably, than did Mr. Leyland. Far be it from me, however, to grudge Branwell his one defender, who returned again and again to his defence with remarkable gallantry.

Into Miss Law's impassioned apology for the character of Branwell I have no space and little inclination to enter. It is a typical instance of that resolute whitewashing, that entire reversal of the verdict of history, which we have noted in so many recent instances. If Miss Law had confined herself to an appeal against the violent condemnation of Branwell's conduct which has been too slavishly repeated, there would be little fault to find.

The Brother of the Brontës 313

But the evidence of the poor youth's distracted feebleness, of his sordid tastes and trumpery ambitions, is too strong to permit us to look upon him as a paragon. According to Miss Law, he never drank too much, he never smelt a drop of opium, he loved his sisters and respected his aunt. He attempted to soften the rigours of Charlotte, who was " gey ill to live wi' "; he presented an unclouded brow to fate, and, although " continual failure in every direction was very depressing to his spirits," yet he never complained.

The incident of Branwell's intrigue with Mrs. Robinson, of Thorp Green, greatly occupies Miss Law. It is true that it was absurdly emphasised by Victorian prudery; it would have been wiser for the sisters to ignore it than for Charlotte to denounce her brother's share in it to Mrs. Gaskell. It was a matter of no real interest to anybody but Mr. Robinson, who lay low, like Brer Rabbit, but, on his death, was found to have known all about it. His will " absolutely precluded his widow's re-marriage, except with loss of the estate." Branwell, like a greater than he, sighed as a lover, but withdrew " in sleepless horror " at the idea of marrying a pauper. Miss Law, who takes up Branwell's cause in this as in everything else, says that his feelings were those of " a young troubadour towards his queen of love and beauty." This is on a par with the emotion of the evening newspapers when something happens to a shopkeeper's wife in the suburbs— " Tragic Fate of a Society Lady ! "

I must, however, push on to what is really the serious object of Miss Law's book. She wants to clear Branwell's character and to ventilate her own extreme dislike of Charlotte and modified contempt for Emily, but her central theme is the authorship of " Wuthering Heights." No doubt whatever was thrown on this until long after the death of everybody concerned, when, in 1879, a Mr.

Grundy asserted that Branwell Brontë had told him that " he wrote a great portion of ' Wuthering Heights ' himself." Mr. Grundy, whose use of English was not impeccable, confessed that it was " well-nigh incredulous " that a refined young girl could have written so coarse a book, and declared that " the weird fancies of diseased genius with which [Branwell] used to entertain me in our long talks at Luddenden Foot reappear in the pages of the novel." Miss Law has brooded over this vague reminiscence, until she has persuaded herself that Branwell not merely contributed some pages to the story, but that " Wuthering Heights " is entirely his invention and composition, and that all Emily did was to send it to press when it was finished, tacitly allowing it to be considered hers until the day of her death. Why she should behave in so astounding a manner, and how she could deceive Charlotte and Anne on a matter of such vital importance, are questions which Miss Law does not shirk, but darkens with an infinitude of oblique comment.

The reasons which Miss Law gives for believing Emily Brontë unable to compose such a book as " Wuthering Heights " will scarcely be read without a smile. Emily was " not an advanced student in the classics," and therefore could never have written the word *penetralium*. Persons in the story are threatened with " the fate of Milo " ; this must be by Branwell, because Emily was not " learned." The curses and brutal language of Heathcliff could never have occurred to the mind of a quiet, reserved young lady. Perhaps the funniest example of this kind of criticism is the remark about the description of the yeoman-farmer in " Wuthering Heights," the man " with a stubborn countenance, and stalwart limbs set out to advantage in knee-breeches and gaiters." This reference to the yeoman-farmer's legs settles the matter for Miss Law. No nice female could possibly have written so

The Brother of the Brontës 315

indelicate a sentence, which " pointedly suggests Branwell's authorship."

Miss Law, who becomes spiritually inebriated with the wine of her own enthusiasm, sums up the matter triumphantly saying that it is a " truly preposterous theory " that Emily Brontë wrote the great novel which has placed her among the masters of imaginative fiction. But she cannot, for all her special pleading and reiterated rhetoric, make the slightest impression on Charlotte Brontë's clear and reiterated statement in her stately preface to the collected edition of 1850. I recommend any reader, shaken for a moment by Miss Law's specious pages, to turn to this document and read it carefully. In the face of what is there deliberately stated no doubt is possible. We have to believe either that Branwell bragged to Mr. Leyland or else that Mr. Grundy's belated memory betrayed him. Let us clearly realise that the only possible alternative is that Charlotte was a liar and Emily a knave. This I absolutely refuse to believe; I am, and shall remain, on the side of the angel-sisters.

Miss Law, whose mounting enthusiasm carries her desperately away, closes on an amazing note. She says that although—

"Emily Brontë did not write ' Wuthering Heights.' In helping her brother to finish and publish it she did a far greater thing, and in so doing surely she has won beneath the eyes of the Eternal Witness a fame more imperishable than any of those earthly plaudits which she so despised."

If this means anything at all, it means that the amanuensis who copies a manuscript is a greater personage than the original writer, and that to carry somebody else's book to the post-office is " a far greater thing " than to have composed it. To such absurdities does an indulgence in paradox ultimately guide the unwary !

LESLIE STEPHEN

LESLIE STEPHEN

OF all the remarkable men whom has it been my privilege to know during my long life, there is not one on whom I look back with more respect than I do on Leslie Stephen. He was the " very perfect knight " of literature, temperate in judgment, strenuous without ostentation, affectionate without sentimentality. When he died, twenty-one years ago, it was generally admitted that we had lost our most distinguished living critic, and, in width of range if not in height, our leading man of letters. Moreover, Leslie Stephen as the editor of a variety of very important composite publications had come into contact with a larger number of persons than any other contemporary author. His personal influence was universal, and his sympathy extended on all sides of him. It is, therefore, as surprising to me as it is painful to find his genius strangely neglected by the current generation. He is not attacked, but he is not mentioned, which is worse. His sane and courageous opinions are seldom referred to, his delicate humour seems no longer to raise a smile, and clever young men dispute about rationalism in the eighteenth century as though the " History of English Thought " had never been written. I hope that I exaggerate this neglect, and that the publication by the Hogarth Press of " Some Early Impressions " may have the effect of recalling serious readers to a noble figure which is worthy of all their attention and all their homage.

Leslie Stephen, who was born in 1832, was seventy-one years of age when he committed these recollections to paper.

Mr. and Mrs. Woolf, who have published the little volume, supply no further information. Leslie Stephen's admirable biographer, F. W. Maitland, who had seen the notes when he wrote his " Life " in 1906, expressed a hope that they would some day be given to the public, and here they are. In the summer of 1903 Leslie Stephen was already a dying man, though dying slowly. He had undergone a dangerous operation and had found relief, but his weakness grew upon him steadily, and on the 5th of February, 1904, he passed away. I suppose that these " Impressions " represent almost his latest thoughts. In writing to an American friend he had said : " The trouble with me is that I do not reminisce. I marvel at my tendency to oblivion of all details. I agreed to write—because one does agree. But instead of reminiscences proper, I have really confined myself to general observations. Therefore, I don't expect to startle the readers."

In fact, he does not " startle " us; and it may be admitted that these " Early Impressions " betray some languor. They are beautiful in their serene simplicity, and to those who are familiar with the temper of Leslie Stephen, and delight in it, they are precious, but the shades of evening press upon them a little. They have the " sober colouring " of which Wordsworth spoke; they come from a mind that " hath kept watch o'er man's mortality," that is ready to depart, and that no longer cares for precise touches of detail. It was my sad privilege at this very time, the autumn of 1903, to be summoned, as were so many other friends, to say farewell to Stephen in the house which had been taken for him in a Wiltshire village. He was still just able to be dressed, and to lie in a long chair, very weak and wasted, and with haggard eyes. I should hesitate after twenty years to speak of so sacred a memory if it were not that my thoughts dwell less on the shrunken features, the withered hands, the wild hair and flowing beard, no longer red but grey; and far more on the dignity, the tenderness, the marvellous spiritual repose. Leslie Stephen, with the sunset light upon his face, uncomplaining, patient, even humorous still in a manner almost heart-rending to those on whom he smiled—that is a vision which will abide with me till I too descend " behind the white wave."

Maitland tells us that his famous father, Sir James Stephen, described Leslie as " a sensitive plant grafted on a Norwegian pine." The illustration offers some botanical difficulty, but describes picturesquely enough the mixture of roughness with delicacy which was so characteristic. The roughness was mainly physical. His bony and attenuated frame, with its incalculable length of limb, gave an impression of something saturnine, and not easily or safely to be approached. I think it was he himself who admitted that when he was climbing in the Alps he was " frequently flattened out against the rock like a beast of ill-repute nailed to a barn." Mr. Thomas Hardy, in a sonnet which he never ventured to show to Leslie Stephen, compared him with the Schreckhorn, that inviolate mountain which he had been the first to conquer, and saw in it a

> semblance to his personality.
> In its quaint glooms, keen lights, and rugged trim.

Gaunt and difficult in his exterior Stephen indubitably was, and formidable in his silences, which were Alpine in their desolation. But underneath this rugged shell there existed a being tremulous in its sensitiveness to every kind of emotion; and, to speak bluntly, what seemed like gruffness proved to be mostly shyness.

As is natural in those who turn to the retrospect of youth in old age, Leslie Stephen dwells fondly on his university days in these last recollections. He was not one of those great men, like Gibbon or Dryden, who look back upon their *alma mater* only to abuse her. He had a passionate and

Y

lasting love for Cambridge, which found frequent expression in his writings and is vocal here. We read of Professor Smyth's lectures which always drew an audience, although they were repeated annually, because it was known that at a certain moment the lecturer would burst into tears upon mentioning the sad fate of Marie Antoinette. Leslie Stephen remarks that this was a spectacle worth taking some trouble to witness. He observes that in his own undergraduate days there was no Carlyle or Emerson or Newman at Cambridge to rouse the slumbering intellect and persuade the undergraduate that he had a soul. Leslie Stephen characteristically asserts that this was no defect, but an advantage, since "spiritual guides are very impressive but sometimes very mischievous persons." There was nothing Stephen deprecated more than the formation of prigs, and perhaps we may perceive something of his eighteenth-century bent of mind in his life-long suspicion of religious "enthusiasm." His advice to students was the purely commonsense one, "Stick to your triposes, grind at your mill, and don't set the universe in order till you have taken your bachelor's degree." This does not preclude an interest in the moral and intellectual questions of the day, which it would be doing the generation of Leslie Stephen a gross injustice to pretend that they neglected.

The impact of one of the greatest of the sons of Cambridge does not, if I remember right, find a record in Maitland's "Life." The following passage, therefore, in the present "Early Impressions" has great value :—

"In my day, the most famous member of the [so-called] 'Apostles' was Clerk-Maxwell, the great physicist, whose mathematical genius was already recognised. He was a fascinating object to me : propounding quaint paradoxes in a broad Scottish accent; capable of writing humorous lampoons upon the dons; and turning his knowledge of

dynamics to account by contriving new varieties of
' headers ' into the Cam."

Stephen speaks of the eminent professor of experimental
physics as though he belonged to an older generation. In
fact, Clerk-Maxwell was only by a few months his senior,
but he had been extraordinarily precocious from the age of
fifteen onwards, and had developed far earlier than his
admirer. Clerk-Maxwell died comparatively young in
1879. Stephen was very anxious to be elected into the
society of the Apostles, but was " not thought worthy of
initiation," he tells us. This appears to have been the
keenest of his university disappointments, but the probability is that his shyness and apparent gruffness had most
to do with it, in addition to the fact that he was not a
Trinity man.

It is impossible to think of Leslie Stephen without a
vision of Swiss peaks towering behind him. He says here
that " Nature has not qualified me for athletic excellence,"
but that is surely a mistake; he may have had no aptitude
for the conventional "games" now so extended as to be
the mechanical tyranny of school life, but his nervous
alertness and muscular endurance were very remarkable.
Even in middle life, his feats as a pedestrian were famous.
I recollect a walk with him—I think, in 1885—when he was
living at St. Ives, which was like a nightmare. I was
asked whether I would like to go over to Redruth to see
the annual meeting of Cornish wrestlers, and, of course, I
said that I should. But the implacable long legs of my
companion, like a pair of brass compasses, with the fierce
sweep of red beard at my side, reduced me to a sad condition before we reached the arena.

It was in the Alpine Club, of which Stephen was, I think,
an original member, that he distinguished himself first as a
climber, and the earliest of his publications was " The Ascent

of the Allelein Horn "; it is notable that he had reached his thirtieth year by that time, and that " The Playground of Europe," his first literary success, dates from his fortieth. He grew up very slowly as a man of letters. He speaks of himself and his Cambridge friends as a set of men, no longer quite young, who " undoubtedly had both legs and stomachs." At the same time, there was no lack of really intellectual intercourse, and in the case of Leslie Stephen himself, if younger geniuses seemed to be racing ahead of him, he was slowly preparing himself for the highest honours by sedulous reading and thinking. The great body of Leslie Stephen's public work belongs to his middle years. His literary criticism practically opened with the first series of " Hours in a Library " in 1874, his ethical and philosophical criticism with the " History of English Thought in the Eighteenth Century " in 1876. As a biographer, his " Samuel Johnson " in 1878 displayed a power and an adroitness which infinite experience continued to strengthen and polish till they produced the " Studies " of 1898. By the side of all this personal activity, there has to be borne in mind the various editorial work in which Leslie Stephen expended an infinitude of labour. From 1871 onwards he conducted the " Cornhill Magazine "; in 1885 he planned and opened that vast undertaking, the " Dictionary of National Biography." Meanwhile, he was superintending endless ventures, exploiting the provinces of literature, philosophy, and athletics, in all which he delighted. The importance of the little 1878 volume cannot be exaggerated; the enforced study of the character of Samuel Johnson to which he had not hitherto been much attracted, revealed to Leslie Stephen his own native bias. He discovered his close kinship to the great eighteenth-century men of letters, and his subsequent career as a critic was consistent with his attitude towards Johnson, Swift, and Pope. He did not care much for kings in the abstract, but he liked to feel that George III was round the corner.

The rather long and close apology which he put into Gibbon's mouth in the first volume of "Studies of a Biographer" should be read with care. It is Leslie Stephen's own analysis and defence of his attitude to life and literature. The great men of the eighteenth century help us appreciate the source of Stephen's charm, which was not brilliance of expression, though he was often brilliant, and was neither dazzlement of intuition nor novelty of approach, since of each of these he was suspicious. As a biographical critic, he is not luxuriant, nor romantic; his style is apt, on the contrary, to seem bare of ornament, while his perception of beauty is keen on the moral and seldom on the physical side. He was the associate of Ruskin and Symonds and Carlyle, but his soul was pre-Revolution.

In these hectic days of ours, when so much incense is burned on the altars of strange gods, it cannot but be salutary to be reminded of a genius so honest and sober as that of Leslie Stephen. I hope that a wide circle of readers will be tempted by the gracious simplicity of these "Early Impressions" to acquaint themselves with the principal works of the author. They will find all that accompanies ripeness of judgment and severity of taste in the writings of a man who is ever ready to temper those qualities with grace and humour. They will find genuine learning, moving with ease under its apparatus; the impassioned love of truth, anxious on all occasions to discern clearly and think directly; a resolute freedom from prejudice which includes some scorn for the intellectual weakness of the half-hearted. One with whom I was associated in our acquaintance with him as an editor fifty years ago, Robert Louis Stevenson, said of him: "I think it is always wholesome to read Leslie Stephen"; and

George Meredith, whose style was at the antipodes of his, considered Stephen's essays as containing " the profoundest and the most sober criticism we have had in our time." I would entreat our youngest pundits to turn to " Hours in a Library " and see whether they cannot recapture for themselves the charm of Leslie Stephen.

THE CENTENARY OF A SPASMODIST

THE CENTENARY OF A SPASMODIST

WHILE everybody is discussing the merits and demerits of the too-famous Pilgrim of Eternity, it is probable that little attention will be diverted to an interesting figure which had its day of notoriety. When Byron died at Missolonghi, the child of an eccentric hide-merchant and Primitive Christian at Cranbrook was a fortnight old. This child was Sydney Dobell, afterwards the author of " The Roman " and " Balder." From early infancy this unfortunate babe was dedicated to an " apostolic misson." His parents were sternly religious, and they were extreme Radicals in politics. It was a moment in England when everybody who was at all serious was beginning to think about the evidences of Christianity and the doom of tyrants. The elder Dobells were united in the hope that their eldest son would distinguish himself in both fields of action, and that infant, who was dreadfully precocious, nervous, and overstrained, ardently responded.

At the age of three, Sydney Dobell announced that he preferred mental diversion to eating and drinking, although his excellent papa had by that time become a wine-merchant like the parent of another precocious infant, John Ruskin. Sydney Dobell grew up at Cheltenham a marvel of morbid sensibility, and, refusing the aid of teachers, buried himself in books, thus absorbing knowledge insatiately from morning to night. His father, in adoring admiration, noted that his young son had " a majestic mind, and was exemplary for piety and virtue." Sydney ate so little that it was a miracle that he did not expire of inanition.

The sect his parents belonged to was small and very unsocial. The members of it had no desire to add to their number, and objected to worldly promiscuity. When Sydney Dobell was ten years old, he was introduced to the infant daughter of another primitive Christian, with a view to ultimate matrimony. These children were held in constant relation, and at the age of fifteen they were formally betrothed, the parents being deeply solicitous that Sydney should be kept "unspotted from the world." Meanwhile he lived a life, otherwise solitary, of what his biographer calls "painful intensity," writing verses which Thomas Campbell saw and encouraged.

When he was twenty years of age Sydney Dobell was married to his bride, who was, if possible, even more neurasthenic than himself. She must have been of the limpet order, since it is gravely recorded that for the next thirty-one years (when Sydney died) she did not permit him on one single occasion to quit her side for twenty-four hours at a time. The life these young people led was so extraordinary that we might expect Sydney Dobell, that learned goblin, to have faded into a lunatic asylum. But no; an "impossible saintdom" ended in a very serious attack of rheumatic fever, on recovering from which he rapidly became comparatively normal. He never lost traces of his early delicacy, but he resumed the use of food, and became moderately athletic. He never ceased to long for poetic fame, nor to write verses which began to attract favourable notice. In 1848, fired with ardour for the destruction of Priests and Kings, he planned a long poem to be called "The Roman," and in 1850 he finished and published it.

No one could have expected that a shapeless kind of epical drama or dramatic epic, put forth by an odd youth at Cheltenham, who had no friends or influence, would attract any notice at all, but " The Roman " was a blazing success. It must be remembered that it reflected many of the enthusiasms of the time, the revolution in France, the Chartist risings, the insurrection of Smith O'Brien, but, above all, the Italian troubles. It was begun when all Europe was brawling for autonomy; it was published just as Mazzini was proclaiming a republic in Rome. Everybody was " throwing off allegiance " to somebody else. Sydney Dobell's generous and shapeless poem appealed to the sentiment of the moment, which was all in favour of impulse and perfectly indifferent to form. He was greeted as " another Shelley, of a manlier, Christian type."

Suddenly we find him, at the age of twenty-six, emancipated from all the social disabilities of his parents' sect, transformed by success into a considerable literary personage, the friend of Carlyle, Tennyson, and Charlotte Brontë, and occupying a position of prominence and authority. These very shy recluses are apt to go to the opposite extreme when once they throw off their reserve, and it is said that Sydney Dobell was considered a little too ebullient in his social raptures. I remember, a great many years ago, being told that he approached Tennyson at Malvern with so violent an exclamation of the introduction being " the crowning honour of his life," that Tennyson shrank back and said, " Don't talk such damned nonsense! " If true, this story would date from about 1852. But what is certain is that Tennyson not merely had a very genuine admiration for Dobell's poems, but was, as I shall point out, positively influenced by them.

Even before " The Roman " was sent to press, Sydney Dobell was at work on another and still more apocalyptic masterpiece. This was " Balder," most of which was written in 1849, but not published till the end of 1853. It was curious that the reception of " Balder " by the critics was as unfavourable as that of "The Roman" was indulgent, since "Balder," with all its terrible faults, is far the more interesting of the two. The reviewers of those days were influenced by scruples which do not affect us now, and to judge poetry on its own merits, without consideration of religion, morals, and politics, was unheard of.

"The Roman" had struck the sentimental key of the moment; "Balder" was harshly opposed to it. It was the most outspoken expression of what was called "the might of poesy" which had been issued, and the hero of it was an epic poet who sacrificed everything, human and divine, to the cultivation of his own genius. "Balder" was intended, by its author, to portray the suicide of extravagant self-culture, of which Dobell now disapproved, but, unfortunately, he painted the imaginative indulgence of his hero in such warm colours, that foolish critics thought the thing to be a portrait of his own soul. Those were days when people identified poetic creators with their own creations, and accused Tennyson of meaning himself by St. Simeon Stylites; they accused Sydney Dobell of meaning himself by Balder, and there was a hubbub of angry indignation. He was charged with believing "scoundrelism" to be "a sacred probation of the soul." As a matter of fact, he was aiming in the opposite direction— he was portraying the monstrous egotism of the artist that he might hold it up to censure.

In spite of the objectors, or perhaps because of them, "Balder" was widely read and discussed. There are probably very few persons who could read it through to-day, when all our habits of thought and outlook upon literature have radically altered. "Balder"—of which only one huge "part the first" was ever written—is a shapeless drama in forty-one scenes of blank verse. There are practically only two persons in it, the hero, whose full name is Mr. Paul Balder, and his wife Amy, a "wan, weeping willow." They have a babe, but it does not appear, and dies during scene sixteen. There is no action whatever, but the personages indulge in vast monologues of self-analysis. Balder is a poet of lofty ambition, and he not merely talks at interminable length, but reads aloud voluminous passages from his own unpublished writings. He is carried along on "an avalanche of thought," and is long-winded beyond all parallel. In the absorption of his egotism he entirely neglects his wife, who sits in an adjoining room, fading away in plaintive lyrics; when the unhappy babe expires, Balder, very calm in a reverie of poetic rapture, does not care at all, and Amy's heart is broken.

Several recent publications had evidently coloured the aspect of the world to Sydney Dobell—Keats's Letters in the form issued by Lord Houghton in 1848 most of all, but also the Autobiography of Haydon, the revelation of "Faust" to English readers, the success of Bailey's "Festus." He believed that "Balderism," that is to say, an overweening estimate of the importance of the poet, was "the predominant intellectual misfortune of our day." To redeem it he wrote his great shapeless drama, and he was encouraged by a little group of other poets who performed similar mysteries. Aytoun, mocking them all, called them "Spasmodists," and the name stuck. Sydney Dobell will always be faintly remembered as the typical Spasmodist.

My bare description of "Balder" may suggest that it is the dreariest and silliest production in the world. On the contrary, while it has every fault, it has one redeeming feature—it is instinct with beauty. In the first place, Dobell was a master of prosody; no bad verse can be pointed out in "Balder." In the second place, although the plot is so thin and foolish, the language often tumid and wearisome, the embroidery of images and symbols exaggerated to the last degree, it yet possesses what Mr. Oliver Elton admirably defines as " the unseizable rainbow quality " which distinguishes good poetry from bad. To read " Balder " continuously is to be bored to death; to dip into it here and there is almost invariably to pick up a bit of mother-o'-pearl. For instance, we open the book, and discover the hero performing upon the harp to a medical man. This is what we read :—

> In the spring twilight, in the coloured twilight,
> Whereto the later primroses are stars,
> And early nightingale
> Letteth her love adown the tender wind,
> That thro' the eglantine
> In mixed delight the fragrant music bloweth
> On to me,
> Where in the twilight, in the coloured twilight,
> I sit beside the thorn upon the hill.

That is all; there is not even a verb; it is not a statement, it is an unrelated impression, but with what delicacy and romantic sweetness noted! Here is another fragment—not, this time, from " Balder " :

> By this the east is red and white;
> The queen of months is seen and known,
> Like flocks of doves that soar and fall,
> Like butterflies that hover and alight,
> Like tears of ecstasy when tear on tear
> From both wild eyes rains through the wreathèd hands,
> The blush of morning drops upon the lands,
> The Rose, the Rose is here.
> And rapture, rapture, crowns the passion of the year.

The " rainbow quality " is manifest here, and if it could have been disciplined and kept in order, it should have made of Sydney Dobell a great poet. Unfortunately, it went to seed, and left him a mere curiosity, an ill-regulated Spasmodist.

But perhaps the most interesting fact connected with Sydney Dobell was the extraordinary and temporary influence which he exercised over Tennyson, already famous and fifteen years his senior. It was a remarkable impetus which led the foremost writer of the day to enrol himself for a moment among the Spasmodist writers of monodramatic lyrics. As a Drama of the Soul, "Maud" was no novelty, but it was so manifestly superior to what had been done by the Baileys and Stanyan Biggs and Alexander Smiths that its kinship with these has been generally overlooked. It was, however, most closely related to "Balder," which may be said to be one parent of "Maud" as the Crimean War was the other. During the long years when the Tennysonian idolatry was rampant this relationship was carefully ignored, and has never been properly examined, but the point is one deserving critical attention. The Spasmodists adored Apollo in an absurd chapel, but Tennyson worshipped there with them in 1854. It is curious that at that particular moment the analysis of a morbid poetic soul should have attracted so many writers. But Spasmodism, even in the glorified form of "Maud," did not outlive the forts of Sevastopol.

Sydney Dobell, in particular, who was only thirty when he published "Balder," can hardly be said to have survived the Crimean War, during which he published two thin volumes of martial lyrics. Then, the victim of a succession of physical misfortunes, he remained silent for nearly twenty years, dying at his Gloucestershire home on August 22, 1874. His motto had been that "verse is an incantation with dominion over the powers of the air," but he had found that the powers of the earth baffled his bewildered talent. His story is a lesson against being over-spiritual, against building our faith implicitly on the basis of a beautiful dream. Even poetry has little abiding value unless it is in essential harmony with experience and common sense.

THE HOUSE WITH THE GREEN SHUTTERS

THE HOUSE WITH THE GREEN SHUTTERS

A LITTLE more than a hundred years ago the publisher Constable firmly remarked, while rejecting a manuscript, " Scottish novels will not do ! " The statement sounds odd on the lips of one who was closely observing the successes of Walter Scott, whose Scottish romances so pre-eminently " did." But Constable was evidently not thinking of books like " The Heart of Midlothian," picturesque pageants of ancient history drawn with all the gusto of imagination. What he meant was what Mr. Oliver Elton has described as " the petty Scottish novel," prosaically occupied with the local humours of a Lowland village. Some day a study will have to be made of " the petty Scottish novel," which for a century past has been alternately appearing and disappearing in a movement not precisely paralleled in English literature. Its own admirers have defined it as fiction of the Cabbage Patch, the Kailyard School, and thirty years ago it was quite inconveniently prominent.

The Kailyard School is no new thing. So far as I can trace its goings and comings, it made its earliest appearance in a novel, still much read when I was quite young, Mrs. Elizabeth Hamilton's " The Cottagers of Glenburnie," now, I suppose, quite forgotten. This was a cheerful tale, in broad Scots, dealing with the reformation of a dirty and dismal village by the ministrations of a retired governess of ample leisure and passing rich on thirty pounds a year. This just preceded "Waverley," if I remember right.

The classic of the Cabbage Patch, however, is John Galt, who survives in the regard of a great many readers, in spite of their annoyance at his prolixity and vulgarity. The truth is that Galt can be so deliciously amusing that the reader is in perpetual bad temper with him for being amusing so seldom. Yet it must be a poor spirit that never rejoices in "The Annals of a Parish." Somewhat later came the famous "Mansie·Wauch," by Delta Moir, a book long read, and perhaps still enjoyed, in Scotland; but to me, I confess, tiresome with the peculiar Kailyard faults of sentimentality, smallness, and a certain incessant "pawkiness" very trying to the Southron temperament.

The "petty Scottish novel" then died down, but was awakened by the success of Sir James Barrie's early studies of life seen from "A Window in Thrums." It is almost blasphemous to name that delicate work of art in connection with the "Stickit Ministers" and "Bonnie Briar Bushes" which presently followed it; but it is only too true that it was Barrie's ploughshare which opened the soil and let the air in to these humbler vegetables. Thirty years ago Scotland went suddenly mad over its Ian Maclarens and its S. R. Crocketts. There was such a brew of pathos and religion and amorousness and humour as never had been seen since the world began, a perfect orgy of local sentimentality in dialect so stiff that a spoon would stand up in it. This plague raged particularly in Galloway, and resembled the invasion of voles which was ravaging that province, when the Small Thessalian Owl was made aware of the situation and dealt promptly with the intruders.

In 1898 an unexpected Small Owl was found for the Cabbage Patch in the person of the author of "The House with the Green Shutters," a novel which, like many of

The House with the Green Shutters

the best satires, has survived, and is likely to continue to survive, all the works which it attacked. A Memorial Edition marks the twenty-fifth anniversary of the publication of this extraordinary work, and is certain of a warm welcome. Mr. Andrew Melrose, in two biographical sketches (which would be improved by being welded together and enlarged), gives us the outline of a pathetic and still rather obscure career. George Douglas Brown was born at Ochiltre, in Ayrshire, in 1869. His mother "was a good and religious woman, but she was just an uneducated, short-coated peasant." His father—but who was his father? Mr. Melrose gives no details, but states that the novelist learned, long before his death, "that he had the good blood in his veins of an old and proud Scottish family." Somebody looked after the boy's education, and sent him to Glasgow, where he graduated in honours, and then to Oxford, where he spent four years "not distinguished for hard work or joyousness."

That is all; and we ask for either less or more, but the scanty tale brings us to 1895, when Brown came to London to live by literature. The next fact about him is that in 1898 there was born in him determination to write a novel which should be a violent counterblast to the Kailyard novels, then at the height of their amazing popularity. The result was "The House with the Green Shutters," Brown's solitary publication. In the summer of 1902 he rather mysteriously died, and was found to have left no manuscripts of importance. He is the author of a single book, but that a very remarkable one.

The fate of "The House with the Green Shutters" is calculated to make us wonder whether books of positive value often, or ever, entirely disappear. For some months the novel seemed to attract no attention, and to be swamped in the flood of mediocrity. Then the procession of appreciators began to move, headed by Andrew Lang and encouraged by Mr. Charles Whibley. Their representations were successful in arousing resentment in Scotland, and the more the worshippers of the " Bonnie Briar Bush " denounced " The House with the Green Shutters " as " coarse " and " brutal " and " disagreeably powerful." the more eagerly it was read.

We return to the reading of the story, after five and twenty years, with calm nerves, and we find the imperfections of it as a work of art as patent as its merits. Mr. Melrose says that George Douglas Brown was planning a second novel, which was to be a love-story of Cromwell's time, " in which he was resolved to express the tender side of his nature." He seems to have been thinking about this for nearly four years without even beginning it, but I cannot pretend to feel any disappointment in the absence of such a romance. The " tender " touch does not seem to me to have been Brown's business at all, and probably he merely talked of such a romantic scheme when he was bored with being told that he was " savage " and " cynical." A " tender " love-tale of tushery—that would, indeed, have been a fatal concession to the Philistines of the Kailyard, at whose leader's forehead Brown had so unerringly aimed his smooth and single pebble.

" The House with the Green Shutters " is a satire, not a parody. It effects its purpose by what it leaves out, not by a burlesque profusion of detail. In fact, the first thing which strikes the reader on reinspection of the tale is its bareness, its severe detachment from all the usual ornaments of fiction. Pathos and religion and humour are excluded, and with still greater austerity all the elements of love. The feature which distinguishes George Douglas Brown most sharply from Galt is his parsimony, his deliberate rejection of everything that is not essential to the matter directly in hand. What that matter was is not left to our conjecture. Andrew Lang, greatly admiring the firm

The House with the Green Shutters 343

draughtsmanship of " The House with the Green Shutters," nevertheless asked the author why he had concentrated his powers on " moral ugliness," and nothing else.

Brown's answer was direct; he said that the sentimental gush of the Kailyard dealt with an imaginary moral beauty, and gave no hint of the realities of Lowland village life, with its " malignancy, hard drinking, and coarse language." He had determined to paint these qualities, and these only, in his unsparing picture of Barbie. He spoke much to his friends about the " malignancy," of the Scottish peasants, by which he seems to have meant their unfortunate tendency to allow the slightest difference of opinion or interest to breed an implacable animosity. This had been speciously ignored by the sentimental novelists, and it forms the central feature of " The House with the Green Shutters," where the village, when once displeased with its leading citizen, pursues him and his family with such unyielding and corporate hostility that the prosperity with which the history opens is reduced to ruin at the end. There is not a touch of human pity or of exoneration in the united, slow persecution of the Gourlays by the relentless inhabitants of Barbie, and yet Gourlay himself is throughout painted in colours which deprive him of our sympathy. What he gets is terrible, yet we feel that he largely deserves it. There is not one chapter in the book which is not thoroughly satisfied with itself and dissatisfied with everyone else.

What Dryden wrote at the death of his young friend, Oldham, can but recur to the memory when we think of George Douglas Brown and his one grim story :—

> O early ripe ! to thy abundant store,
> What could advancing age have added more?
> It might (what Nature never gives the young)
> Have taught the numbers of thy native tongue,
> But satire needs not those, and wit will shine
> Through the harsh cadence of a rugged line.

It is perfectly idle to conjecture what Brown might have done had he lived to maturity. But he will be remembered because of the stern originality and the sincere bitterness of his solitary study of life as he had seen it around him in his childhood. The opening scene of his novel, where Gourlay, in the plenitude of his pride, sends his pomp of carts streaming down the dazzled village, and the final scene, where the House of the Green Shutters closes around its inevitable and awful tragedy, give us reason to believe that Brown would have displayed a master-touch in everything he afterwards undertook. But what really inspires us most with respect and regret is the unflinching spirit in which he pursued the spirit of Truth in moral observation.

THÉODORE DE BANVILLE

THÉODORE DE BANVILLE

FRANCE has been celebrating the centenary of one of its once most beloved and still most characteristic poets, for Théodore de Banville was born on March 14, 1823. It should be interesting to observe how the Paris criticism of to-day greets the memory of one with whose work the bitter and morose spirit of much current French literature is intensely out of sympathy. We shall see; the French have a marvellous gift for throwing aside momentary prejudice, and reviewing the great figures of their literature in perspective. At all events, in the few words I can dedicate to Banville to-day, I shall disregard contemporary neglect. I shall try to recover something of the passionate admiration with which we regarded him forty years ago, and to prove that our admiration was not founded on a delusion.

His influence on the *technique* of verse, when I was young, would alone justify a particular attention to his merits to-day. His theories and practice bore fruit in the writings of English poets as diverse as Swinburne, Austin Dobson, and Andrew Lang, not to speak of one who is still the laureate of our Parnassus. The " Petit Traité de Poésie Française," of 1872, was a revelation to the men who were then young, and whose part in the evolution of English poetry, though greatly undervalued to-day, will inevitably recover its honourable prestige. When the next revulsion to beauty and melody arrives, Théodore de Banville will be read once more, for diamonds are sure to be retrieved, even though for a generation they are lost in the mire.

Théodore de Banville was born in the pleasant city of Moulins, still charming, but no longer the idyllic place that it was a hundred years ago. It was full of gardens then, and in one of these a dreamy little boy used to sit, as he tells us, under the mulberry trees, and accompany the song of the birds on a small red fiddle. He could not really play, but he made a noise which passed for music in his chimerical mind. Anatole France has said that the soul of Banville was like a garden full of flowers, and we may add that in that garden was an imp pretending to make melodies on a violin that was a toy. His whole life was spent in playing imaginary music, but when he was older the instrument grew to be a real one; it grew to be a lyre, not the majestic *phorminx* of Milton and Hugo, but a little *chelys* of tortoise-shell, held tight against the heart while Banville twanged it.

This became part of the poet, became, indeed, himself; "la lyre, c'est vous," his admirers used to assure him. No other French poet has lived who has showed so prodigious a skill in versifying; he was "le roi des rimes," and to understand the magic which he exercised we have to go back to the frenzy created here by Swinburne's "Dolores" and "Faustine" in 1866. The new Georgians do not understand it, nor do their brethren in France. The "Odes Funambulesques," with their flamboyant and excessive dexterity, produced a species of delirium. Even Victor Hugo felt the intoxication, and reeled along the shore of his island. Nor was it only the melody of the sparkling odes which set folk dancing. Banville, extremely unlike the author of "Atalanta" in other respects, had Swinburne's faculty for recalling to poetic diction worn and superannuated words, and endowing them with new life. This is a gift which presently meets with ingratitude, since these words, once recovered soon cease to give the pleasure of surprise. No one, I suppose, under the age of sixty can realise what we felt when we first read

> Leaves pallid and sombre and ruddy,
> Dead fruit of the fugitive years,
> Some stained as with wine and made bloody,
> And some as with tears,

nor reproduce the impression of "Le Saut du Tremplin." The typical word to describe Banville is "funambulesque," and he so named the most characteristic of his poems. A *funambule* is a rope-dancer, and no versifier has ever lived who achieved more marvellous feats on the lyrical trapeze than he. He even did himself an injustice by his extreme agility, since the public is volatile, and soon grows tired of an exhibition of mere nimbleness. An incredible performance in the air may become wearisome through its own apparent lack of effort, and a reaction comes in favour of walking slowly on flat ground, even with the aid of a stick.

It was a fault in Banville that he carried his mastery of form to such an extreme perfection that an ungrateful audience turned away from him at last as from a clown that attempts too many somersaults. This was doing a wonderful talent great injustice, but it may be admitted that the artist himself was partly to blame. He combated the popular error with dignity. He says: "I do not regard Rhyme, as fools pretend to think I do, as a thing uniformly dazzling and sumptuous, but as being varied, diverse, amorously wedded to thought, transfigured by close attention to the nature of the subject, and uniform only in its faithful and constant concordance with harmonic propriety." This was true; but a satiated public would persist in seeing nothing in Banville but a clown in spangled tights.

For so gentle and inoffensive a bard, Banville suffered much at the hands of detraction. Somebody has always to be the last, and it was Banville's fate to close the great Cénacle, so that he inherited some of the abuse of the Philistines. His earliest volume of poems, "Les Cariatides," was published in 1842, when he was a law-student just nineteen; it long preceded the earliest issues of Leconte de Lisle, who was his senior by five years and has therefore been inaccurately supposed to have influenced Banville. "Les Cariatides," on the contrary, is of the long-haired, crimson-waistcoated order, voluptuous and capricious, carrying on the early enthusiasm of Gautier in the full-blooded tradition of the Cénacle. The little book was fiercely attacked, and the young bard was told that his poems "smelt of tobacco and rum, and reflected the ill-regulated passions and sensuous appetites of a society without law and without manners." But the noble Alfred de Vigny, out of the "ivory tower" of his retirement, sent him a letter of warm approval, and from the first Banville was accepted by his fellows, whatever the harsh reviewers might say.

It is odd, or would be if we did not recognise the instinctive hatred of any new kind of beauty which animates the ordinary man—it is odd that anyone, in the first instance, should have failed to respond to Banville's appeal, since his freshness of spirit was untouched by the despair and darkness which are the cankers of an old society. He came, as I have said, at the close of the Romantic movement, but he bore none of the stigmata of decay. The central emotion in his poetry is joy. Baudelaire, whose temperament was the antithesis of his, was fascinated by a happiness he could not share, and could hardly comprehend. He said of Banville that he was the symbol of all the happy hours in life. It was a strange phenomenon, this apparition, in the autumn of the deep Romantic sadness, of a spirit in whom the sap of April seemed to leap. In the "Odes Funambulesques," in the little flower-like comedies, most of all perhaps in the masterly "Trente-Six Ballades Joyeuses" of 1875, Banville revealed a whimsical sympathy with all that was sumptuous and delicate. His poems were peals of laughter, heard out of the provoking shelter of the boskage.

Anatole France has said that the Muse of Théodore de Banville is a " Venetian Venus." This phrase happily sums up the curious mixture of the rigidly antique and the frivolously modern which we meet with in his writings. He had much of Watteau in his nature, and something of Aristophanes. In his plays, which are as artificial and as exquisite as old Dresden china, Aphrodite seems to be playing the part of Columbine, and flirting outrageously with an Indian Bacchus, who is disguised as Harlequin. The odes of Banville may be called Pindaro-comic; they treat of the varnished slipper of Madame Panache in language and metre worthy of the most high gods of Hellas. This is an attitude which provokes the rage of the implacable enemies of a joyous lyrical inspiration, for whom nothing ought to be written which does not expand the American maxim that " Life is real, Life is earnest." Théodore de Banville is the extreme type of those outcasts of the higher seriousness who determine to be poets before everything, and to be nothing but poets. He has expressed his aim in verses which were once on everyone's lips :—

> Plus haut encor, jusqu'au ciel pur !
> Jusqu'à ce lapis dont l'azur
> Couvre notre prison mouvante !
> Jusqu'à ces rouges Orients
> Où marchent des dieux flamboyants,
> Fous de colère et d'épouvante.
>
> Plus loin ! plus haut ! je vois encor
> Des boursiers à lunettes d'or,
> Des critiques, des demoiselles
> Et des réalistes en feu.
> Plus haut ! plus loin ! de l'air ! du bleu !
> Des ailes ! des ailes ! des ailes !

Unhappily, the very magnificence of the effort is its own destruction; the audience grows tired, and turns away at last from so extravagant an apotheosis.

In 1882 Théodore de Banville published a volume of reminiscences, "Mes Souvenirs," in which he speaks of all his chief contemporaries, whom he saw through a haze of rose-colour. His very irony is amiable. Unfortunately, the reader turns the pages in vain for much revelation of his own aims and temperament, for he was too modest to expatiate on himself. He was always gentle and transfigured with admiration; he was Melicertes with the mouth of honey. Of his plays, "Gringoire" is the best known, but others are still occasionally acted on select occasions. When he died on March 15, 1891, the day after his sixty-eighth birthday, the poets laid garlands of verse on his tomb, but the public had already deserted him. More than thirty years have passed since then, and the dust has gathered over his name. Perhaps the event of the centenary may blow some of it away.

1923.

HERMAN MELVILLE

A A

HERMAN MELVILLE

SOME quarter of a century ago, a critic, intelligently surveying the literature of seventy years since, observed with regret that fortune "seemed to have deserted" Herman Melville. He was consigned to partial oblivion, in company with Montgomery Bird, Gilmore Sims, and Sylvester Judd, whose romances have completely ceased to fill the trump of fame. But the statement has not been justified. A marvellous revival has lately attended the author of "Typee" and "Moby Dick," who has recovered a position in the forefront of nineteenth-century literature.

Like Borrow, after being buried, Melville has been dug up and transfigured; from being nobody he has become a classic. When Stevenson went to the Pacific, he read "Oomoo," and pronounced its author to be "a howling cheese," an expression which should attract the notice of future Stevensonian annotators. The works of Melville have recently been collected in many volumes; a capable, though too-copious and gaudy Life of him has been published by an ardent admirer. Fortune, that fickle jade, has returned to the man she had deserted, and heaps her benefits upon him. He must now be taken very seriously by criticism, and this has hardly been realised by his former detractors or by his present adulators.

The contents of the two new volumes before me to-day have not found a place in the collected edition of which I have just spoken, but I suppose that they will ultimately do so. Mr. Chapin, who contributes introductory notes, gives us but scanty information as to the circumstances, but states categorically that none of these sketches " have heretofore been gathered into a book." The prose volume, which is by far the most important, consists of a grotesque story, " The Apple-Tree Table "; a critical review of or rhapsody over the early writings of Nathaniel Hawthorne; and nine short tales or sketches belonging to the same period. Among these sketches, the most interesting autobiographically is "I and my Chimney," in which Melville gives a veiled description of Arrowhead, the farmhouse near Pittsfield, in New England, where he settled with his family in the autumn of 1850.

He was now writing " Moby Dick," and was, therefore, at the highest point of his imaginative attainment; he published that famous book in the course of the following year. Hawthorne, who was finishing " The House of the Seven Gables," had just settled close by at the Red House in Lennox. Mr. Chapin gives no indication of date, but I observe that Melville speaks of Hawthorne's " Mosses from an Old Manse " as having been published four years earlier. As the " Mosses " appeared in 1846, this gives us 1850 as the date of Melville's essay. But he also speaks of having as yet no personal knowledge whatever of Hawthorne, with whom, before the beginning of 1851, we find Melville in close neighbourly relations. He had passed through a violent mental and physical crisis, " ploughing and sowing and raising and printing and praying," and was at length able " to enjoy the calm prospect of things from a fair piazza." The tales and essays in this new volume bear the stamp of a season of still weather in the summer of 1851.

This element of unusual calm must be borne in mind by whoever reads " The Apple-Tree Table " and its companions. Nothing is here of the sea or of the whirlwind; not the smallest fluke of the fin of a whale can be detected from cover to cover. Nor does the musky voluptuousness of

Polynesia leave a trace of perfume over these New English and even strictly Puritan pages. The neighbourhood of Hawthorne, rather icily repressive, has moderated for the moment the flame in Melville's burning veins, a flame, indeed, through the rest of his long life, never to blaze out again with the fury of " Moby Dick " or the intoxicating spice of " Typee." For that very reason, perhaps, the peculiarities of Melville's mind and manner are the better observed, because they create less agitation here than they do in his more characteristic works.

Melville had the faculty of exciting and almost of intoxicating a sympathetic reader, and he exercised this gift without the least hesitation, heaping logs of resinous pine-wood, indeed, on the fire that he had recklessly set blazing. The philosopher may meditate with pleasure on the spectacle of the two illustrious romance-writers of America, sitting almost side by side in the pastoral desolation of the Berkshire hills, and simultaneously composing " The House of the Seven Gables " and " Moby Dick " the one so delicate and cold, the other so violent and catastrophic. And yet, the influence of Melville upon Hawthorne is not difficult to detect in what is audacious in " The Scarlet Letter," although not nearly so obvious as is the influence of Hawthorne upon Melville in such a story as " The Apple-Tree Table."

Herman Melville's admiration for his friend's genius inspires him in this volume with a critical study which is well worthy of attention, less from its intrinsic value than for its bearing upon the state of literary emotion in America seventy years ago. Hawthorne had been before the world for twenty years, and had produced some of his finest books. They had been praised, but imperfectly understood, and, above all, they had not escaped from grudging and invidious comparison with English imaginative work of a slightly previous age. Melville had gone through the same experience, and although, between 1846 and 1851, his romances, in a quite surprising number, had been republished in London, he was not accepted in America for much more than a writer of stories for schoolboys.

This comparative neglect exasperated him, and, mingled with the desire to enlarge the circle of Hawthorne's auditors, there naturally and pardonably existed a wish to extend his own. His essay is a plea for the honourable recognition of American romance, on its own merits, and not as an offshoot of English literature. The author of "The Scarlet Letter" had shot "his strong New England roots into the hot soil in " Melville's " Southern soul," and he dreamed of a generalship in the army led by Hawthorne. It is singular that he makes no mention whatever of Poe, who was a field-marshal in that army. The name of Poe was not one to conjure with in New England, especially since his recent ignominious death. But the careful reader will not fail to observe how much Melville owed to Poe, who was ten years his senior. The "Tales of the Grotesque and Arabesque" were the obvious precursors of Melville's stories of mystery and bewilderment. The younger man has even adopted some of Poe's tricks of language, with the use of such words as " Plutonian." Yet, so far as I can discover, the name of the elder writer does not once occur in any of Melville's books or correspondence.

In the strictest sense "The Apple-Tree Table" is a "tale of the Grotesque." Like most that Melville wrote, fancy seems in it to be woven inextricably into the texture of experience. At the top of a very old house in one of the oldest towns of America, the author explores a staircase leading to a garret which has been closed for years. The rusty key is found, and the tenant enters. He finds it "festooned and carpeted and canopied with cobwebs," and, what is more singular, thousands of insects are clustered on the skylight, while " millions of butterfly moles " are swarming " in a rainbow-tunnel clear across the darkness of the garret." I know not what is a " butterfly mole," and I leave it to the entomologists to decide how such profuse insect-life could have been fed through so long a seclusion. The whole description of the garret is extremely characteristic of Melville's perfervid and rather tormented imagination, and of his eloquent verbosity. The long and short of it is that the author discovers in the garret an old-fashioned table made of apple-wood, which he dusts and drags downstairs into the cedar-parlour, where his wife and daughters take their breakfast. The ladies do not much relish the intrusion of so unfashionable a piece of furniture, which makes them, they know not why feel nervous.

The author, however, is charmed with his apple-tree table; but one night as he sits at it, like the gentleman in " The Raven," reading " many a quaint and curious volume of forgotten lore," the table begins to tick. There follow amusing, if somewhat preposterous, scenes in which this sound, repeated day after day and night after night, successively freezes the blood of the author, of his wife, of his daughters, and of Biddy, the maid-of-all-work. We are strung up to suspect a supernatural energy concealed, but the noise proves to be strictly zoological. It arises from a century-old beetle, which the warmth of the room has awakened, and which is forcing its way out of the wood. At last, while the author is watching in the darkness of the night, it escapes from its prison. It is radiantly lovely, luminous, and coloured like a fiery opal, " a beautiful bug, a Jew jeweller's bug, a bug like a sparkle of a glorious sunset." (Again, I must call the entomologists to the support of my little faith !) And that is the end of the matter, since the beetle (or " bug ") continues to flash in death from a box " on the apple-tree table in the pier of the cedar-parlour."

The tale is somewhat spun out, but told with great vivacity, and spirit, with that curious breathless air of being in a terrible hurry yet magically rooted to the spot, which is one of Melville's peculiarities as a narrator. It would, of course, be extremely unfair to pit a trifle like " The Apple-Tree Table " against such massive enterprises as " Moby Dick " and " Typee," but the elements of style are the same in each.

Another instance, almost sought at random, may continue our impression of Herman Melville's cumulative vehemence, almost hysteria, of description. It is taken from a shorter story. In a mountain-village of New England, against a background of pines and hemlocks, the author meets a hero of the poultry-yard and this is how he sees the gallant bird. (Note the rising excitement !) :—

" A cock, more like a golden eagle than a cock. A cock, more like a field-marshal than a cock. A cock, more like Lord Nelson with all his glittering arms on, standing on the Vanguard's quarter-deck, going into battle, than a cock. A cock, more like the Emperor Charlemagne in his robes at Aix-la-Chapelle than a cock. Such a cock ! "

And then the ecstasy flags a little. Melville finds it necessary to justify his rapture, and this is how he does it :—

" He was of a haughty size, stood haughtily on his haughty legs. His colours were red, gold, and white. The red was on his crest along, which was a mighty and symmetric crest, like unto Hector's crest, as delineated on ancient shields. His plumage was snowy, traced with gold. He walked in front of the shanty, like a peer of the realm; his crest lifted, his chest heaved out, his embroidered trappings flashing in the light. His face was wonderful. He looked like some Oriental king in some magnificent Italian opera."

Some of this is very good (the sentence about the "peer of the realm ") : some very bad (the sentence about the " crest along "); on the whole, it exemplifies the extreme difficulty of estimating the real value of Melville's style, with its vividness, its exultation, and its unfortunate tendency to repetition and over-emphasis. One perfect sentence about the extravagantly heraldic bird would doubtless produce a more lasting effect than does this chain of vehement hyperboles. Nevertheless, the image, if too garrulously insisted upon, is fine, and remains in the memory. Here is all Melville, in his baffling inconsistency.

Such a nature as Melville's, radically indisposed to submit to the discipline of selection, was little likely to succeed in pouring his enthusiasm into poetic form. He was a master, though a capricious and insecure master, of a glowing and torrential prose, but he had little command of verse. Hence the second of the volumes on my table, called " John Marr and other Poems," is almost entirely without value. The principal pieces deal with the sea, and even with whales, but in tantalising fashion. A group are dedicated to soldiers who fell in the war of 1864, and these are sincerely felt, if not artfully expressed. A set of songs is taken from Melville's " Mardi," a romance which I have not read, but which a devoted admirer describes as offering a " dangerous predominance of imagination." Another set is from " Clavel " a work still less known, containing several hundred pages of " intricate philosophical verse." Life is short, and I am convinced that I shall never read " Clavel." Here is the best passage of Melville's poetry that seems to be extant :—

> How sweet, how sweet, the Isles from Hind :
> 'Tis aye afternoon of the full, full moon,
> And ever the season of fruit,
> And ever the hour of flowers,
> And never the time of rains and gales,
> All in and about Marlena.

> Soft sigh the boughs in the stilly air,
> Soft lap the beach the billows there;
> And in the woods or by the streams,
> You needs must nod in the Land of Dreams.

Here is a faint revival of the ecstasy of voluptuous lotus-eating among the Pacific Islands in the 'forties. But we turn back to the prose of " Oomoo."

A BELATED CAVALIER

A BELATED CAVALIER

QUITE twenty years ago, in the London room where I write these lines, my dear and lamented friend, Walter Raleigh, speaking of the strange ways in which poetry reveals itself, bade me listen to the following anonymous lines which he had met with in a newspaper, and could not get out of his head :—

> When on the marge of evening the last blue light is broken,
>   And winds of dreamy odour are loosened from afar,
> Or when my lattice opens, before the lark has spoken,
>   On dim laburnum blossoms, and morning's dying star,
>
> I think of thee—O mine the more if other eyes be sleeping—
>   Whose greater noonday splendours the many share and see,
> While, sacred and for ever, some perfect law is keeping
>   The late and early twilight alone and sweet for me.

I was able to tell him that the author was an American girl then just settled in Oxford, and to show him the modest volume, " A Roadside Harp," in which the lines were first published. He expressed a warm determination to learn more, but whether, in the proximity of the Cherwell beloved by them both, he pushed the relation to a personal acquaintance I know not. I miss his name from Miss (or Mrs.) Tenison's biography. But he was one of the little band, now rapidly enlarging since her death, who recognised in Miss Guiney a figure of charm and originality.

Louise Imogen Guiney was born in Roxbury, a suburb of Boston, on January 7, 1861. In her odd way, in writing the memories of her childhood, she said that " a young person " twenty-four years her senior had preceded her to the war, whereas she herself did not volunteer until she reached the age of four. This means that her father, General Patrick Guiney, who had been fighting in Virginia since April, 1861, called her up to share his life in camp. She seems to have been alone among the "bearded and epauletted guests of our exceptionally elegant log-house," who "spoiled" her to the top of her bent.

This visit, like the Civil War itself, soon came to an end, but the impression it made on the mind and temperament of Louise was indelible. She was a soldier at heart all the rest of her life, and, gentle as she grew to be, there was always the flash of the blade behind the smile. "The smell of powder is sweeter to me than Oriental lilies," she says; and, again, "An it please you, I aspire to Mars!" She took Nelson for her hero, and became an incorrigible tomboy. Drum-beat and sword-flash were part of her being. Her genius was an odd creation of the great national war, acting without logic, and purely from its magnanimous and scenic sides, on a romantic imagination. As a baby— a "war-baby"—she refused the solace of coral-and-bells, and insisted upon a small flag, such as was waved in battle by "her" brigade of the 5th Corps of the Army of the Potomac. Her father, the general, received a wound in the engagement of the Wilderness, which, although he survived it, ultimately killed him. The youthful gracious soldier, adored by his men and his officers, who was Louise Guiney's father, was at once her idol and her mirror. Her devotion to him explains her character; he represented to her imagination the mixture of religion and gallantry which she found when she was older in the heroes of the seventeenth century, on whose minds she modelled her own.

Her father was a Catholic, and Louise spent six years of her childhood among the nuns of the Convent of the Sacred Heart at Elmhurst, in Rhode Island. The moral atmosphere in this school was of a kind fitted in every way to encourage her idiosyncrasies. The convent had been founded by some noble Frenchwomen, who emigrated to New England in 1818; the memory of Marie Antoinette was preserved there in the lavender of a courageous and infatuated devotion. Louise utterly repudiated the Black Arts, as she called them, of mathematics and sewing, with an obstinacy which was pardoned because of her remarkable aptitude for history and literature. When she was punished by the patient nuns, she consoled herself by becoming a martyr of the Vendée or a Jacobite in exile. She had arrived at Elmhurst armed with a gun. She has described her own absurd, charming and chimerical girlhood with delicious mock-gravity, and perhaps with a touch of exaggeration, but it is easy to understand how her character, as she accurately describes it—

> All youth, all force, all fire, all stress,
> In her impassioned gentleness,
> Half-exhortation, half-caress.

was moulded by the unusual conditions of her early life.

Her father, who had lingered long, died, suddenly at last, when she was sixteen; and this event brought about a crisis the effects of which were permanent. The various friends who have written about Louise Imogen Guiney since her death, always affectionately, but sometimes too redundantly and sentimentally, have, doubtless from discretion, failed to emphasise the fact that all her life she was very poor. The death of her father seems to have left her mother, of whom we hear little, almost without resources. There are many cases in which lack of money is a stimulus, and no ultimate loss, to a young man and even to a young woman of energy. But in the case of Miss Guiney it was a positive disqualification, checking and almost paralysing her peculiar gifts. Her generous and romantic nature, which dwelt habitually in the past, and was only at ease in the atmosphere of a chivalrous and antique dreamland, was starved at the outset. She was obliged to take to journalism for a livelihood, and, as Miss Tenison puts it :—

" She whose mind was full of vivid dreams, and whose spirit was now beginning to feel its wings and crave eagle-like flights, saw before her no splendid warfare, no great opportunities, but a dreary struggle for the pence she despised."

No particulars are given to us, and the curtain falls across seven dismal years, at the close of which, in 1884, she put forth a slender volume of verse, called " Songs at the Start." We only know that through the darkest hour she preserved her romantic ambition, her *panache*, and that she wrote with her father's sword and spurs, and his cap and scarf as Colonel of the Ninth Massachusetts, hanging always over her desk.

This earliest venture was quickly followed by others, which gradually secured for her some local reputation, and, as one cannot but hope, some alleviation of her financial anxiety. These first poetical volumes, however, were remarkable more for the spirit of chivalry which inspired them than for their executive skill, which was faint. But in 1893, at the age of thirty-two, she made a notable advance in the book called " A Roadside Harp," which contains some of her best and most characteristic verse. She now came into a sort of gossipy prominence, which had its effect upon her career.

In America the office of Post Mistress is one which is in the gift of politicians. By this time the talents and charm of Miss Guiney had made her an object of interest to the literary coteries of Boston. Among her admirers were Oliver Wendell Holmes, E. C. Stedman, R. W. Gilder, and Thomas Bailey Aldrich, all names to conjure with in the United States of thirty years ago. It seems strange that these influential friends should have contrived no better employment for an enthusiastic poet than that of selling postage-stamps in a Massachusetts village, but this seemed better than nothing. Louise Guiney was appointed postmistress at Auburndale, a hamlet without a history. The emolument was very small, but she liked the name, which reminded her of Goldsmith's " Deserted Village." She proceeded to Auburndale, with her great St. Bernard dog, her mother, and a kit of books; and all was to be well.

But all was not well. The actual salary of the postmistress being small, it was eked out by a percentage on the stamps she sold. I have mentioned that Miss Guiney was a Catholic; the inhabitants of Auburndale, to a man, were Puritans, who regarded the " Scarlet Woman " with abhorrence. The innocent poetess, carrying out her duties conscientiously, noticed with horror that Auburndale appeared to have abandoned the habit of correspondence : not a soul bought postage-stamps. When she mentioned this fact to friends in Boston, inquiries were set on foot, with the result that a painful discovery was made. All the inhabitants of Auburndale had entered into a conspiracy that, sooner than buy stamps from a Papist, they would send, in a body, to a neighbouring town for this commodity. Their hope was that Louise and her dog, those insidious emissaries of the Vatican, would be starved out and would have to resign.

But Auburndale had not reckoned with the great beating heart of the American Press, which had been indifferent to Miss Guiney's poetry, but now spoke out boldly like a man. The " criminal bigotry " of the Puritans was denounced from Maine to Texas, and " the persecution of our General's daughter for her hereditary creed " set a hundred pens wagging. From all parts of the United States people sent orders for packets of postage-stamps to the poetess, a lady of " perfect official rectitude." The inhabitants of the village continued their fanatical boycott, but could not contend against outside enthusiasm. Presently the glad tidings rang forth tautologically that " the salary of Miss Guiney has not only been restored to the original figure, but bids fair to reach a higher figure "; and so Auburndale had slapped its nose to spite its face.

The postage-stamps had made her famous, but the cold Massachusetts village was hateful to her, and she accepted a post in the Public Library of Boston. But her heart was in England, and she determined " to emigrate to some hamlet that smells strong of the Middle Ages, and put cotton-wool in my ears, and swing out clear from this very smart century altogether." In 1895 she was in England, and had plunged into the work of the remainder of her life, her study of the literature of the seventeenth century. She made some stay in the Silurian haunts of Henry Vaughan, the mystic poet, and we find her in many Western cities, but finally in Oxford, which seemed to her to be shining still with the glory and sorrow of its Royalist heroes. She cast off America altogether, not from any unpatriotic prejudice, but because it was not, and never had been, the home of her instincts and her aspirations. Her own words on this subject, written in 1907, define her attitude :—

" I came to England, not for excitement, not for vogue, but for the velvety feel of the Past under foot, like moss of the forest floor to a barefooted child; or for the hardly less gentle feel of the present, whence noise and worry seem miraculously to have vanished away."

Already in 1925, as Browning says : " How are we so far out of that minute!" But the gentle exile from Auburndale found the murmur of Oxford a quarter of a century ago " no more agitating than a dove's note."

She lived in Oxford in extreme retirement, and few were conscious of the presence of this admirable poet-scholar. She published much about her beloved cavaliers; she edited Vaughan, and the Matchless Orinda, and Thomas Stanley, the philosopher, whose life was as quiet as her own. She had a devotion for Blessed Edmund Campion, whose temperament reminded her of a world of mysteries. She revived forgotten worthies of the age of Charles I., such as Alabaster and Edward Sherburne. Above all, she put forth slender and unobtrusive pamphlets of her own verse, in which her gaiety and passion found adequate, if sometimes rather strained and alembicated expression. She lived so completely in the past, and in that little section of it which fought and fell between 1640 and 1650, that the world passed her by, bewildered. Here is one of her most characteristic lyrics :—

> How life has cheapened, and how blank
>   The World is ! like a fen
> Where long ago unstainèd sank
>   The starry gentlemen :
> Since Marston Moor and Newbury drank
>   King Charles's gentlemen.
>
> If Fate in any air accords
>   What Fate denied, O then
> I ask to be among your swords,
>   My joyous gentlemen;
> Towards Honour's heaven to go, and towards
>   King Charles's gentlemen.

The gentle soul of this spiritual sister of Lady Rachel Russell was little spoken of four years ago, when it rose to join her saints and heroes from the little house at Chipping Campden where she had retired in failing health. But since her death her fame has constantly expanded, and Miss Tenison's careful and pious labours will largely extend the circle of Louise Imogen Guiney's admirers.

THE SAVILE CLUB

THE SAVILE CLUB

THE initials S. C. appear to be propitious. More than two hundred years ago they indicated the Society Club, of which Swift was some time President; and they spell " Sodalitas Convivium." The original social company was founded in 1711 " to advance conversation and friendship, and to reward deserving persons with our interest and recommendation." Can we not, with the ear of imagination, hear Swift propounding the latter clause, while his azure eyes go flashing round at the blank faces of the Lord Chancellor and the Solicitor-General? I know not whether the earlier words—" to advance conversation and friendship "—were in the minds of the gentlemen who met early in May 1868 to found a new club, and we shall never know, since almost all of them have passed away; but I am sure that something very similar was present to them when they urged, as the central purposes of the club, " a thorough simplicity in all arrangements " and " the mixture of men of different professions and opinions."

I know of only two survivors of the sixty-four original adventurers, Mr. J. S. Phillpotts, and Mr. Henry Lee-Warner. Both were at the time conspicuous members of a rather conspicuous body of men—Dr. Temple's staff of Rugby masters. Mr. Phillpotts was afterwards for nearly thirty years famous as the head-master of Bedford School, and adds to the distinction of being the grandson of " Henry of Exeter " that of being the father of Miss Bertha Phillpotts, lately Mistress of Girton College. Another survivor when the History of the Savile Club first appeared was Lord Morley of

Blackburn. He might have told us something of the sentiments of his first colleagues, but he left the club so long ago as 1870, by what must have been an impulsive act which I hope he sometimes regretted. I am sure that our arms were open to this prodigal, even after fifty-two years of infidelity, and I think that if he had come back he would have found the Savile Club as much as, if not more than, any other national institution essentially unchanged by the passage of the half-century. It still cultivates, though in more comfort, an easy simplicity, and it still is remarkable for its " mixture of men of different professions."

It is widely known that the late war exercised a disturbing, and in many cases a critical, influence on the London clubs. In each instance the several committees had to face fresh conditions, and to put their houses in order. No doubt, in almost every club of good standing, arrangements tending to economy had to be made, and it became a question of stability whether the body could bear a heavy increase in subscription. This last has been an unpleasant necessity, " forced " upon the Savile Club, as the volume before me puts it, " by the condition of the country." It was a moment for desolating quidnuncs to shake their heads and murmur " Dissolution ! " But the crisis, in all healthy cases, merely stirred the committees to that administrative ingenuity in which Englishmen seldom fail if they are put to it. The Savile Club may have had, like the rest, its anxious hour, but the danger is past, and now " all members have the right to contemplate the future with courage and hope."

At this moment of tempered elation nothing could be more timely, and few things more encouraging, than a record, which may almost be described as " stately," of its unblemished history and eminent services to society. When it is remembered that more than two thousand five hundred selected persons have at one time or another been members of the Savile, it is not extravagant to claim a certain national importance for it, although this volume, which is conspicuous for its modesty, never hints at such a claim.

This History of the Savile Club, which extends to 206 pages, and is compiled with accurate and laborious fullness, has one defect. There is not the slightest indication of the hand to which we owe such a monument of our existence. This is to carry self-abnegation too far, and therefore, without a blush at my betrayal of confidence, I give honour where honour is due. The work is the compilation of Sir Herbert Stephen, than whom there is no living man to whom the Savile Club owes more of its continuous welfare. Sir Herbert Stephen was elected in 1879, became a member of the committee in 1883, honorary secretary in 1885, and honorary librarian in 1904. In a very busy life he has found leisure through forty years to support the interests and increase the amenities of the club. If he thinks these facts of no general interest, I must beg leave to differ from him in this instance only. He has done a large number of younger men a service in recounting to them what they may so easily forget, the history of a social institution which it is natural to take for granted, and I do not think that the interest of the record is by any means limited to those who are, or who have been, members of the club.

The founder of the Savile was Auberon Herbert, later on widely known as " the Politician in Trouble about his Soul." In May, 1868, Auberon Herbert, not yet thirty years of age, was private secretary to Sir Stafford Northcote at the Board of Trade. The second in Parliament command at that office was Sir Robert Herbert, who was persuaded by his kinsman to become an original member, as was Lord Carnarvon himself. The Herbert interest, therefore, was strong in the infant club. Auberon, who in this year 1868 abruptly turned from Conservative to Liberal, was an eccentric, but extremely vivid and social man. He was eagerly interested in bringing his friends into the club, but himself left it and them six years later, when he retired from Parliamentary life.

It was doubtless in consequence of his wish to be near Whitehall that the first dwelling-place of the new Club was at No. 9, Spring Gardens, in a set of pleasant rooms overlooking Trafalgar Square. Here the vivacious M.P. for Nottingham was close to the House of Commons, and in the centre of his friends. Auberon Herbert was in the chair in June, 1871, when the decision was taken to move to No. 15, Savile Row, when the club adopted its present name. Of those who were associated with the house in Spring Gardens, I think that only five still remain members of the club; of these are Sir Sidney Colvin, Sir Edwin Ray Lankester, and the venerable Rector of Exeter College, Oxford. Sir Sidney Colvin, ever since 1871 an officer of the club, of which he is still a trustee, is undoubtedly its present father. Young members are sometimes persuaded to believe that he was its founder as well, the initials S. C. being confidently pointed to.

On such a subject as the Savile Club it is difficult not to be tempted into the garrulity of reminiscence. The first time I penetrated, even as a visitor, to the house in Savile Row was in the winter of 1874, when Andrew Lang and Mr. George Saintsbury entertained Mr. Thomas Hardy and myself to dinner there. Robert Louis Stevenson had just been elected a member, but I cannot recollect whether we found him in the drawing-room when we went upstairs. Probably not, for he would be in Edinburgh at that season. But in 1876, when I was myself elected, my meetings at Savile Row with R. L. S. became incessant, whenever he had occasion to be in London. It was not until 1878 that Mr. Hardy joined us. When I look back on the symposia of those years, and see, besides those whom I have already named, the vanished faces of so many men eminent in literature and science, and not less eminent in friendship,

I ask myself whether there are many social bodies of the nineteenth century which have added as much useful pleasure to their age as the Savile Club.

Memories crowd upon an ancient mind, but must be severely restrained, since I have no ambition to be an autobiographer. One little scene it may be amusing to recover, because it illustrates that " mixture of men of different professions and opinions " which the founders of the Savile laid down as a principle. In its present house in Piccadilly the double drawing-room on the first floor runs through the whole breadth of the building. At least thirty years ago I happened to be alone between the divisions of the room, and saw a pleasing sight. In the front room Mr. Herbert Spencer was sitting at the fireplace, reading a book; in the back room a young writer, already celebrated—whom I will not name, since he has left the club —was regaling a circle of admirers with stories. At the close of each story there was a burst of laughter, at which Herbert Spencer lifted a pale face, tortured with disapprobation. At last a supreme story provoked in the back room a more explosive hilarity than ever. The philosopher, hurriedly feeling in his pockets, produced two padded ear-protectors; these he clapped to the two sides of his head, and fixed them; and then calmly resumed his book. There was a popular song in those days, " The Old Obadiah and the Young Obadiah," and this was an illustration of it.

The conversations in the 'eighties in which the two Stevensons—R. L. S. and his wonderful cousin R. A. M. S.— took the predominant part, were not so vociferous nor so purely anecdotal. Day after day, these met at the luncheon-table with, to name only the dead, Andrew Lang, W. E. Henley, William Minto, H. J. Hood, sometimes Coventry Patmore and Austin Dobson. Cambridge sent its occasional contingent, A. W. Verrall, Frank Balfour, A. G. Dew-Smith, W. Robertson Smith. The talk was not noisy when these men met in the absolute liberty of 15, Savile Row, but it was worthy of the finest traditions of eager, cultivated communication. R. L. S. has left a picture of certain features of it in his famous double essay in " Memories and Portraits."

Lest anyone should think, as some fool-outsiders have been known to say in their hearts, that the Savile has always been a mere haunt of the high-browed, I am glad that the author of this history has made the geniality of the club life apparent, and in particular has given an account of that characteristic annual event, the Club Birthday. I can do no better than quote his account of it :—

" It began with a dinner-party, for which the existence at Piccadilly of a guest's dining-room afforded special facilities. At this feast, evening dress was not, as at the *table-d'hôte*, ' optional,' and both the food and the wine had to be of the best, quite regardless of expense, that the club could provide. After dinner the company repaired—comparatively late—to the cardroom, and for that night, with the connivance of the committee, all rules were suspended, and those present indulged in gambling. Any game might be played except whist—and afterwards bridge—but the most popular was a form of loo introduced by Hood, and capable of producing much excitement. In later years it was almost entirely superseded by poker. Between twelve and one o'clock large supplies of sandwiches appeared, and alcoholic drinks continued to be served as long as anyone stayed. The party never finally broke up until about 4 a.m., and it is believed that once or twice the last revellers did not depart until something like 6 a.m."

This fearless old fashion was continued for a great many years until legislation stepped in with grandmotherly supervision by magistrates and policemen. But " the days of our youth were the days of our glory," as Byron remarked.

MORALS AND MANNERS

MORALS AND MANNERS

A GREAT Whig lady, recently deceased, who was distinguished by the dignity of her manners and the austerity of her conduct, shortly before her death said to a friend: " If I could live my life over again, I should devote a part of it to the defence of Lord Chesterfield." The task was worthy of an indomitable spirit, since it would have run counter to the preconceived opinion of every class of reader. For a century and a half Chesterfield has laboured under the stigma of being " a bold, bad man, my dear," as Charles Kingsley said of Heine. Not the religious and didactic classes only, but all sorts and conditions of people have united in defaming him, and in speaking of the celebrated " Letters " as being no less subversive of every true emotion and honest principle than, let us say, the " Liaisons Dangereuses."

Chesterfield has been treated as the helot of the eighteenth century, as being, in the words of one admirer, " profoundly immoral, profoundly selfish, profoundly cynical." No less a person than Dickens asserted, by the voice of Mr. Chester, in " Barnaby Rudge," that " on every page of this enlightened writer I find some captivating hypocrisy which had never occurred to me before," and nobody has troubled to ask how many pages Mr. Chester could have read. And then there was that masterpiece of sarcasm, the Johnson letter. It is true that occasionally a faint voice of deprecation has been raised, as by Chesterfield's careful editor, Charles Strachey, but no matter. Chesterfield remains a byword for impropriety, with the celebrated definition of him by a man of the highest genius, who had earnestly desired his patronage, and who on losing it declared that "he teaches the morals of a whore and the manners of a dancing-master." And yet, on honest examination, he does neither.

When Chesterfield died, in 1773, he was known merely as an aged politician of liberal views and practical wisdom, whose private and diplomatic career had been eminent for tact and politeness. But in the following year Mrs. Eugenia Stanhope, the widow of his illegitimate but constantly beloved and protected son, published in two magnificent quartos the letters which the Earl had written to that son during thirty years or more. Mrs. Eugenia Stanhope had the naïveté to believe that she was " being of some use to her country " in publishing a correspondence which displayed " a scrupulous adherence to the strictest morality." She was being of some use to herself, for the " Letters " enjoyed a prodigious success, and brought her in the sum of £1,575, but there was immediate diversity of opinion about their morality. There was a strong reaction at that moment throughout English society, in favour of enthusiasm and passion. Rousseau was in the air; the asceticism of the Wesleys was rousing the emotions of the public. The torpor of the preceding age was being shaken up with violence, in religion, in the arts, in literature, in the canons of conduct. To widely opposed sections of society the Frenchified *laissez-faire* of the past generation had grown detestable. No victim to the new zeal could be found more acceptable than the cool and unsentimental Chesterfield, and he was offered up on every altar. Cowper was one of the first to speak out :—

>Petronius ! all the Muses weep for thee,
>But every tear shall scald thy memory. . . .
>Thou polished and high-finished foe to truth,
>Grey-beard corrupter of our listening youth.

The note of exaggeration was thus loudly struck—the " grey-beard " was only forty-five when the " Letters "

Morals and Manners 385

began—and the hue and cry was started. Everybody took it up; everybody read (and, in private, enjoyed) the incomparable letters, but declared to everybody else that they were "dazzling and diabolical." And then came Boswell, in 1791, dragging that moral athlete, Dr. Samuel Johnson, into the arena with his magnificent letter of invective.

The champion who should snatch up the gauntlet for Chesterfield—and much as I love the "Letters," I do not presume to take that honour upon me—will certainly begin by asking the conventional detractor to read them. Let us consider what they are. Philip Dormer Stanhope, having succeeded as the fourth Earl of Chesterfield, was sent to The Hague as Ambassador in 1728. There he met a beautiful girl of good family, Mlle. du Bouchet, of whom very little is known. They became warmly attached, but, for some reason not explained, they could not marry. In 1732 she bore him a son, and about the same time he returned to England. The son received the family names of Philip Stanhope, and was brought up by his father with a devotion that ended only with the son's comparatively premature death. As early as he could read, the child received affectionate, playful, and wise letters whenever circumstances divided him from his father; sometimes this correspondence was repeated daily; it extended over thirty years. When so much is said about Chesterfield's "selfishness," it might be remembered that his ambition could obtain no advantage whatever from cherishing a young man who could never adorn the title or add anything to the pride of the family.

Young Philip Stanhope carefully preserved all the important letters, and out of these his widow Eugenia formed her two massive quartos in 1774. We have, therefore, in the famous " Letters to his Son " an entirely private and confidential record of a lifelong attachment. They

c c

were not written for publicity, or to dazzle the frivolous world with paradox, but to direct the education, in the largest sense, of a young man for whom the writer felt a parental devotion. That Chesterfield's ideas of education were not those usually adopted by school-boards and the clergy must be conceded, but also that he was not a common-place person. He had his own ideas of the action of morals on conduct, and they may not have been those of the Society of Methodists, but the point is that they were expressed by him to a person and in a manner which prove them to have been, in the strictest sense, sincerely intended for the edification of that person. Chesterfield is compared with Machiavelli, but it is difficult to see a parallel between the subversive publicity of the one and the instructive privacy of the other. Chesterfield wished his son to be a happy and prosperous man, cutting a fine figure in the world, and he gave him confidential advice directed to that end. He was neither trying to seduce the Courts of Europe nor to lay down a system of ethics.

The reader who has been trained to regard Chesterfield as a kind of serpent may be recommended to turn to the long letter he wrote on September 12, 1749. He was in London; young Philip, aged seventeen, was in Rome, making the Grand Tour under the tutorship of a distinguished clergyman, the Rev. Walter Harte. The reader conjectures that Mr. Harte has written home to say that Philip is idle, neglects his classics, and is easily led away by loose society. The Earl is all anxiety and prudence, and he writes the youth a letter which is a masterpiece of tenderness and wisdom. Not a word betrays that the tutor has been complaining, but the necessity of discipline and self-improvement is put forward with the most persuasive delicacy. The father invents a dialogue, in which Philip rebuffs the temptations laid before him by a dissolute companion; nothing could be more amusing, nothing more calculated, in every flexible phrase, to suggest that the youth himself is of the same opinion as the father and the tutor. The Earl avoids anything like censure; he appeals entirely to "piety and affection towards me; regard and friendship for Mr. Harte; respect for your own moral character, and for all the relative duties of man, son, pupil, and citizen." The very mode of address, "My dear friend," points to the tact of the father, who, incessantly occupied with the social improvement of the son, never allows the relation between them to become didactic. "I am not now preaching to you like an old fellow, but I am advising you as a friend, as a man of the world."

Men of the world had not quite the same outlook a hundred and eighty years ago as they have now, or had even in the decade after Chesterfield's death. A person of Chesterfield's habits, carefully abstaining from what was just beginning to be called "sentiment," put good nature and good breeding very high among the virtues. The model gentleman of middle age was to be calm, graceful, and unobtrusive; he was, like Bolingbroke, to "join the deepest erudition with the most elegant politeness." He could not achieve this purity of style without making some sacrifices of literal accuracy. If you wished to emulate Diogenes in his tub, or Timon of Athens, well and good, but then you must relinquish any ambition to be a man of the world. The practice of bluntly sticking out your elbows and shoving a path for yourself through society must be abandoned, and you cannot learn too soon to cultivate the little "*agrémens*" which are the oil of life. "I sacrifice such a convenience to you, you sacrifice another to me." What have to be aimed at are the polishing artifices and last burnishing strokes of good breeding. You cultivate these graces, of course, for your own ultimate advantage, and if this is immoral, then Chesterfield's teaching is immoral. It was not very successful in the case of poor boorish Philip Stanhope. But surely it is no mere hypocrisy —the peculiar hypocrisy of which the French accuse us— to pretend that to sacrifice some exactitude to the art of pleasing is not in itself atrociously wicked.

A great part of the indignation poured out upon Chesterfield was founded on the report that he recommended to his son certain gallant " arrangements " which were fashionable in Paris and Rome. Here, also, British prudery has asserted itself with some excess. A novel, " The Pupil of Pleasure," was written by a dissipated clergyman, the Rev. Samuel Pratt, who called himself Courtney Melmoth. It is a clever book and enjoyed considerable success, and did much harm to the memory of Chesterfield. It openly professes to illustrate the Earl's principles by describing, not without talent, a series of seductions carried on by an admirer of the Earl's letters at Buxton. Nothing could be more perfidious, and that " The Pupil of Pleasure " could ever have been accepted as a truthful commentary shows how Chesterfield has been shot at with poisoned arrows from every side. It was truly said of his unlucky genius that " the wit hath had his joke at it, the versifier his parody, the moralist his opposing sentiment, and the divine his grave dissertation." The only thing missing has been a judicious estimate of the actual import and tendency of the " Letters."

The latest instalment of correspondence is not highly important, but welcome, and skilfully introduced. It consists of a packet of letters recently found in the possession of the Countess of Loudoun. They are all addressed, between 1749 and 1769, to Francis Hastings, tenth Earl of Huntingdon, a very lively and polite young nobleman, whom Chesterfield liked extremely for his own sake, and cultivated in the hope that he would be a useful patron for Philip Stanhope. Mr. A. F. Steuart tells all that is known of Lord Huntingdon's history, which was blameless but not very distinguished. He does not, however, give Mrs. Piozzi's impression of the good man, which I will therefore venture to quote. Writing in the " Gentleman's Magazine" after Lord Huntingdon's death in 1789, she remarked on his " perfect good breeding," and added that he

" combined every talent to instruct, every power to please, and every grace to charm in conversation; and this, too, after sixty years and a long series of ill-health had dreadfully impaired a person which in its best days could never have been better than barely not disagreeable."

The terrible Eighteenth Century, how merciless were its personal observations! But this is not the picture of a man upon whom the affection and the correspondence of Lord Chesterfield can have had any deleterious effect.

THE CARPET AND THE CLOCK

THE CARPET AND THE CLOCK

FROM the list of Mr. George Moore's works, which is printed opposite the title of his new volume, " Avowals," published in 1919, is omitted. If this is an accident, it is an unfortunate one, for these two books are closely allied, and serve to explain one another. They form a section of Mr. Moore's authorship by themselves, and they present his bland and undaunted figure in a new atmosphere. We are accustomed to meet with this novelist on the Parisian boulevards, on the slopes of the Mount of Olives, in the recesses of the Wicklow Hills, by Irish lake or Provençal orchard or garret of the Bou' St. Mich', but always far from home, always in exile, always garrulous in lonely places.

In " Avowals," and now in " Conversations in Ebury Street," we see him for the first time at home. No secret is withdrawn from our scrutiny. We learn that he lives in Pimlico, in a certain street, at a certain number. At that house he receives, or pretends to receive, various living persons of more or less prominence in letters, and with them, or with their unresisting wraiths, he carries on vehement and artless dialogues on subjects connected with literature. In the course of these dialogues Mr. George Moore invariably gets the best of the argument, but the dummies have nothing else to complain of. He treats them with the utmost courtesy, and tells stories about their private life with no less nonchalance than if he were feeding them with custard.

In the course of each of these unsolicited interviews Mr. Moore draws the attention of the visitor to two pieces of furniture. He is proud—justly proud—of an Aubusson Carpet and of a Lyre-shapen Clock. It is a matter of etiquette for the visitor to look on the floor and exclaim, " So this is the Aubusson Carpet! And can that be the Lyre-shapen Clock? " The interview thus started, invariably proceeds to a harmonious close. The penates are appeased; the rigour of the game has been preserved. The objects I have mentioned will, fifty years hence, form the central attraction of the George Moore Museum to countless visitors. At present they are reserved for a selected few, but they animate the text of the " Conversations." In each of the dialogues—there are nineteen of these, more or less—we feel that our shoes are planted on the Carpet, and our eyes, if for a moment they quit the features of Mr. Moore, are fixed upon the Clock. With modest pride I may mention that of all the visitors introduced, I am the only one who has been able to drag Mr. Moore from his armchair. In Dialogue XVI., I am astounded at my own audacity in leading Mr. Moore to " a pleasant seat " by " a lake at the other end " of " some gardens." But the triumph is a physical, not a spiritual, one. In the discussion which ensues (if discussion it can be called when one party incessantly agrees with Mr. Moore) the atmosphere is exactly that of 121, Ebury Street. The turf at our feet is the Aubusson Carpet, and the " handsome beech-tree " above our heads no other than the Lyre-shapen Clock.

A genuine originality may be admitted for the critical method pursued in " Avowals," and with still greater audacity in " Conversations." But it is not quite the originality claimed by Mr. Moore, who bases his appeal on that of Landor, whom he proposes to imitate, and of whom he speaks as though no dialogues but the Landorian had ever been produced. Yet an army of illustrious Greeks had been followed by author after author before Landor began to pour out the stores of his reading and his reflection in the shape we know so well. The eighteenth century had delighted in the dialogue, and Bishop Berkeley, in the famous passage of his " Hylas and Philonous," where the fox-hunters ride by under the terrace where the philosophers are seated, comes closer to Mr. Moore than Landor does. Mr. Moore is an idolater of Landor; he prefers him to Shakespeare, in so many words; and in this he resembles Landor himself, who says of his own " Imaginary Conversations," that they contain " as forcible writing as exists on earth." Something of the same kind was said seventy years ago by admirers of Helps' " Friends in Council," a book of dialogues no longer read with much exhilaration.

But the originality of Mr. Moore's " Conversations " does not consist in their being written dramatically, but in the nature of their treatment. What is new in these pages is their curious emancipation from all the traditional bonds of criticism. They run hilariously from theme to theme, they lay down the law with complete irresponsibility, they make no reference whatever to tradition or principle or accepted rule. They record, with unprecedented rawness, the impact of masterpieces on an impulsive mind. The result is exceedingly interesting, because the mind of Mr. Moore is the very original mind of a highly-gifted man. But I confess that its vagaries bewilder me. It will be remembered that Dr. Johnson, who highly esteemed Poll Carmichael, nevertheless complained that when he talked to her " tightly and closely," she " was wiggle-waggle, and I never could persuade her to be categorical." That is the case with Mr. Moore; he cannot be persuaded to be categorical. He is pre-eminently " wiggle-waggle."

If the reader is resolved not to be made angry by Mr.

Moore's critical extravagances, he will find them very diverting. They will probably not amuse his imaginary interlocutors, such as Mr. Walter de la Mare, Mr. Cunninghame Graham and Mr. Granville Barker. They cannot but be disconcerted to find themselves dragged at the tail of Mr. Moore's fiery chariot. If I were not a philosopher, I might myself resent the surprising opinions with which I am credited. Mr. John Freeman, who, besides being an accomplished poet, is a sound and liberal critic, will certainly be shocked to see attributed to him the opening line of page 87. When Mr. Moore—for it is all Mr. Moore, whatever distinguished visitor pretends to utter a reply —when Mr. Moore praises, he speaks the language of generous hyperbole. But when he blames, and he blames too readily and too recklessly, his hyperbole is not at all generous. He is unable to see merit in the most honoured names in his department of our profession. Why?

I think the reason is to be sought in Mr. Moore's almost infantile candour. To attribute his judgments of Conrad and Henry James and Mr. Thomas Hardy to jealousy would be to fall into a coarse and baseless error. Perhaps no novelist ever quite sincerely admires the work of another leading novelist, and for a reason which is worth bearing in mind. To the ordinary reader the main affair is the entertainment to be found in the story. But the novelist, if he be a man of any genius, is an artist. He has his own theory of approach, his own methods of construction. When he begins to read a novel by a fellow-artist, his first impression is that if he himself had the material in hand he would treat it quite differently. The further he penetrates the work of his rival, the more conscious he is of this dislocation, until he throws down the book in disgust, simply because it is not conducted as he himself would conduct it. Other novelists politely conceal this instinctive repulsion; Mr. Moore is constitutionally unable to conceal anything.

It will be regrettable if these exhibitions of flightiness prevent us from appreciating the merits of Mr. Moore's writing. It was never more vivid or more individual than in the present instance. Not to recognise in Mr. Moore one of the finest living writers of English prose is to fall a victim to a prejudice as peevish as his own. His recollections of French scenes and persons occur frequently, and are invariably marked by that sinuous intensity, that long-drawn punctilious observation which is characteristic of his admirably personal style. " Is not every memory intermittent ? " he pertinently remarks; and it is in the record of these broken scenes that Moore excels. " We spoke of other things, myself holding forth," he says on one page, and could anything be better descriptive of the manner he affects and adorns ?

But I must come to close quarters with the portion of " Conversations in Ebury Street " which it is most difficult to analyse with judgment. I mean the singular gallery of " portraits " which occupy a space of eighty pages in the centre of the book. Mr. Freeman and Mr. de la Mare have been paying a visit to 121, Ebury Street, and the time has come when they are dismissed from the Presence. Mr. Moore, who has been giving to their remarks only " a semblance of attention," now points to the Lyre-shapen Clock and bids them depart. They are to return to discuss Wordsworth, asparagus, and grouse. For an hour or more Mr. Moore will be alone—alone upon the Aubusson Carpet. In that solitude there will crowd upon him the dear remembered faces of eminent artists with whom he was once intimate, and who seem to welcome him no more. We wonder at that ! But without a vestige of resentment he paints their figures, repeats their words, betrays their innocent foibles, and belauds their talents, until, one by one, they rise before us in all their naked majesty. Every victim is still alive. How does each appreciate this searching portraiture? Probably not so much as we strangers may enjoy the powerful brush-work and the unflinching impressionism.

The customary phrases die upon our lips as we try to define the action of Mr. Moore. Reticence, privacy, reserve—what have these to do with the revelations of Ebury Street? If there were the slightest tincture of ill-nature, so much as the twinkling of a tail or the whisper of a hiss, we should denounce the serpent and be all on fire with indignation. But how are we to face an innocency which resembles nothing so much as Sterne's naked infant rolling on the carpet—the Aubusson Carpet under the Lyre-shapen Clock? Not only does Mr. Moore mean no harm by his indiscretions, but he has no idea what it is to be discreet.

The conception of such a quality is not present to his mind. If he betrays the embarrassments of a friend who is widely known and still moving among us, it is because his plastic sense has been violently affected by the circumstances in question, and because he cannot imagine a social state in which the misfortunes of the living are not as much the property of the public as are Desdemona's little accident with the handkerchief or the surprising bloodiness of King Lear. He pays his acquaintances the compliment of treating them as though they were imaginary personages described by some genius of three hundred years ago. " Out of these create he can forms more real than living man," as Shelley says, because to Mr. Moore life is only interesting when it can be translated into literature, and the literary aspect of a fact or a situation is infinitely more actual to him than its attitude to the wilderness of useless instances which we call life.

If we would explain why Mr. George Moore, while apparently breaking every law of decency and every rule of good conduct, is still never detestable and rarely disagreeable, we must largely attribute it to his imaginative candour. He is making pictures the whole time; why should anyone be vexed at having served as model to so marvellous a portrait-painter?

INDEX

INDEX

"ABSOLOM and Achitophel" (Dryden), and Claudian's "Rufinus," 7
Addison, Joseph, 149, 150, 158
"Adolphe" (Benjamin Constant), 98, 99
"Adone" (Marini), Chapelain's analysis of, 88
Adrian, Earl of Windsor ("The Last Man"), portrait of Percy Bysshe Shelley, 234 *et seq.*
"Affliction of Margaret, The" (Wordsworth), 178
Akenside, Dr., 252
Alabaster, William, 371
Aldington, Mr., 134–140
Alexinsky, Gregor, 292
Alpine Club, 323
"Aminta" (Tasso), 37
Andree, Bernard, 15, 16
"Angel in the House, The" (Patmore), 183
"Angola" (La Morlière), 138
"Annals of a Parish, The" (Galt), 340
Annunzio, Gabriele d' (Duke of Montenivoso), 36
"Apostles," the Society of, 322, 323
"Apple-Tree Table, The" (Melville), 356, 357, 358–360
Arbuthnot, John, 150
Arcadian Academy, the, 86, 87
Arcadius and Honorius, division of the Roman Empire under, 5, 9
Aristotle, 84, 87
Arnold, Matthew, 204, 214, 215
"Art of Love, The" (Ovid), 243, *et seq.*
Ascham, Roger, prose of, 13

Asquith, Oxford and, Earl of, 278
"Assertion of the Seven Sacraments, The" (Henry VIII), 14 *et seq.*
Ataide, Catarina de, and Camoens, 34, 35
Aubertin, J. J., translator of Camoens' "Lusiads," 38
Aubigné, Agrippa d', 36
Augustine, St., 19
Augustus Cæsar and Ovid, 242 *et seq.*
Austen, Jane, 54, 196
"Avowals" (Moore), 393, 394
A'Wood, Anthony, 65
Aytoun, William Edmoundstone, 333

"BABYLONISH Captivity of the Church" (Luther), 16, 17
Bailey, Philip James, 333, 335
"Balder" (Dobell), 329, 331 *et seq.*
Ballads, Border and American, compared, 299, 301, 304
Banville, Théodore de, 167–168, 186, 347–352
"Barbary Allen," 301
Barker, Mr. Granville, 396
"Barnaby Rudge" (Dickens), 383
Barrie, Sir James, 340
Baruzi, Dr. Jean, work on St. John of the Cross by, 45, 47 *et seq.*
Bashkirtseff, Marie, 97
Baudelaire, Charles, 177, 350
Beauclerk, Lady Diana, 118
Beerbohm, Mr. Max, 203–204
Behn, Aphra, 63

404 Index

Bell, Mr. Aubrey, 33–39
Belleau, Rémy, 167
Bellegarde, Marquis de, 97
Beresford, Mr. John, editor, Woodforde's Diary, 153–159
Bergerac, Cyrano de, 134
Berkeley, George, Bishop, 143, 144, 149, 395
Bible, Cranmer's and Tyndale's versions of, 13
Biggs, Stanyan, 335
Bird, Montgomery, 355
Bisland, Miss Elizabeth, biographer of Lafcadio Hearn, 222, 225
Black, William, 193
Blackstone, Sir William, 155
Blunden, Mr. Edmund, Poems of John Clare, edited by, 103–109
Boccaccio, 28
Bodmer, 89
Boileau, Nicolas, 56, 57, 84
Boleyn, Anne, 19
" Bonnie Kilmeny " (Hogg), 124
" Books of the Little Souls " (Couperus), 265
"Border Minstrelsy" (Scott), 124
Boswell, James, 94, 97, 98, 385
Brewer, John Sherren, 19
Bridges, Dr. Robert, 36, 169–170, 227
British Museum, poets connected with, *circa* 1870, 173 *et seq.*
Brontë, Anne, 310, 312
Brontë, Charlotte, 310, 312, 313, 315, 331
Brontë, Emily, 310 *et seq.*
Brontë, Patrick Branwell, 309–315
Brown, George Douglas, 341–344
Brown, Lancelot (" Capability"), 143
Browne, Sir Thomas, 79
Browning, E. B., 35
Browning, Robert, 166, 227, 370
Buchanan, George, 34
Buchanan, Robert, 227
Buckingham, Duke of, 19, 63, 89–90

Buckinghamshire, Duke of, 89–90
Buffon, 135
Burney, Fanny, 153
Burns, Robert, 9, 124
Burton, Sir Richard, 38
Bury St. Edmunds, trial of witches at, 79
Byron, Lord, 36, 54, 118, 231, 380; portrayed as Lord Raymond in " The Last Man," 234 *et seq.*

CAILLAUX, M., 295
Calderon, Pedro, 54
Caliban (" The Tempest "), 255, 256
Cambridge University, Leslie Stephen's recollections of, 321–323
Camoens, Vasco Perez de, 33–39
" Campaspe," play (Lyly), 29
Campbell, Thomas, 330
Campeggio, Lorenzo, 18
Campion, Edmund, 371
" Candide " (Voltaire), 117
Canning, George, 106
Canopus, birthplace of Claudian, 5
" Cariatides, Les " (Banville), 349, 350
Carlyle, Thomas, 325, 331
Cary, Henry Francis, 53 *et seq.*
Castiglione, Baldassare, 28
Castle Cary, 154, 158
" Castle of Otranto, The " 113–119
" Cato " (Addison), 158
Catullus, 245
Cénacle, the, 349, 350
Cervantes, 38
Ceuta, Camoens at, 36
Chamberlain, Mr. Basil, 224
Chapelain, Jean, 88
Chapin, Mr., notes on Herman Melville by, 355–356
" Characteristics " (Lord Shaftesbury), 147
Charenton, Protestant conferences at, 65

Index

Charrière, M. de, 98
Chatterton, Thomas, 119
Chaulieu, 187
Chesterfield, 4th Earl of, 383–388
Child, Professor, 299
Christina, Queen of Sweden, 87, 88
Clairmont, Claire, 232, 234, 236, 237
Clare, John, 103–109
" Clarissa Harlowe " (Richardson), 133, 134, 139
Claudian, 3 *et seq.*
Clerville, 273
Clive, Mrs., 119
Coimbra, claimed as Camoens' birthplace, 34
Coleridge, S. T., 55, 177–178
Colvin, Sir Sidney, 378
" Confessions of a Justified Sinner, The " (Hogg), 123–130
Congreve, William, 63, 66
Conington, John, 311
Conrad, Joseph, 8, 144, 396
Constant, Benjamin, and Zélide, 94, 95, 98–99
Conti, Antonio, 89–90
" Conversations in Ebury Street " (Moore), 393–399
Cook, Eliza, 184
Coppée, François, 177
Corneille, Pierre, 86
" Cornhill Magazine," Leslie Stephen as editor, 324
" Corrected Impressions " (Saintsbury), 213
Corvinus, Messalla, 243
" Cottagers of Glenburnie, The " (Mrs. E. Hamilton), 339
" Country Wife, The " (Wycherley), 65, 66, 68, 69
Couperus, Louis, 261–267
Cowley, Abraham, 84
Cowper, William, 384
Cranmer, Thomas, 13
Crashaw, Richard, 45, 47, 84
Crawford and Balcarres, Earl of, Rectorial address on John Lyly by, 23 *et seq.*

Crébillon, Claude Prosper Jolyot de, 135
Creighton, Mandell, 206, 209
Crescimbeni, 83, 87
Cunningham, John, persecution of, for witchcraft, 76 *et seq.*
Cyprianus, Dr. Abraham, 146

" DÆMONOLOGIE " (James I), 75 *et seq.*
Danou, 56
Dante Alighieri, 34, 53, 55
" Dark Night of the Soul, The " (St. John of the Cross), 45
Défaitisme, the term, 291–292
" Defender of the Faith," Henry VIII's title of, 15, 19
Deffand, Mme. du, 118
Defoe, Daniel, 123
De La Mare, Mr. Walter, 396, 397
Dennis, John, 64
De Quincey, Thomas, 8–9, 55, 221
Descartes, René, 88
Dew-Smith, A. G., 379
" Dial of Princes " (A. de Guevara), and Lyly's " Euphues," 27
Dickens, Charles, 383
" Dictionary of National Biography," planned by Leslie Stephen, 324
" Discoverie of Witchcraft " (Reginald Scot), 73, 74
Dobell, Sydney, 329–335
Dobson, Mr. Alban, 189–190
Dobson, Austin, 168, 183–190, 347, 379
" Dolores " (Swinburne), 227, 348
Dorset, Earl of, 89
Drinkwater, Mr. John, 310–311
Dryden, John, 67, 84, 86, 321, 343
Dumur, M. Louis, 290–295
Dunbar, William, 8
Duncan, Geillis, 76

" EARLY French Poets " (Cary), 53 *et seq.*

406 Index

Eeden, Frederik van, 264
Elephant Man, the (Robert Merrick), case of, described by Sir F. Treves, 253–256
" Eliduc " (Marie de France), 176
" Eline Vere " (Couperus), 262, 263
Elizabeth, Queen, her attitude to Witchcraft, 73, 75; and John Lyly, 25
Elton, Mr. Oliver, 334, 339
Elyot, Sir Thomas, prose of, 13
Emerson, Ralph Waldo, 198
" Endimione," 88
" Epic of Women, An " (O'Shaughnessy), 173, 176
Erasmus, 15
" Eros and Psyche " (Bridges), 169–170
Erskine, Professor John, 225–226
" Essays in Criticism " (Arnold), 204
" Essays in English Literature " (Saintsbury), 213
Etherege, Sir George, 67, 68
Ettrick Shepherd, The (James Hogg), 123–130
" Euphues, the Anatomie of Wit " (John Lyly), 23 *et seq.*
Euphuism, 23 *et seq.*, 84
Eutropius, 6–7
Evelyn, John, 69
" Extasy " (Couperus), 263

" Fable of the Bees, The " (Mandeville), 143–150
Fanshawe, Sir Richard, translator of Camoens' " Lusiads," 34, 38, 39
Farington's " Diary," 153
" Fasti " (Ovid), 243
Fenton, Elijah, 118
Fielding, Henry, 116, 154
Filicaja, 86
Firkins, Mr., biographer of W. D. Howells, 194–199
Fitzmaurice-Kelly, Professor, 43

Flaubert, Gustave, 264
" Foddering Boy, The " (Clare), 105–106
Folk-Song, American, 299–305
Fontenelle, Bernard de, 275
Fontiveros, 46
" Footsteps of Fate " (" Noodlot "), (Couperus), 261–262
France, Anatole, 292, 348, 351
France, Early French Poetry, 53 *et seq.;* Poetical taste in, *circa* 1820, 56; eighteenth century novel in, 134 *et seq.;* Vauban and the fortifications of, 271–278; *Défaitisme* in, 290 *et seq.*
" Frankenstein " (Mrs. Shelley), 237
Freeman, Mr. John, 396, 397
" Friends in Council " (Helps), 395
Froude, J. A., 33

Gairdner, James, on Henry VIII's Latin, 14
Galen, 257
Galt, John, 340, 342
Garland of Julie, the, 64
Garnett, Richard, 173
Garrick, David, 119
Gaskell, Mrs., " Life of Charlotte Brontë," 310
Gautier, Théophile, 189
" Gentleman Dancing-Master, The " (Wycherley), 66
Gibbon, Edward, 3 *et seq.*, 155, 321
Gilder, R. W., 368
Giustiniani on Henry VIII, 15
Gladstone, W. E., 207, 209
Goa, Camoens at, 36
Godet, Philippe, biographer of Zélide, 94, 95 *n.*
Godwin, William, 218, 234
Goethe, 188, 252
Gonzalo de Yepes, 46
Gordon, Adam Lindsay, 303
Gosson, Stephen, 28
Graham, Mr. R. B. Cunninghame, 396

Index 407

Graham, Mrs. Cunninghame, biographer of St. Teresa, 43
Granada, St. John of the Cross at, 48–49
Grasset, 187
Gravina, Gian Vincenzo, 83, 87–89
Gray, Thomas, 19
Greene, Robert, 24
Grierson, Professor, 86
" Gringoire " (Banville), 352
" Grumbling Hive, The " (Mandeville), 146
Guevara, Antonio de, " Dial of Princes," 27
Guiney, Louise Imogen, 365–371
Guiney, Patrick, 366, 367, 368

Hale, Sir Matthew, 79
Halévy, M. Daniel, 271–278
Hamilton, Mrs. Elizabeth, 339
Hardy, Mr. Thomas, 321, 378, 396
Harte, Bret, 302
Harte, Rev. William, 386, 387
Harvey, Gabriel, 28
" Hasard au Coin du Feu, Le " (Crébillon), 135, 136
Hawkins, A., 3
Hawkins, Sir John, 146
Hawthorne, Nathaniel, 196, 197, 284, 356–358
Haydon, Benjamin, Autobiography of, 33
Hazlitt, William, 55, 215
Hearn, Lafcadio, 221–227
Henley, W. E., 379
Henry VIII, 309; " Miscellaneous Writings " of, 13 et seq.
Herbert, Auberon, 377–378
Herbert, Sir Robert, 377
Hermanches de Rebecque, 97, 98
" Hero and Leander " (Wycherley), 69
Hippocrates, 257
" Historical Essay concerning Witchcraft with Observations upon Matter of Fact " (Bishop Hutchinson), 79–80
" Historiettes," Des Réaux, 64

" History of English Thought in the Eighteenth Century " (Stephen), 319, 324
" History of Prosody " (Saintsbury), 214
Hodgkin, Thomas, 3, 5
Hogg, James, " Confessions of a Justified Sinner," 123–130
Holbein, portraits of Henry VIII by, 15
Holmes, Oliver Wendell, 197, 368
Homer, Lang's translation of, 167
Honorius, 7, 9; and Arcadius, 5
Hood, H. J., 379, 380
Horace, 9, 242; " Odes " of, 186 et seq.; Mr. Drinkwater on Branwell Brontë's and other translations, 310–311
Houdon, bust of Zélide by, 94
Houghton, Lord, Keats's Letters edited by, 333
" Hours in a Library " (Stephen), 324, 326
" House of the Seven Gables, The " (Hawthorne), 356, 357
" House with the Green Shutters, The " (Brown), 339–344
Houville d', Mme. Gérard, 223
Howells, William Dean, 193–199, 216
Hughes, John, 118
Hugo, Victor, 56, 177, 348,
Huguenots, the, 65
" Human Understanding, The " (Locke), 96
Hume, David, 143
Hunt, Leigh, 163
Huntingdon, 10th Earl of, Lord Chesterfield's Letters to, 388–389
Hurd, Richard, 115
Huss, John, 17
Hutchinson, Bishop Francis, Essay on Witchcraft by, 79–80
" Hylas and Philonous " (Berkeley), 395

Ilchester, Earl of, copy of the " Lusiads " owned by, 38

"Imaginary Conversations" (Landor), 395
Indio, Fray José, on the death of Camoens, 38
"Ingénu, L'," Voltaire, 117
Inquisition, the, persecution of St. Teresa and St. John of the Cross by, 47 *et seq.*

JAMES I, his "Dæmonologie" and attitude towards Witchcraft, 75 *et seq.*
James, Henry, 25, 223, 396
Jammes, M. Francis, 223
Jerome, St., 19, 247
Jewel, John, Bishop of Salisbury, 73
Jewett, Sarah Orme, 196
John, St., of the Cross, 43–49, 137
Johnson, Samuel, 98, 150, 173, 222, 395; biography by Stephen, 324; and Lord Chesterfield, 383, 385
Jowett, Benjamin, 165, 209
Juan de Yepes, real name of St. John of the Cross, *q.v.*
Judd, Sylvester, 355
"Julius Cæsar" (Duke of Buckinghamshire), 90
Juvenal, 4

KAYE, Mr. F. B., editor of "The Fable of the Bees" (Mandeville), 143–150
Keats, John, 57, 124, 333
Kerensky, 292
Kingsley, Charles, 383
Kipling, Mr. Rudyard, 303
Kittredge, Professor, 299
"Kleine Johannes" (Eeden), 264
Knight, Joseph, 176
Koizumi, Yatumo, adopted name of Lafcadio Hearn, 224–225

LA BRUYÈRE, Jean de, 277
Laclos, Choderlos de, "Les Liaisons Dangereuses," 133–140

Lamartine, 36, 56
Lamb, Charles, 215
La Morlière, Chevalier de, 138, 139
Landmann, Dr., 27–28
Landor, Walter Savage, 55, 394–395
Lang, Andrew, 163–170, 215, 341, 342, 347, 378, 379
Lankester, Sir Edwin Ray, 378
"Last Man, The" (Mrs. Shelley), 231–238
Latimer, Hugh, prose of, 13
La Tour, portrait of Zélide by, 94
Law, Miss Alice, on Branwell Brontë, 310, 311–315
"Law is a Bottomless Pit" (Arbuthnot), 150
Law, William, 143, 149
"Lays of France" (O'Shaughnessy), 176
Lecky, William E. H., 154
Lee, Nathaniel, 118
Lee, Sir Sidney, 309
Lee-Warner, Mr. Henry, 375
Leland, Dr., 116
Leo X, Pope, and Henry VIII, 16, 18–19
"Letters to his Son" (Chesterfield), 384 *et seq.*
Lettsom, Dr., Memoirs of, 252
Lewis, Mr. David, 49
Lewis, "Monk," 114
Leyland, Mr., 312, 315
"Liaisons Dangereuses, Les" (Laclos), 133–140, 383
Lisle, Leconte de, 177, 350
Livia, 245, 246
Locker, Frederick, 185, 186
Lockhart, John Gibson, 125
Lodge, Thomas, 24
Loeb Library, 3, 241
Logé, M. Marc, 224
London Hospital, the, 252
Longfellow, H. W., 198, 299
Loti, Pierre, 223
Louis XIV and Vauban, 273
Louvois, François, Marquis de, 273

Index 409

"Love in a Wood" (Wycherley), 66, 67
Lowell, James Russell, 194, 197, 198
Lubbock, Mr. Percy, "Roman Pictures" by, 281–286
Luis de Granada, 45
Luis de Leon, Fray, 43, 49
"Lusiads, The" (Camoens), 33, 35, 37, 38
Luther, Martin, 43; and Henry VIII, 16, 17
Lyly, John, and Euphuism, 23–29, 84
Lytton, Edward Bulwer, Lord, 175

MAARTENS, Maarten, pen name of J. van der Poorten-Schwartz, 261
Macaulay, Lord, 54, 154
Mackail, Mr., on Claudian, 4, 6, 7
McKenna, Mr. Stephen, 264, 267
Maclaren, Ian, 340
Macnamara, Mr., editor of Henry VIII's "Miscellaneous Writings," 13–20
Magdalena, Mother, of the Holy Ghost, 48
Maitland, F. W., 320 *et seq.*
Malherbe, François de, 56
Mandeville, Bernard, "The Fable of the Bees," 143–150
Manoel I, King of Portugal, 33
"Mansie Wauch" (Delta Moir), 341
"Marcus Brutus" (Duke of Buckinghamshire), 90
Maria, Infanta, daughter of Manoel I, and Camoens, 35
Marie de France, 176
"Marie Roget" (Poe), 129
Marini, Giambattista, 86
Marinism, 84, 88
Marivaux, Pierre, 135, 136
Marot, Clement, 56, 57
Martial, 245
Martin, Sir Theodore, 311

Martinique, Lafcadio Hearn in, 223–224
Marzials, Théophile, 173
Mata-Hari, 295
Mather, Cotton, 301
Mattos, Teixiera de, 262, 265, 267
Maupassant, Guy de, 196
Maxwell, Clerk, 322–323
Mazzini, Joseph, 331
Melmoth, Courtney, pen-name of Rev. Samuel Pratt, 388
Melville, Herman, 355–362
Mendès, Catulle, 177
Meredith, George, 164, 326
Merrick, Robert (The Elephant Man), case of, described by Sir F. Treves, 253–256
"Mes Souvenirs" (Banville), 352
Metastasio, Pietro, discovery of, by Gravina, 88–89
Mickle, translator of Camoens' "Lusiads," 38
"Midas," play (Lyly), Songs in, 29
Milton, John, 348
Minto, William, 379
"Miscellany Poems" (Wycherley), 68, 69
"Moby Dick" (Melville), 355, 356, 357, 360
Moir, Delta, 340
Molière, Jean, 67, 68, 129, 130; and doctors, 257
Montaigne, 74
Montausier, Julie de, 64, 68
Montégut, Emile, 214
Moore, George, "Monks of Madrid" by, 116
Moore, Mr. George, "Conversations in Ebury St.," 393–399
Moore, Thomas, 163
"Moral Philosophy" (Hutchinson), 156
Morley, Henry, revival of "Euphues" by, 25
Morley of Blackburn, Viscount, 375–376
Morris, William, 166, 227

"Mosses from an Old Manse" (Hawthorne), 356
Moulton, Mrs., 174
"Mourning Bride, The" (Congreve), 118
Muratori, Lodovico, 54
"Murders in the Rue Morgue, The" (Poe), 129
"Music and Moonlight" (O'Shaughnessy), 176
"Mysterious Mother, The" (Walpole), 118, 119
Mysticism in Spain, sixteenth century, 43

"NACH Paris" (Dumur), 290
Nantes, Edict of, 274–275
Nash, Thomas, 23
Newman, Mr. Ernest, 83
"News from Scotland" (James I), 76
Newton, Sir Isaac, 89, 96
"Night of the Soul" (St. John of the Cross), 48
"Noctes Ambrosianæ," 124
"Noodlot" ("Destiny"), (Couperus), 261 et seq.
Northamptonshire, Clare's poetry of, 103–109
"Northanger Abbey," 114
Northcote, Sir Stafford, 377
Norwich, in 1775, 158–159
"Nouvelle Héloïse" (Rousseau), 133, 137, 139

"ODES Funambulesques" (Banville), 167, 348, 350
Oldham, John, 67
Olybrius, 6
Orinda, the Matchless (Katherine Philips), 371
"Orlando Furioso" (Ariosto), 55
"Orphan, The" (Otway), 158
O'Shaughnessy, Arthur, 173–179
Ossian, 119
Ovid, 241–247
Oxford, university life at, circa 1760, 154 et seq.

"PACCHIAROTTO" (Browning), 166
Pace, Richard, composition of the "Seven Sacraments," attributed to, 15
Palgrave, F. T., 174
Parr, Dr., 54
Patmore, Coventry, 49, 136, 173, 183, 379
Peacock, Thomas Love, 232
Peele, George, 23
"Petit Traité de Poésie Française" (Banville), 168, 186, 347
Petrarch, 28, 34
Philip II of Spain, 47
Phillpotts, Miss Bertha, 375
Phillpotts, Mr. J. S., 375
"Pindar," translation by Cary, 55
Pindar, Peter, 218
Piozzi, Mrs., on Lord Huntingdon, 389
"Plain Dealer, The" (Wycherley), 63, 66, 68, 69
Platnauer, Mr. Maurice, translator of Claudian, 3 et seq.
"Playground of Europe, The" (Stephen), 324
Pléiade, the, 86, 167
Poe, Edgar Allan, 123, 128, 129, 358
Pollard, Mr., on Henry VIII, 15
Poorten-Schwartz, J. van der, 261
Pope, Alexander, 66, 84, 149, 324
Porphyry, 54
Porter, Mr. Alan, Poems of John Clare edited by, 103 et seq.
Pound, Professor Louisa, 299–305
Praed, W. M., 159, 184 et seq.
Pratt, Rev. Samuel, "The Pupil of Pleasure," 388
"Précieuses Ridicules, Les" (Molière), 67
Pre-Raphaelites, the, 176, 184
Pringle-Pattison, Professor, 44
Prior, Matthew, 89, 242
Probinus, 6

Index 411

Probus, 6
Propertius, 242
" Pupil of Pleasure, The "
  (Pratt), 388
Puritanism, 66

RACINE, Jean, 85
Radcliffe, Mrs., novels of, 114
Raleigh, Walter, 217, 365
Rambouillet, Hôtel de, 64, 69
" Rape of Proserpine, The "
  (Claudian), 7–9
Rapin, 84
" Raven, The " (Poe), 359
Raymond, Lord (" The Last Man "), portrait of Byron, 234 et seq.
Redi, 85
Reid, Sir Wemyss, 312
Richardson, Samuel, 95, 116, 133, 134, 137, 139
" Rise of Silas Lapham, The " (Howells), 199
" Roadside Harp, A " (Guiney), 365, 368
" Robert Elsmere " (Ward), 207
Robertson, Professor John G., Study of the Italian sources of Romanticism, 83–90
Robinson, Mrs., and Branwell Brontë, 313
Rolland, M. Romain, 292
" Rolliad, The," 218
" Roman, The " (Dobell), 329, 330–331, 332
" Roman Pictures " (Lubbock), 281–286
Ronsard, Pierre de, 56, 167
Rossetti, Christina, 49
Rossetti, Dante Gabriel, 176, 217, 227
Rousseau, Jean Jacques, 98, 133, 136, 290, 384
Rudler, Professor, 99
Rufinus, 6–7
Ruskin, John, 325, 329

ST. ANDREWS, 166
" Saint Jean de la Croix " (Baruzi), 45
St. Osyth, Essex, witchcraft persecution at, 73
St. Thomas's Hospital, 252
Saint-Victor, Paul de, 214
Sainte-Beuve, Charles-Augustin, 56, 215
Saintsbury, Professor George, 133–134, 213–218, 378
Sanchez, Miguel, 43
Sanquhar Declaration, 126
Santarem, claimed as Camoens' birthplace, 34
" Sara Burgerhart," 95
" Sasper " (Shakespeare), origin of the term, 89
Savile Club, the, 375–380
" Scarlet Letter, The " (Hawthorne), 357, 358
Scarron, Paul, 69
Scot, Reginald, " Discoverie of Witchcraft," 73, 74
Scott, Mr. Geoffrey, " The Portrait of Zélide," 93–99
Scott, Sir Walter, 124, 125, 196, 339
" Seven Sacraments " (Henry VIII), see under " Assertion of the Seven Sacraments, The."
Shadwell, Thomas, 68
Shaftesbury, 3rd Earl of, 147, 149
Shakespeare, William, 29, 37, 89, 104, 255, 256, 395; and witchcraft, 78, 79
" Shaving of Shagpat, The " (Meredith), 227
Shaw, Mr. G. Bernard, 149, 257
Shelley, Mary Wollstonecraft, 231–238
Shelley, Percy Bysshe, 54, 197, 227, 231 et seq., 398; portrayed as Adrian, Earl of Windsor, in " The Last Man," 234 et seq.
Shelley, Sir Timothy, 231
Sherburne, Edward, 371
Sidney, Sir Philip, 54
Sims, Gilmore, 355
" Sister Helen " (Rossetti), 227

Index

Skylark, The, odes to, by Wordsworth, Shelley, and Clare, 107
Smith, Adam, 143
Smith, Alexander, 335
Smith, Charlotte, sonnets of, 106
Smith, W. Robertson, 379
Smyth, Professor, 322
Society Club, the, 375
" Sopha, Le " (Crébillon), 135
Southey, Robert, 103
Spain, mystical theology in, during sixteenth century, 43
" Spasmodists," origin of the term, 333
Spencer, Herbert, 379
Spenser, Edmund, 24, 214
" Spiritual Writings " (St. John of the Cross), 45
Staël, Mme. de, 94, 99
Stanhope, Mrs. Eugenia, 384, 385
Stanhope, Philip, son of Lord Chesterfield, 385 et seq.
Stanley, Thomas, 371
Stedman, E. C., 368
Stephen, Sir Herbert, History of the Savile Club compiled by, 377
Stephen, Sir James, 321
Stephen, Sir Leslie, 149, 214, 319–326
Steuart, Mr. A. F., on 10th Earl of Huntingdon, 388
Stevenson, R. A. M., 379
Stevenson, R. L., 325, 355, 378 et seq.
" Stickit Minister, The " (Crockett), 340
Stilicho, 5 et seq.
Strachey, Mr. Charles, 383
Summers, Mr. Montague, 63 et seq., 113–119
Swift, Jonathan, 68, 146, 150, 324, 375
Swinburne, Algernon Charles, 164, 166, 168, 176, 184, 227, 347, 348
Sydenham, Thomas, 256
Symonds, J. A., 325
Symons, Mr. Arthur, 49

TAINE, H., 214
" Tartuffe " (Molière), 129
Tasso, Torquato, and Camoens, 37
" Tempest, The " (Shakespeare), 256
Tennyson, Alfred, Lord, 9, 166, 177, 186, 187, 332; and Sydney Dobell, 331, 334–335
Teresa, St., of Jesus, 43, 46 et seq.
Tetzel, 16
Texte, M., 133
Thackeray, W. M., 196, 216, 281
Theocritus, Lang's translation of, 167
Theodosius, Emperor, 5
Thompson, Francis, 222
Throckmorton, Robert, 78–79
Tiberius, 309
Tibullus, 242
" Titus Andronicus " (Shakespeare), 29
Tokio, University of, Lafcadio Hearn's lectures at, 225
Toledo, imprisonment of St. John of the Cross in, 48
Tomis, Ovid at, 244, 247
Tompson, Agnis, 76–77
Trapassi, Bonaventura, 89
Trefusis, Lady Mary, Henry VIII's music printed by, 20
" Trente-Six Ballades Joyeuses " (Banville), 168, 350
Trevelyan, Mrs. George, 203–210
Treves, Sir Frederick, Recollections of, 251–258
" Tristia " (Ovid), 244, 245
Trollope, Anthony, 189
Trotsky, 292
Tuyll, Isabella van Sersoskerken van, 93–99
Tyndale, William, 13

UNITED States of America, Folk-Song of, collected by Professor Louisa Pound, 299–305
University life, circa 1760, 154 et seq.

Index

VALERIUS, Flaccus, 54
"Valperga" (Mrs. Shelley), 237
Vatican Library, the, 19
Vauban, Sébastien Le Prestre de, 271–278
Vaughan, Henry, 370, 371
Vega Carpio, Lope de, 38
"Venetian Life" (Howells), 198
Verrall, A. W., 379
Vers de société, use of term, 185
Versailles, Library of, 57, 274
Vico, 83
Vigny, Alfred de, 56, 350
Villon, François, 36
Virgil, 242
Voiture, Vincent, 242
Voltaire, 97, 98, 117
"Voyage of Maeldune, The" (Tennyson), 9

WALPOLE, Horace, 113–119
Warboise witchcraft case, the, 78–79
Ward, Mary Augusta (Mrs. Humphrey), 203–210
Watts, Isaac, 242
Welby, Mr. T. Earle, 53 *et seq.*, 123 *et seq.*, 183
Wells, Mr. H. G., 233

Wemyss, Lord, 97
Wesley, Charles and John, 384
Wheeler, Professor A.L., 241–247
Whibley, Mr. Charles, 342
Whittier, J. G., 299
Wilcox, Ella Wheeler, 184
Wise, Mr. Thos. J., 231
Witchcraft, 73–80
Wolsey, Thomas, 15, 16, 18
"Woman in the Moon," play (Lyly), 28
Women, Lyly's treatment of, in "Euphues," 26–27
Woodforde, Rev. James, 153–159
Wordsworth, William, 104, 106, 107, 177–178, 320; and T. Moore, 163
"Wuthering Heights" (E. Brontë), 310, 313–315
Wycherley, William, 63 *et seq.*

"YOUMA" (Hearn), 221, 223–224
Young, Edward, 118

ZÉLIDE (Isabella van Sersoskerken van Tuyll), 93–99
Zola, Émile, 196, 284